Worlds Within Worlds

A Journey into the Unknown

Worlds Within Worlds

A Journey into the Unknown

Michael Marten, John Chesterman,
John May and John Trux

Holt, Rinehart and Winston
New York

Published simultaneously in Canada
by Holt, Rinehart and Winston of
Canada, Limited.

Library of Congress Catalog Card
Number: 77-71380
ISBN Paperback: 0-03-019416-4

Printed in Great Britain
10   9   8   7   6   5   4   3   2   1

Worlds Within Worlds was
conceived, researched, written
and edited by Michael Marten,
John Chesterman, John Trux
and John May of Clanose
Publishers Ltd., 2 Blenheim
Crescent, London W11 1NN:—

Production – Michael Marten
Captions – John Chesterman,
John Trux
Photo research – Michael
Marten, John May
Diagrams – John Chesterman

Designed by Richard Adams

Special thanks to Lee Torrey of
Cape Cod, Maggie
Murphy-Ferris in San Francisco.
And to Nigel Press of Nigel
Press Associates
(Photogeology & Remote
Sensing) and H.J.P. Arnold of
Space Frontiers Ltd. for
supplying remote sensing and
space photographs.

We have been able to include
only a fraction of the pictures
we received from individual
scientists and photographers,
corporate and government
research departments around
the world. They are the real
authors, and artists, of this
book.

Contents

Introduction

In September 1608, a new Dutch toy went on sale at the annual Frankfurt fair. It was a tube which enabled one to see further than one could with the naked eye, and was called a telescope. It could also be arranged in a different way, as a device called a microscope, to make invisible things visible. For the first time in human history the observable universe suddenly expanded, not just once or twice but a hundredfold. It made visible new realms in outer space and inside ourselves, and laid the foundations of modern astronomy and medicine.

For 300 years the limits of the observable universe slowly expanded. Optical techniques improved. The invention of photography in 1839 made it possible to record what was seen. But there was nothing to compare with that first headlong breakthrough – not until our own century. For in the last few decades we have been experiencing a paradigm as extraordinary as the one Galileo stumbled upon when his friend brought him a toy telescope from Frankfurt and he turned it on the heavens.

With or without a telescope, from ancient civilisations to the Victorian era, the limit of our universe depended on what we could *see* – and that depended on light. The human eye is a remarkably accurate device, but it has the drawback of being tuned to a narrow band of the electromagnetic spectrum. The lightwaves which our eyes are designed to receive are only a fraction of the radiation around us. This has blinkered our image of the world and given us a kind of "tunnel vision."

Take colour, for instance. It only exists as an image in our brains. Objects themselves are not "coloured" (unless they glow, like phosphorescence). Colour is just a convenient code for certain wavelengths of radiation. But try to imagine a *new* colour and you soon realise how limited imagination is. We know that snakes can "see" in infrared and certain insects in ultraviolet, but what exactly is it that they see? What are the colours of radio and radar and x-rays?

We cannot experience these radiations directly. But during this century we have learnt to translate most of them into the familiar code of light and colour. Of course, something is inevitably lost in the translation. The results are two-dimensional ghosts of those other worlds, and the colours are substitutes picked from our experience to stand in for the real ones. Television is at the centre of this revolution. Not TV with its much discussed social implications, but the television tube itself, which can translate any kind of radiation into pictures we can understand. Every kind of sensing device is today being linked to the ubiquitous video-screen.

We can now look up into the huge luminous x-ray sky, or convert hailstorms of electrons smaller than the wavelength of light into detailed photographs. Infrared cameras monitor heat emissions from cities, factories, hurricanes and the human body. Radio telescopes map cosmic events 10,000 million light-years away. Electron microscopes photograph genes and viruses, even atoms.

In addition to the breakthrough of electronic vision, there are also techniques for manipulating light in new ways. It can now be "amplified" like sound, to give night-vision. The stress patterns in the fabric of a gothic cathedral can be made visible by polarised light. Strobes produce high-speed photographs that "freeze" a bullet in flight.

All these new techniques are windows into alternative realities. Each level of structure is supported by a scaffolding of substructures. Each system is part of a larger one: worlds within worlds.

Most startling to those who think of themselves as "unique" individuals is the view scientific photography gives us of ourselves. A microworld exists inside us. Indeed, it *is* us. Life originally evolved from a primal ocean and, in a sense, our bodies are still a replica of it – a mobile salt-water environment with controls to regulate the salinity and thermostats to keep a constant temperature. Within this privileged environment millions of organisms live, reproduce and die. Like their prototypes in that ancient sea, they develop hierarchies of mutual aid, mark their territories and repel invaders. They go about cleaning our lungs, filtering our blood supply and fighting our diseases without our ever being aware of them. Just as we can pollute and destroy the ecosystems of our environment, so these organisms can pollute our internal world. The lymphocytes and blood cells and macrophages that swim through the liquid jungle of our bodies are part of a "homosphere," in the same way that we, in turn, are part of a biosphere.

Just as micrography has transformed the traditional view of our interior world, the new techniques of satellite and aerial photography are giving us a radically different image of the world about us. We can now *see* geology and geography, instead of depending on maps. Abstract diagrams and statistics turn into swirling weather systems, sharp corrugations of the planet's crust, or glowing red networks of vegetation.

This new "world view" could turn out to be a major cultural achievement. It complements the long overdue realisation that Earth is one system, and all its problems are interrelated. Throughout the spectrum of existence, the same fundamental patterns are repeated. The spiral shape of a diminutive marine organism reappears in the clouds of a cyclone and the structure of a galaxy. The branching pattern that distributes blood to our lungs is repeated in trees and rivers. Common forms of organisation seem to hold the universe together. We hope so.

The photographs in this book come from many different sources all over the world, and the result is a personal choice. We have not attempted to cover every technique or application, but simply to explore some of the more beautiful, exotic, and revolutionary results.

M.M., J.C., J.T., J.M. London, 1977.

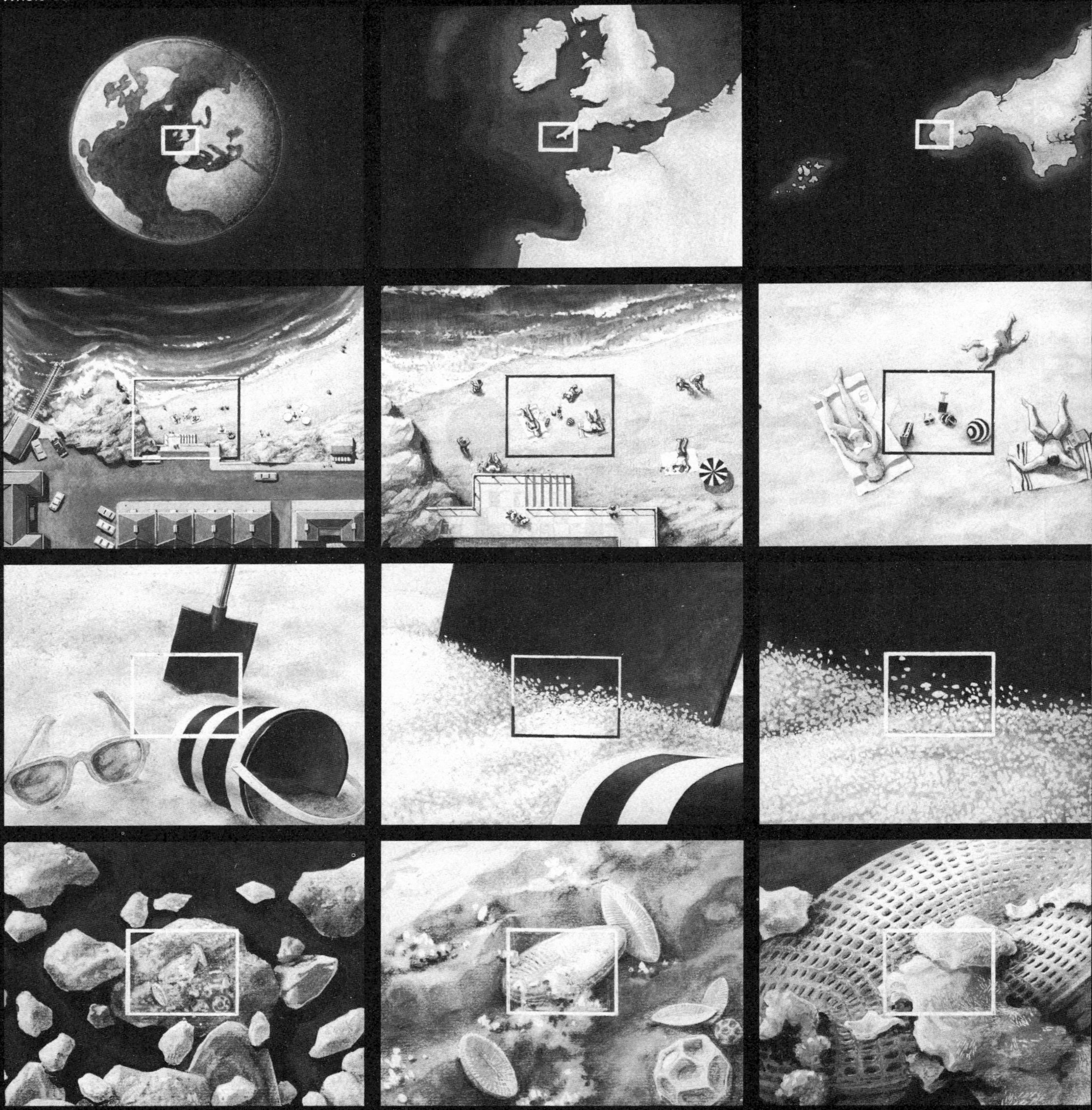

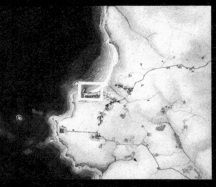

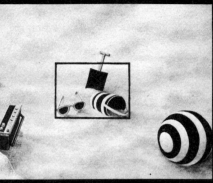

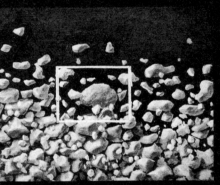

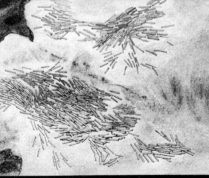

...teria feeding on organic debris on a
...om.

SPACE SCALE

There are vast changes of scale
in this book and it is sometimes
difficult to believe that they are
all part of the same system. A
diagrammatic "zoom" in to Earth
gives some idea of how they
relate, although it would take at
least twice as many pictures to
cover the full range.

Each of the top line of pictures
is enlarged one hundred times
the area of the preceding one.
The other pictures are in
increments of ten.

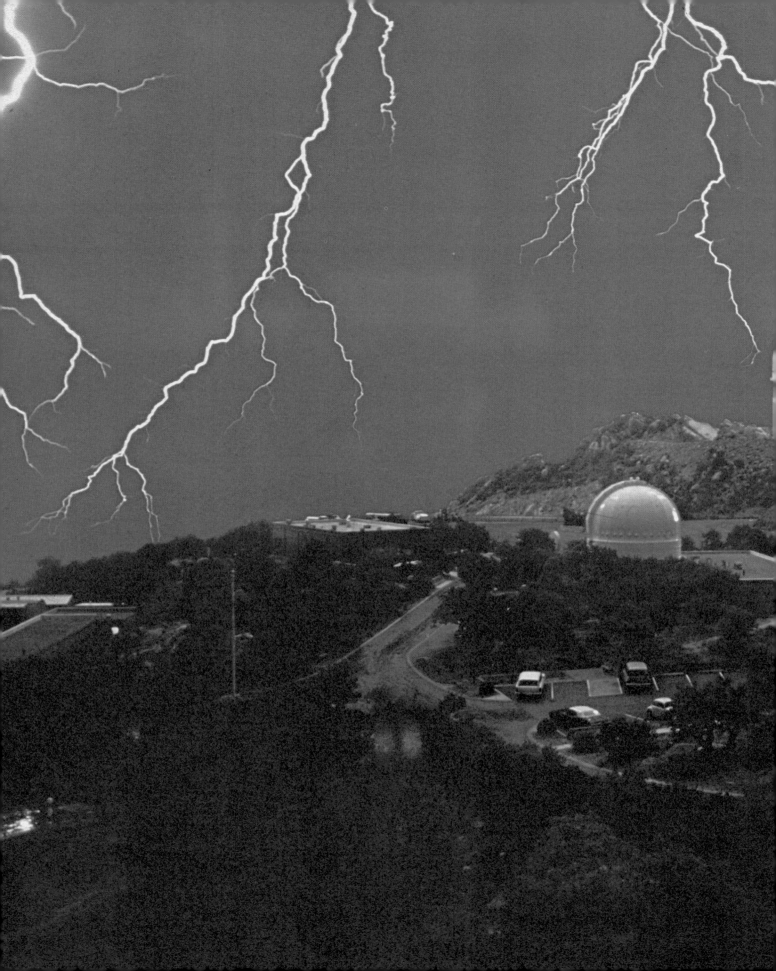

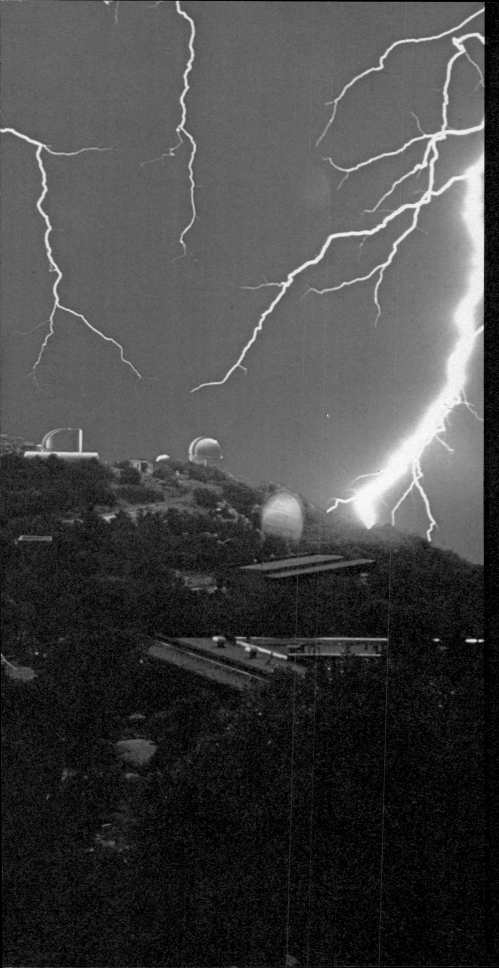

Energies

Millions of volts of electricity are discharged over Arizona's Kitt Peak National Observatory, flooding the landscape with an eerie light.

The flashes are not instantaneous. Lightning pauses for 50 microseconds between each change of direction as it works out a path to the ground. About half way down, another flash leaps upward to meet it. Only then can the main charge, of up to 300 million volts, be released in a return stroke. So when a person is struck by lightning, it first flows up through his body and out of the top of his head!

Photographer Gary Ladd spent eight cold nights on the mountain to get this crisp 60-second exposure. The chances of similar conditions occurring again? By Ladd's own reckoning—one in a million.

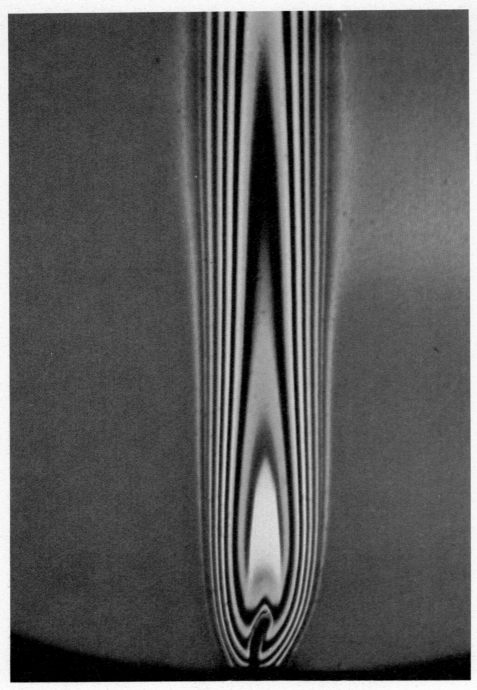

If the radiance of a thousand suns
Were to burst into the sky,
That would be like
The splendour of the Mighty One.
  —Bhagavad Gita

A silent nuclear fireball devours the air over the Nevada Desert.

At first the explosion is distorted by the heavy materials of the bomb's detonating mechanism. Neither sound nor shock wave have yet emerged. Nothing has burnt or melted or collapsed. The tower on which the bomb was placed remains intact. But in another millionth of a second the fireball will grow into a smooth greedy sphere, expanding at thousands of feet per second, and vaporising matter instantly. The landscape will be lit up by its fierce glare, many times brighter than the sun.

Professor Harold Edgerton, one of the pioneers of ultrafast photography, developed a special camera protected by elaborate shutter mechanisms to record the first moments of the atom bomb's life. The first shutter opened mechanically one second before the explosion, and was followed by an electronic shutter which exposed the film for a few millionths of a second. But this alone was not sufficient. Even though the camera was ten miles from "ground zero," a third shutter had to be added to prevent the film from being fogged by the fireball's light. This shutter consisted of a glass plate crisscrossed with thin lead wires which were vaporised by a pulse of electricity so that an opaque coating of lead guaranteed the film's safety.

HAROLD E. EDGERTON, MIT, CAMBRIDGE, MASSACHUSETTS.

The anatomy of a candle flame is revealed by imitating the natural effect of rainbows in oil slicks and soap bubbles.

This effect occurs when light is reflected off a very thin surface. Part of the light bounces off the top of the film and part off the bottom, so that when the wavelengths are combined they are slightly out of step with each other and produce the typical stripes of an "interference" pattern.

Such patterns can be reproduced, as in the candle flame, with an instrument called an "interferometer," which artificially slows down part of the light. Where the peaks of the lightwaves match, the colours are brighter; where they do not, the waves cancel each other out, producing darker areas.

It was the "interference" effect which originally led to the discovery that light travels as waves of radiation.

COURTESY OF CARL ZEISS.

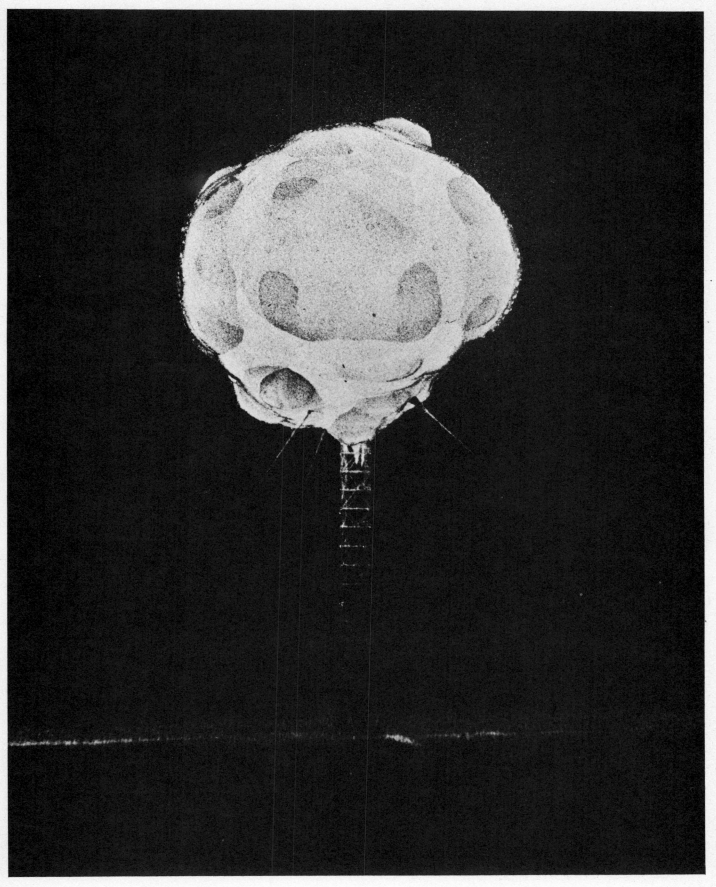

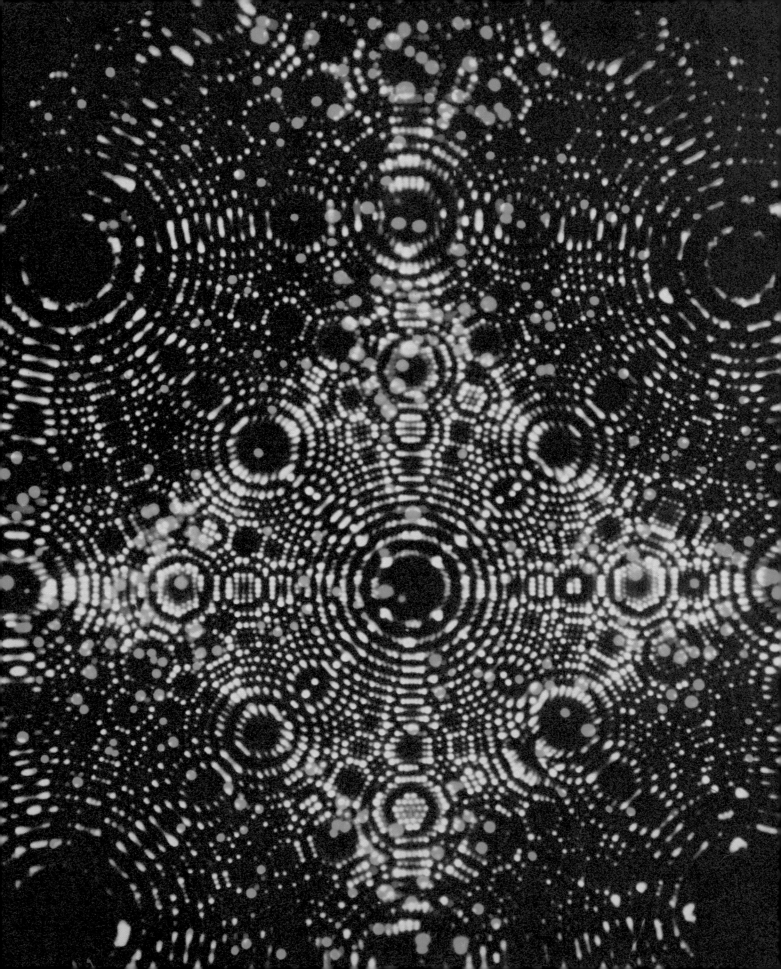

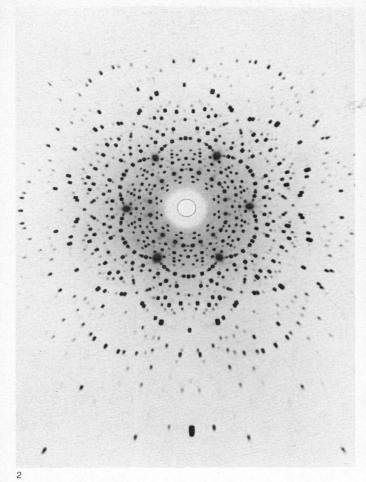

2

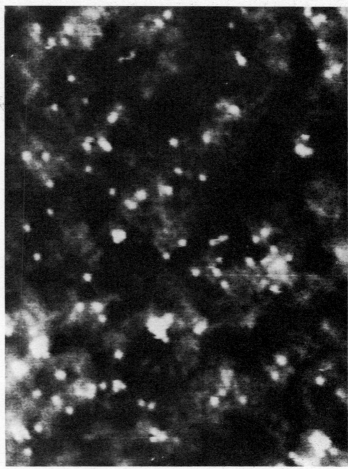

3

"We had passed the first half of the 20th century, which in science may well be called the century of the atom, yet no one had ever seen one, even with the most sophisticated electron microscopes."

—Professor Erwin W. Mueller, inventor of the field-ion microscope.

Atoms are invisible, for the simple reason that even the smallest wavelength of light is 5000 times larger than atoms themselves. But there are other ways of "seeing." Though these are not photographs in the usual sense (and use very different techniques), they are undoubtedly "pictures" of atoms.

1. The tiny dots of light on Mueller's micrograph are the locations of individual atoms of iridium. The ring-like shapes are facets of a single crystal of the metal.

The picture was made by superimposing successive photographs, taken with different colour filters, to show minute changes on the surface. The red dots are atoms which have evaporated or been corroded away, while the green ones are probably atoms of gas which have been absorbed.

Using the technique of field-ion microscopy, Mueller placed a needle of iridium in a gas-filled chamber, and then passed a high voltage through it. When the drifting ions of gas bumped against the charged atoms, they were pushed violently away at right angles to the surface, forming this pattern on a fluorescent screen.

DR ERWIN W. MUELLER, EVAN-PUGH PROFESSOR OF PHYSICS, PENNSYLVANIA STATE UNIVERSITY.

2. Like the revolving mirrored ball that reflects a spotlight on a dance floor, a crystal of beryl fragments a beam of x-rays. The narrow beam was projected through the beryl, and the black spots reflect the regular lattice of atoms within the crystal.

This technique of x-ray diffraction is used to work out the atomic structure of different elements. A similar technique was used to decode the double-helix spiral of DNA molecules.

REPRODUCED BY KIND PERMISSION OF THE EASTMAN KODAK COMPANY AND KODAK LTD.

3. Today the most sophisticated electron microscopes *can* photograph individual atoms. This is a picture of atoms of uranium, magnified an incredible seven and a half million times. The micrograph was made at the University of Chicago, using a technique which rapidly scans a beam of electrons backwards and forwards to build up a TV-like image.

This is roughly the largest direct magnification we are ever likely to achieve, because only electrons have a wavelength comparable to the size of an atom.

DR ALBERT V. CREWE. ©1970 BY THE AMERICAN ASSOCIATION FOR THE ADVANCEMENT OF SCIENCE. FROM "VISIBILITY OF SINGLE ATOMS." CREWE, A. V., *SCIENCE*, VOL. 168, pp.1338-1340, 12 JUNE 1970.

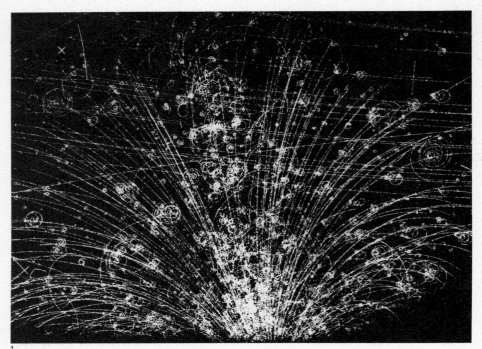

1

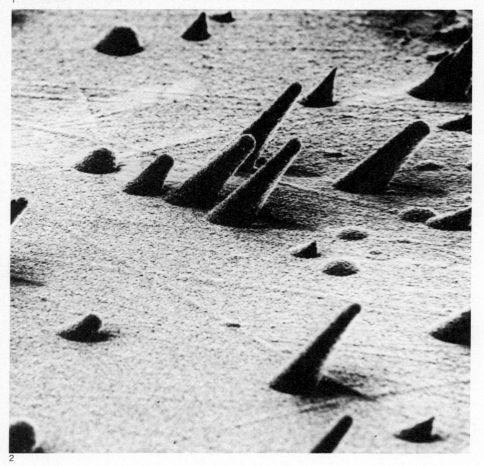

2

One of the most powerful, and mysterious forms of energy we know are cosmic rays; the high speed particles or bursts of radiation which constantly bombard the Earth from outer space. Fortunately most of them break up when they collide with the upper atmosphere. Some of those which reach the surface have been recorded by the vapour trails they leave in bubble-chambers, though seldom with such dramatic effect as this rare photograph from the CERN laboratories in Switzerland.

1. A particularly high-energy ray smashed into a molecule somewhere in the piston mechanism of the bubble chamber (off the picture), spraying a hundred or more particles of atomic debris into the chamber itself.

CERN PHOTO

2. Though we are relatively safe from cosmic rays, they represent a long-term threat to astronauts since they can easily pass right through a spacecraft. When the Apollo crews returned from the moon with dents like these in their helmets, laboratory tests were carried out, using artificial cosmic rays, to design adequate shielding for future trips. The photograph is of a silicone rubber replica (magnified 800 times) of the tracks etched in one of the test helmets.

COURTESY OF THE GENERAL ELECTRIC COMPANY. FROM "COSMIC RAY TRACKS IN PLASTICS: THE APOLLO HELMET DOSIMETRY EXPERIMENT," COMSTOCK, G. M. ET AL, *SCIENCE*, VOL. 172, PP. 154-157, 9 APRIL 1971

these four frames the swift flight
a rifle bullet and the instantaneous
lse of a high-energy spark are frozen
film. Each event, occurring in less
an a millionth of a second, results
a photograph of that most elusive
subjects: air itself.

A speeding bullet passes over the
of a lighted candle, preceded by
e equivalent of a ship's bow-wave
een crescent).

A second bullet pierces the fragile
in of a soap bubble. Again, the
shaped shock waves are clearly visible.
e bright spots on the bubble are
rmally invisible droplets of soap
lution, reflecting light from the
otographer's flash-gun.

An underwater spark flashes for a
ction of a second—long enough to
m the vapour bubble at centre. The
loured bands to the right of the bubble
tray the presence of a series of
panding shock waves.

The revolving blade (top) of an
ectric fan is frozen midway through
e flame from an alcohol lamp (bottom).
e fan's speed—1200 revolutions per
nute—forms a vortex of hot air at
e tip of the flame.

ese photographs are the first to be
en of air-flow at ultra-high speed—
hout the benefit of additives. Previous
dies had always used smoke or chemicals
"dye" the air currents.
These pictures show the density levels
air, and they were made possible only
er scientists at the famous Massachusetts
stitute of Technology combined three
novative techniques: an instrument
led a "schlieren interferometer,"
ich records relative densities in
-flows; a high-speed light source
ich can "freeze" the schlieren patterns;
d lastly, an apparatus to colour code
e frozen patterns, allowing them to be
curately measured.

OFESSOR J. KIM VANDIVER, MIT

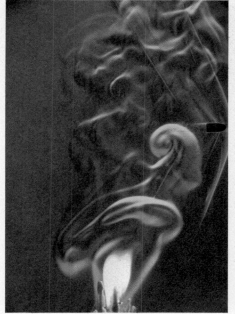

1

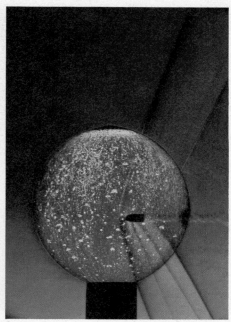

2

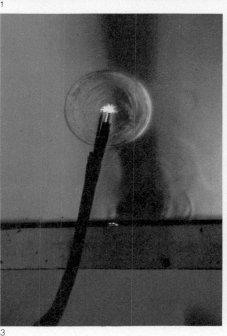

3

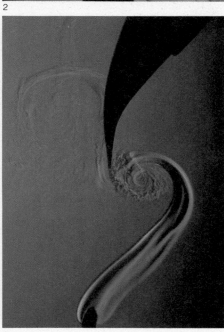

4

A new adage amply proven—"what comes down must go up."

This sequence of pictures, taken with a high-speed camera at Cambridge University's Cavendish Laboratory, shows the slow-motion impact of a water droplet.

The droplet, dyed red, falls approximately eight inches into a container of water to which blue colouring has been added. The resulting splash blossoms out into a "coronet." As the splash subsides, the well formed by the falling drop expands and then rapidly collapses, driving a central jet upwards. When the jet has risen to a considerable height, surface tension constricts the top of the column and produces a spherical drop which seems to defy gravity. But the drop *does* fall back—into the disturbed water below.

We begin and end with the same red drop! The explanation is a phenomenon known as "reversible laminar flow." During the short duration of the event (150 milliseconds) fluid from the red drop does not have time to mix with the blue water. Consequently, the red water is reformed as the drop at the top of the emerging jet.

It happens every time a tap drips.

DR DAVID GORHAM AND DR IAN HUTCHINGS,
CAVENDISH LABORATORY, UNIVERSITY OF CAMBRIDGE.

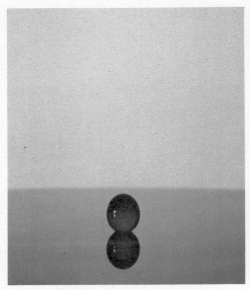
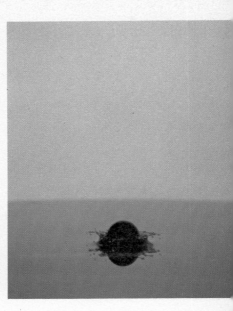
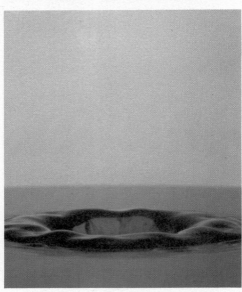
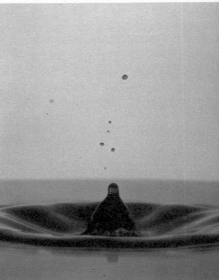
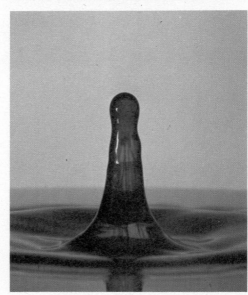
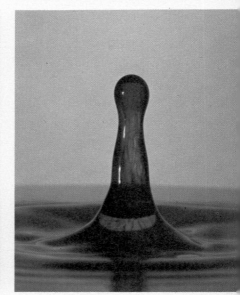

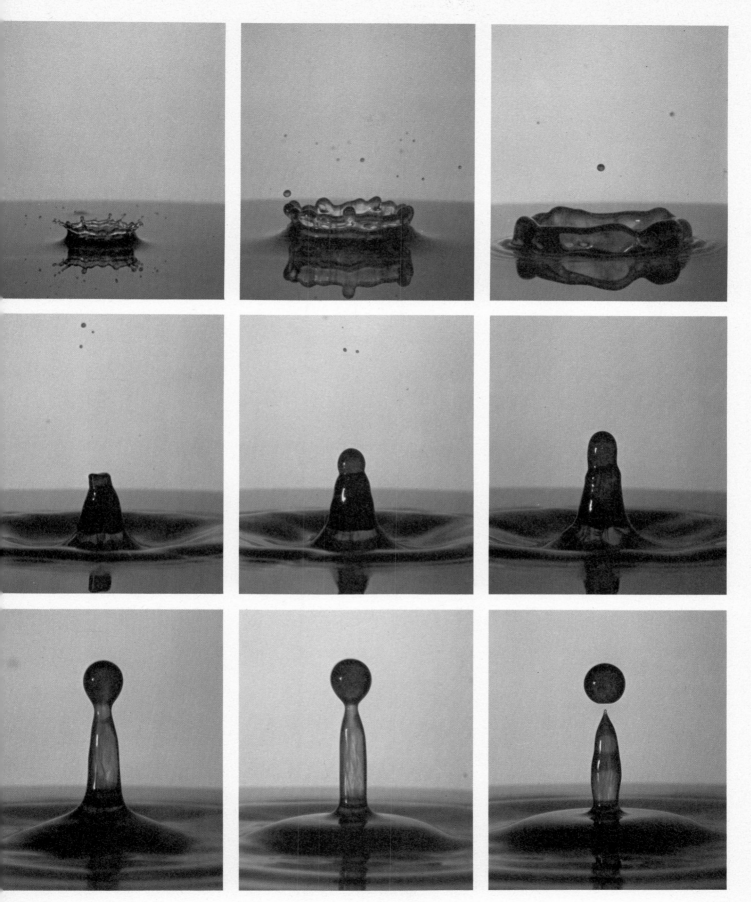

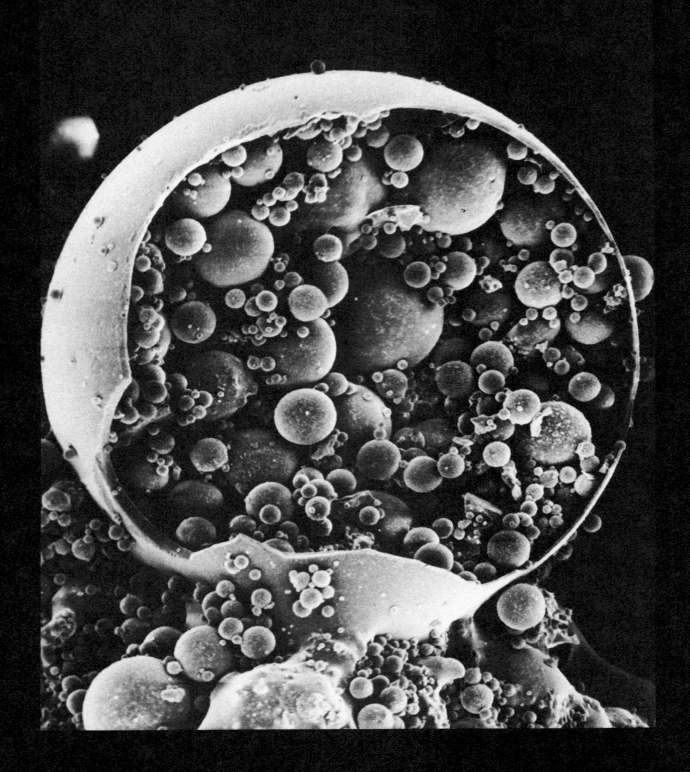

Spheres within spheres—the unique structure of fly ash, a common atmospheric pollutant. Collected from the chimney of an American coal-fired power station, this particle measures less than one hundredth of a millimetre in diameter. Yet the hollow outer sphere contains hundreds of smaller spheres, and researchers at the University of California's Davis campus found that many of these inner spheres contained, in turn, even tinier spheres. It has been suggested that this extraordinary structure is due to a combination of heating and gas pressure.

Millions of such particles are pumped into the atmosphere daily as part of the unburnt residue of coal-fired plants. They are composed of glass, iron, calcium, sodium and magnesium, and may be a health hazard.

The Davis researchers used a scanning electron microscope to take this fly ash portrait.

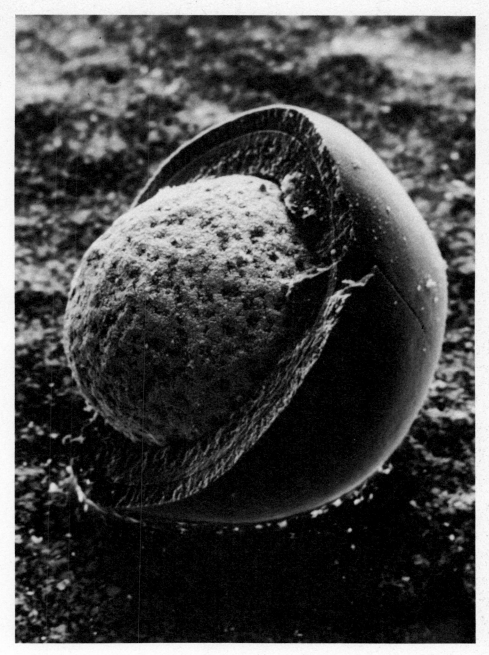

The power of the atom, contained within a sphere no larger than a grain of sand.

Millions of these fuel particles—less than 0.2 of an inch across—are used in a new development in atomic power: the high-temperature gas-cooled reactor. The particles have a core of uranium (though a plutonium/thorium mixture may also be used) and a tough, layered outer shell made of ceramics. The spheres are bonded with carbon to make "fuel compacts," which are then inserted into the reactor's core.

Because such large numbers of particles are used, the reactor's output can be closely controlled. As a result, the reactor can work at extremely high temperatures— around 900°C—without danger. One benefit of this type of reactor may be the direct generation of heat for chemical processes like steelmaking. Also, the conventional steam cooling reactor system, which discharges heat pollution into rivers and coastal waters, can be dispensed with in favour of closed systems using helium gas. X 112.

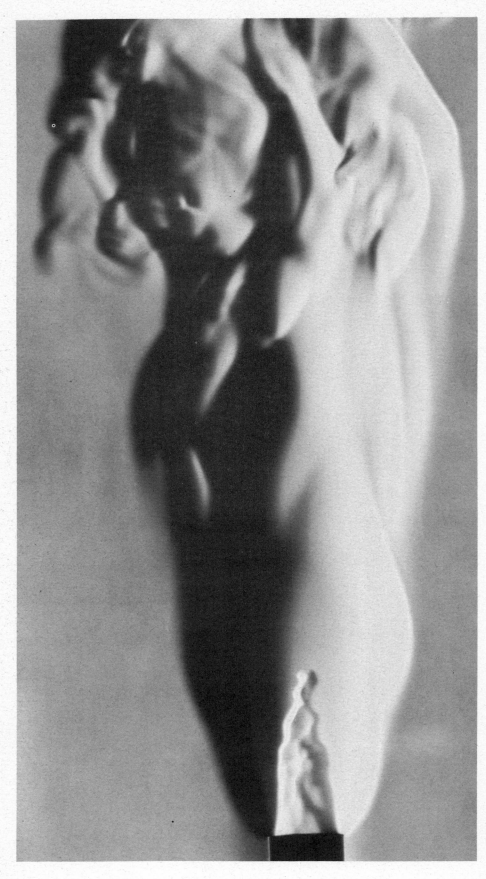

The lady in the flame—heated, turbulent air over a bunsen burner is sculpted into a still-life by schlieren photography.

The technique exploits the behaviour of light as it passes through currents of air or gas. Employing an instrument known as a "schlieren interferometer," parallel rays of light are beamed through the subject. Some of them are slightly bent, or "refracted," by temperature and pressure differences in the fast-moving current. The heart of the interferometer, two sharp knife-edges, partially intercepts the beam of light both before and after it passes through the turbulence, and this allows the distortions in the beam to be recorded on film. Because the currents of air and gas are themselves in rapid motion, an ultra-high speed shutter is used to "freeze" their movement.

WILLIAM T. REID. BATTELLE. COLUMBUS LABORATORIES.

Electro–, or Kirlian, photography is the result of an accidental discovery made some years ago by Semyon Kirlian, a Russian electrician and amateur photographer. The technique was at first ignored by Soviet science, but has now achieved recognition as a useful scientific tool.

In Kirlian photography, the object to be studied is placed between a high-energy electric field and a photographic plate—a process analogous to field emission techniques.

Introduced into the USA in the late sixties, electrophotography immediately became the centre of scientific controversy. Scientists agreed that the results were spectacular, but differed in their interpretations of what, exactly, the technique revealed: a new form of energy, or an interesting (but valueless) electrical side-effect.

This miniature Kirlian "lightning storm" was created by dropping a steel ball-bearing into a high-energy electric field.

COURTESY OF H. S. DAKIN, 3101 WASHINGTON STREET, SAN FRANCISCO, CALIF. 94115. AS ORIGINALLY PUBLISHED IN *ELECTROPHOTOGRAPHY* BY E. LANE. AND/OR PRESS, BERKELEY, CALIFORNIA.

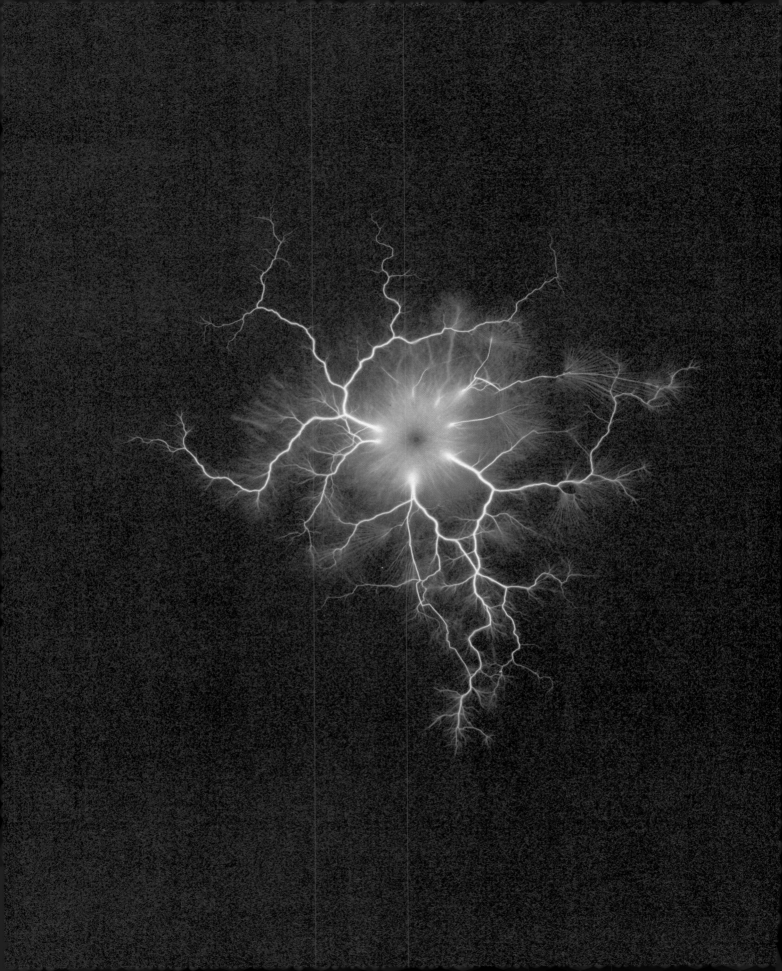

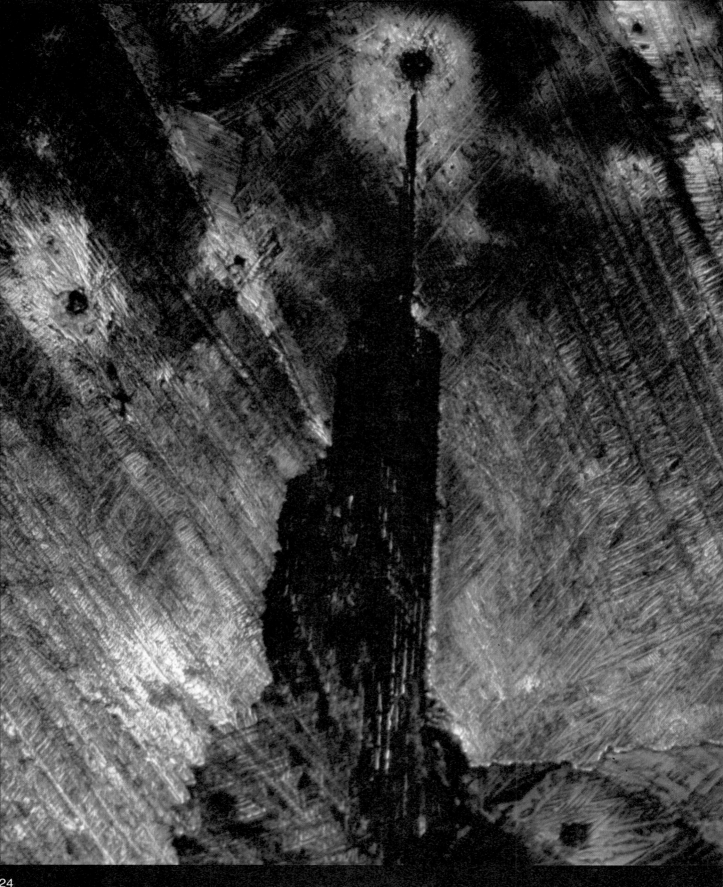

Crystal World

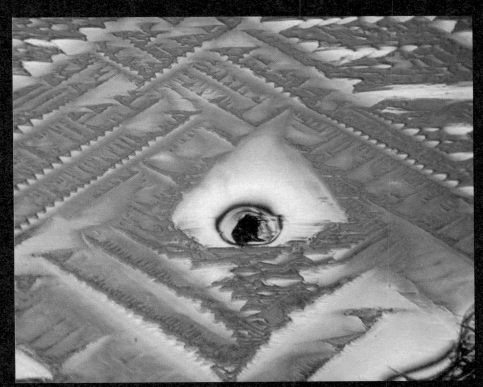

The vivid, microscopic light-show within chemical crystals.

James Bell, who took these photographs, works in the laboratories of Union Carbide in Chicago, but he spends his leisure hours exploring what he calls "inner space"—the internal structure of crystals as it is revealed under polarised light.

The method is simple. The specimen is placed under a microscope, sandwiched between two filters similar to those in Polaroid sunglasses. Light is bent at different angles as the filters are rotated, and is reflected off the planes and fractures inside the crystal, producing a kaleidoscope of patterns.

These pictures, which Bell calls "The Empire State" (far left) and "The Third Eye" (left), illustrate the astonishing variety that can be obtained from crystals of a single chemical, in this case resorcinol, which is widely used in dyes, adhesives, shampoos and as a treatment for acne.

But the technique, properly known as polarised light photomicrography, is not only a visual adventure. It is also a valuable scientific tool, enabling the molecular structure of a substance to be mapped by using the known wavelength of different colours.

JAMES M. BELL

Overleaf: The fantastic landscape formed by crystals of an unknown chemical substance produced at the Leverkusen laboratories of Bayer, the international chemical conglomerate. It is known simply as "Preparation Clont."

MANFRED KAGE. REPRODUCED FROM *FAKTUM FARBE* WITH PERMISSION OF CARL ZEISS.

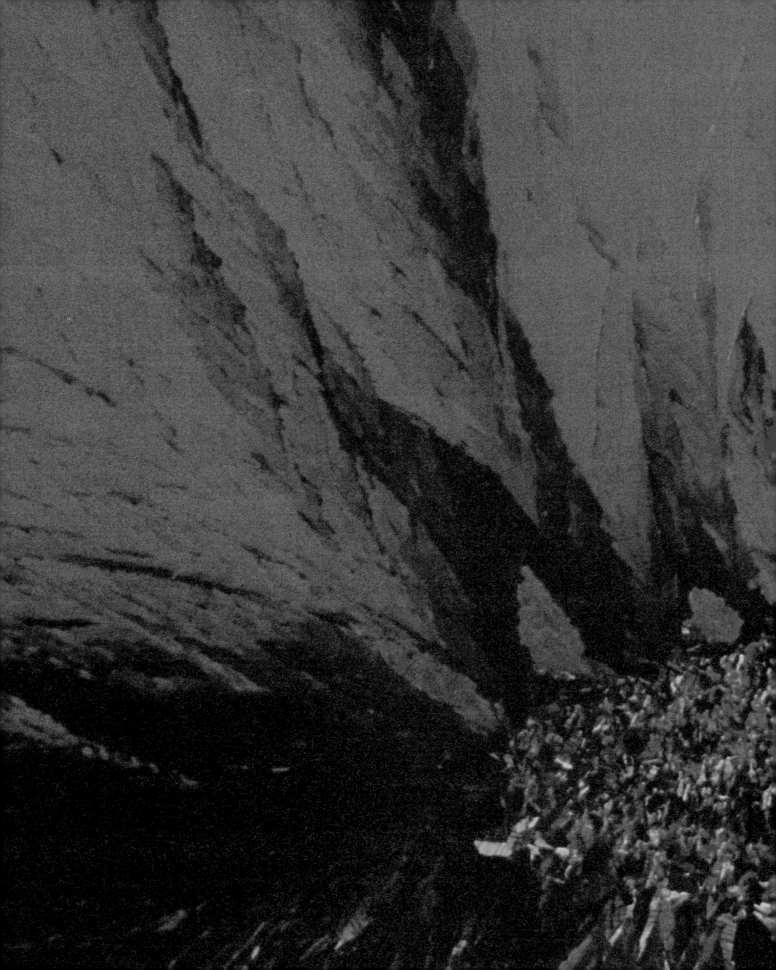

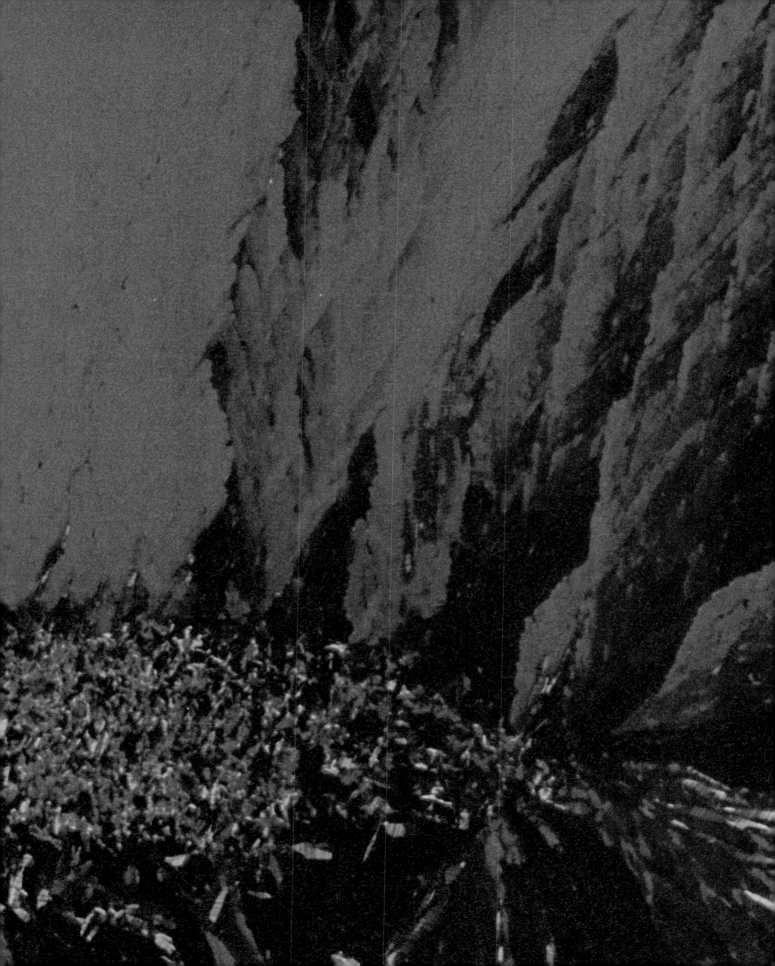

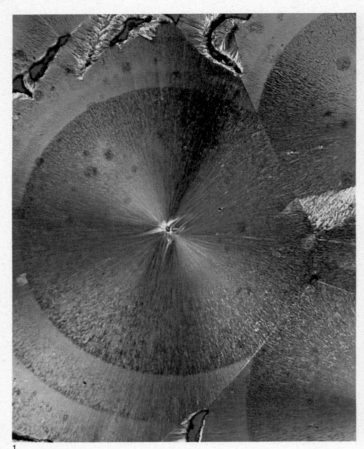

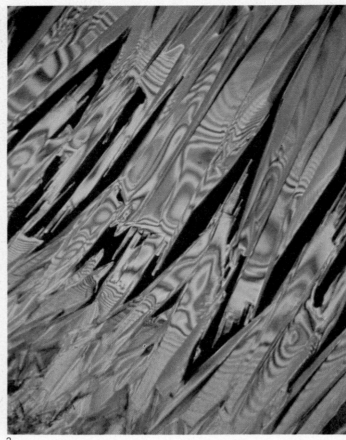

1. DDT was at one time regarded as a wonder chemical. A contact poison which disorganises the nervous systems of insects, it scored spectacular successes in controlling major diseases like malaria and typhoid. Between 1942 and 1952, according to one estimate, public health use of DDT prevented 100 million incidences of disease and saved 5 million lives worldwide.

But the DDT panacea was exploded in 1962 with publication of Rachel Carson's *Silent Spring*. Widely regarded as the catalyst of the ecology movement, Carson's book demonstrated that DDT was indiscriminately killing beneficial as well as harmful insects; that it was accumulating in food chains and even appearing in human tissues in disturbing amounts; and that mutant insect strains had evolved which were immune to its effects. As a result use of DDT has now been banned in Sweden and severely restricted in most other countries, including the USA and Canada.

MORTIMER ABRAMOWITZ, SUPERINTENDENT OF SCHOOLS, GREAT NECK, NEW YORK.

2. These rainbow-coloured slivers are crystals of ketone, a substance which accumulates in the blood when the chemical combustion of fat in the body is disturbed, for instance by starvation or severe diabetes. Analysis of blood samples for ketone is used by doctors to check whether the treatment of a diabetic is proving effective.

One of the effects of ketone accumulation is to make the breath smell of acetone. This may account for the "odour of sanctity" which saints were described as exuding after prolonged fasting.

JAMES M. BELL.

3. These exploding shafts of colour are produced by crystals of hippuric acid—a substance found in the urine of cattle and horses.

DR JOSEF GAHM. REPRODUCED FROM *ZEISS INFORMATION* NO. 61, BY PERMISSION OF CARL ZEISS.

4. Crystals of 2,4,6-trinitrotoluene, better known as TNT, the most effective of modern explosives.

TNT is derived from the petrochemical toluene, itself named after a small town in South America where "balsam of Tolu" was found as a natural resin. The explosive was first developed in the 19th century. Contrary to popular belief, TNT is remarkably resistant to impact and its inherent stability allows it to be stored for up to 20 years.

MORTIMER ABRAMOWITZ, SUPERINTENDENT OF SCHOOLS, GREAT NECK, NEW YORK.

5. Crystals of sulphur, one of the most versatile and essential elements on the planet. Early cultures used burning sulphur—or brimstone, as it was then called—to ward off evil spirits. The acrid fumes and ethereal blue flame were regarded as supernatural.

This mystical use of the element in temple sacrifices and rites is a probable origin of the belief that hellfire is fuelled by brimstone: a notion which, among certain fundamentalists, persists to this day.

MANFRED KAGE, COURTESY OF CARL ZEISS.

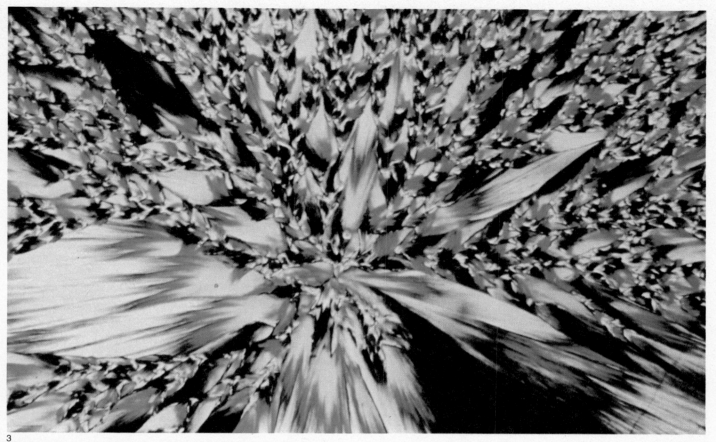

3

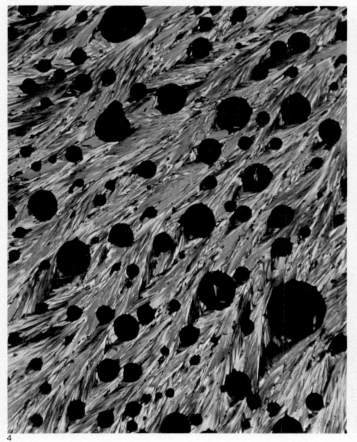

4

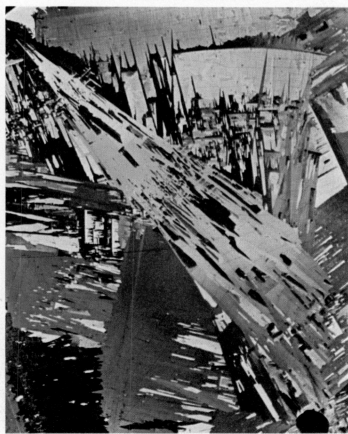

5

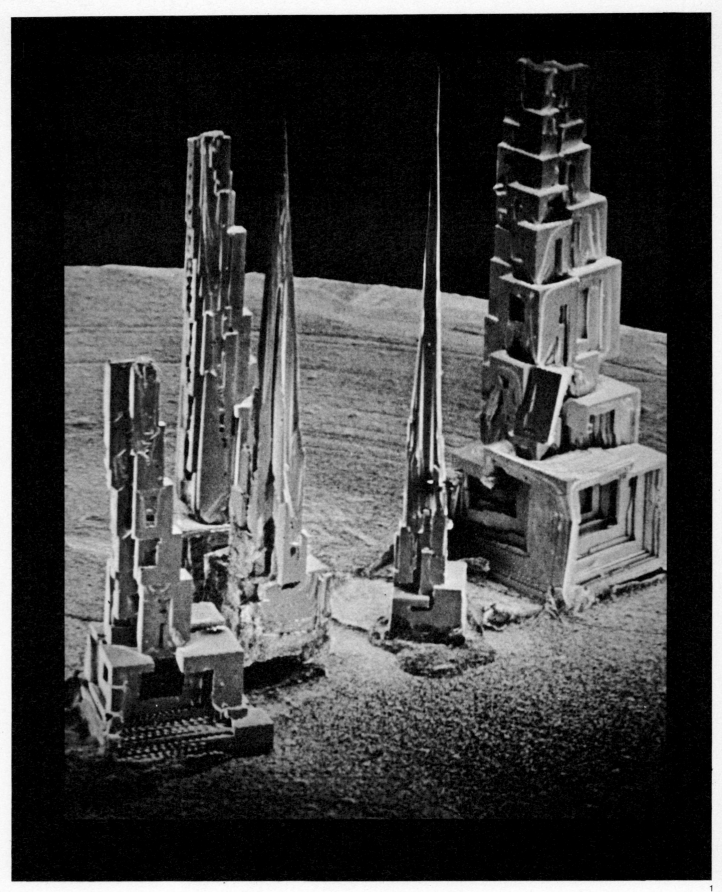

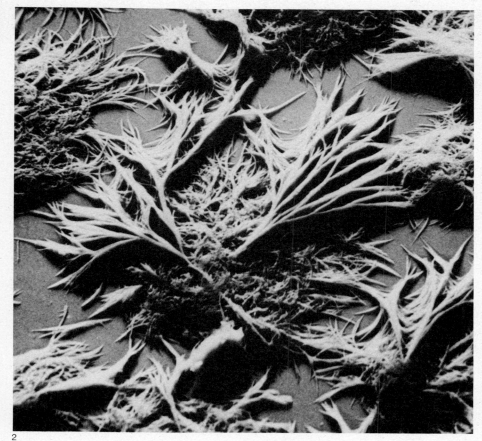

Whereas photography with light microscopes reveals the inner structure of a substance, the scanning electron microscope (or SEM) reveals its surface form and texture. The two instruments operate on entirely different principles. The ordinary microscope shines light through a very thin specimen. The SEM scans electrons bounced off the specimen's surface. Because it employs electrons, which have a much smaller wavelength than light, the SEM can achieve much higher magnifications.

1. These intricate spires and skyscrapers are a microscopic freak of nature. Magnified 60 times, they are crystals of lead tin telluride, an alloy used in the semi-conductor industry. Normally, such crystals grow in simple, uncomplicated shapes—so when researchers at Plessey's Allen Clark Research Centre spotted these unusual growths, they immediately remounted and photographed them. The reason for their extraordinary form remains a mystery.

COURTESY OF CAMBRIDGE SCIENTIFIC INSTRUMENTS. PHOTO BY PLESSEY LTD.

2.

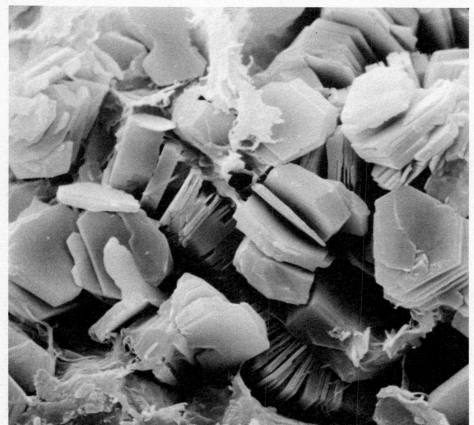

2. The delicate fronds of a crystal of sodium benzoate, a food preservative used in fruit juices, sauces, pie fillings and jams. Because of its low toxicity, up to 25 grams of sodium benzoate can be eaten per day without ill effects. It is one of the few food preservatives permitted in the USA—with the proviso that it cannot be used in ketchup. Oddly enough, sodium benzoate is also a powerful agent against corrosion in car radiators. X 850.

REPRODUCED BY KIND PERMISSION OF THE EASTMAN KODAK COMPANY AND KODAK LTD.

3. Flakes of kaolinite, the principal constituent of china clay and one of the three major clay minerals. The six-sided structure of the flakes is a unique crystal lattice formed by two separate crystal sheets becoming "welded" together. X 3000.

COURTESY OF THE EXXON PRODUCTION RESEARCH COMPANY. HOUSTON. TEXAS.

3

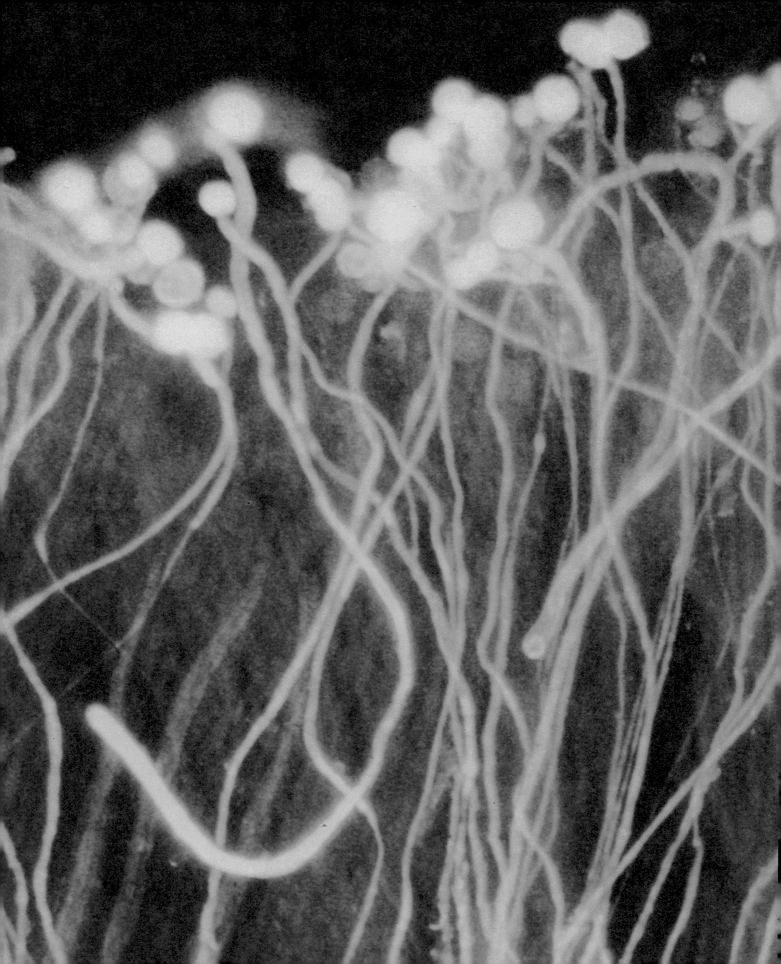

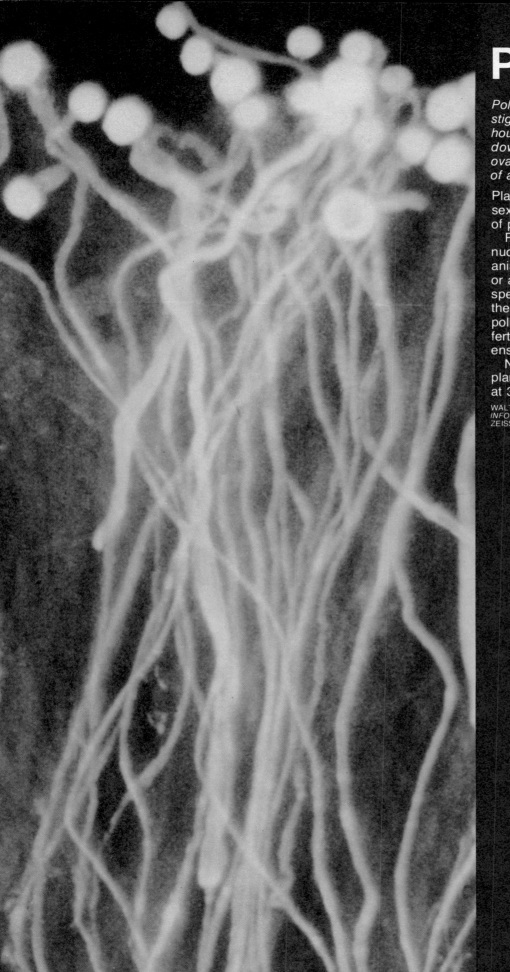

Plant World

Pollen grains have landed on the stigma of a tomato plant. Twelve hours later, they are sending tube downwards to search for the pla ovary: the first steps towards the of a new tomato plant.

Plants, like humans, reproduce sexually. Unlike humans, the sex of plants occurs at a distance.

Pollen grains, containing male nuclei (analogous to sperm in animals), are carried by wind, ins or animal to other plants of the sa species. If pollination is successfu the male nuclei travel down the pollen tubes to meet the ovules, a fertilisation is the result. From the ensuing seed, the new plant grow

Note: the world's tallest tomato plant grew to 20 feet and weighed at 34 lbs.

WALTER PREIL. REPRODUCED FROM *ZEISS INFORMATION* NO. 75 WITH PERMISSION OF CARL ZEISS.

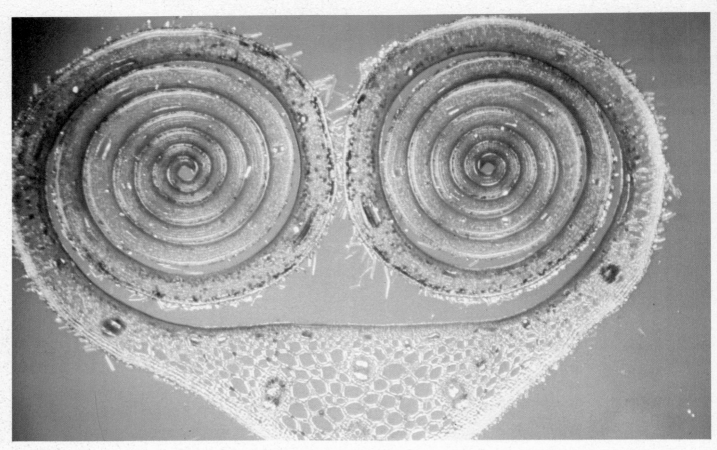

Not the head of an organic electric shaver, but the spiral pattern (in cross-section) of the bud of a waterlily leaf.

Man has often been accused of imitating nature. From the lifestyle of the humble waterlily—order *Nymphaeales*—we can learn much. Waterlilies have existed on Earth for over 100 million years and, because of the relative lack of environmental stresses in their aquatic habitat, have made few evolutionary changes from their ancient forms, save for the introduction of devices to protect their seeds from insect attack. Nymphaeales pollute not (except for their tendency to reproduce wildly, clogging lakes and rivers) neither do they consume more than is necessary for survival.

GENE COX, MICROCOLOUR LTD.

Much of Earth's surface is covered by vegetation. Essentially devices for converting the energy in sunlight into life-sustaining organic raw materials, such as sugar, these natural chemical factories also help maintain the planet's atmospheric balance by converting carbon dioxide into oxygen. Without the help of the plants, our oxygen-dependent species could not survive.

Leaves are the "lungs" of the plant. Pores on the leaf's outer layer allow the passage of gases directly from the atmosphere to the leaf's interior, where photosynthesis takes place. These pores–stomata–are controlled by a pair of guard-cells, one on either side of the pore. As valves, regulating the flow of carbon dioxide inwards and oxygen outwards, the stomata are remarkably efficient.

1. The underside of a carrot leaf. Each of the oval shapes is a stoma with its complement of two guard cells: some of which have responded to command. The result is the opening of several of the pores. The wavy lines are surface cell walls. In passing, it should be mentioned that the humble carrot originated in Afghanistan. X 785.

2. The lower surface of a sweet potato leaf. The sweet potato (which has been so changed by cultivation that botanists are unable to identify its wild ancestors) has evolved an intriguing defence against predatory insects. Hairs on the leaf surface exude a sticky substance, which traps the incautious insect. One of these stem-like natural snares, capped by its sphere of glue, is seen at centre of the picture. X 400.

3. Surface of a calceolaria petal. The curious "fingers" are extended surface cells, known as *papilli*. X 570.

4. Not fans at a Rolling Stones concert, but the papilli on the petal surface of the common wallflower. The ridges on the papilli give the flower its peculiar velvety texture. X 1050.

SCANNING ELECTRON MICROGRAPHS REPRODUCED BY COURTESY OF LONG ASHTON RESEARCH STATION. UNIVERSITY OF BRISTOL.

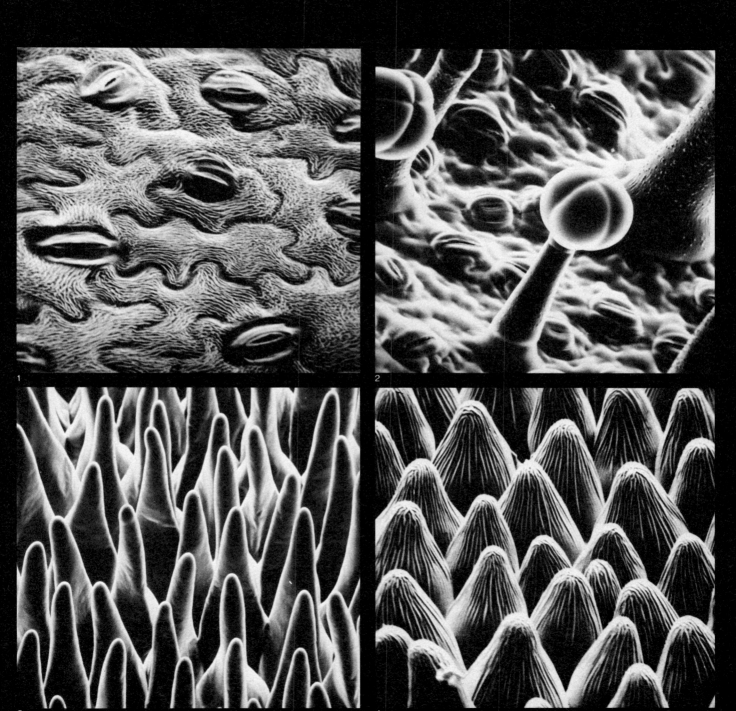

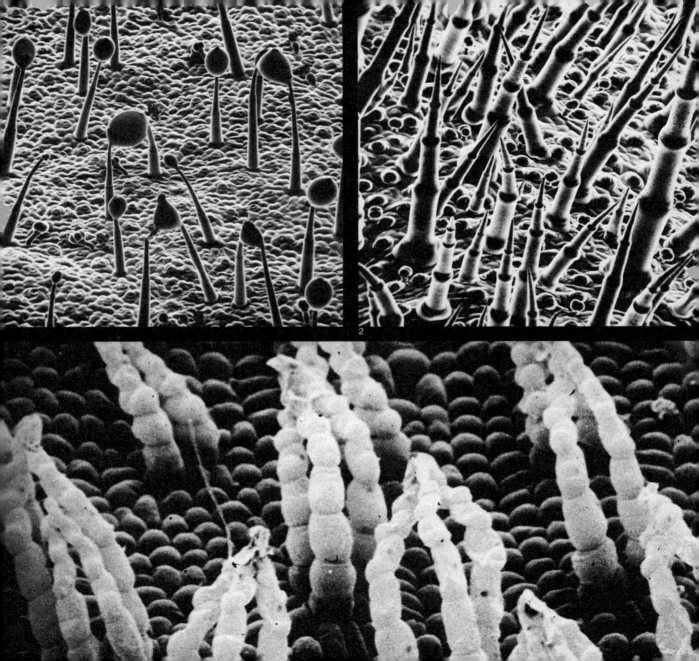

1. The underside of a thorn apple leaf. The thorn apple—*Datura stramonium*—is also known as Jimson Weed, a powerful psychedelic long used for religious purposes by American and Mexican Indians. Jimson Weed contains a number of strong alkaline poisons, one of which—scopolamine—is the "truth drug" beloved of spy dramas. X 100.

2. A microscopic forest of plant hairs covers the underside of a gloxinia leaf. These hairs, or *trichomes*, have a variety of uses for plants: as aids to climbing for more adventurous species, as containers for fragrant oils in plants like lavender, and as "hypodermics" for injecting poisons into marauding insects—the stinging nettle is an example. X 115.

3. Plants have developed many evolutionary mechanisms to ensure survival. Kariba weed is an African water weed which needs to stay on the surface of its aquatic habitat. Waterlogging is a problem for Kariba, but the plant copes in two ways. First, a coating of wax prevents Kariba's surface from wetting. If this device fails, mechanism number two comes into action: air pockets are trapped by the weed's surface hairs (shown in this micrograph) and restore its buoyancy. Unfortunately, Kariba has adapted so well that it is becoming something of a nuisance, clogging waterways and blocking dam sluices in reservoirs. X 260.

4. Scanning electron micrograph of hairs on a leaf of *Cannabis sativa*. Forensic scientists can identify microscopic amounts of cannabis by the characteristic effervescence of carbon dioxide from the leaf hairs after the addition of dilute acid. The result of such tests, for the cannabis user, are rarely pleasant. X 500.

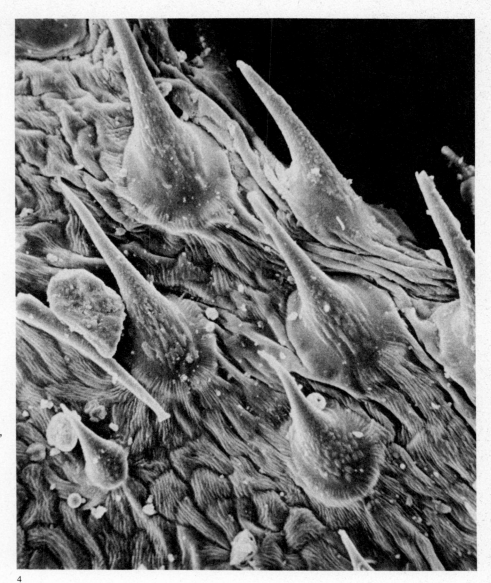

4

"Today the word cannabis *suggests not the centuries-old importance of hempen rope and hempen tissue, but the drug variously called hemp, cannabis, bhang, hashish, marijuana, pot, grass, etc. This, however, is due to a fortuitous circumstance, the very belated discovery by west European and American youth of the mildly intoxicating qualities of the hemp-leaf and seed . . .; and to the hysterical excitement of the authorities in those parts of the world at the growth of a habit of smoking hemp, a practice which, provided the leaf used be free from such dangerous impurities as opium, is demonstrably less dangerous from the health point of view than the smoking of tobacco.*

"But hemp is much more important as a fibre-plant than as a drug-plant . . . In the East, where its use as a stimulant has been tolerated for many centuries, it is clearly ancient in cultivation, since the names for it in Oriental languages—bhang, ganga, hashish—are all derivatives of the Sanskrit names bhanga *and* gangika.*"

Edward Hyams, *Plants in the Service of Man*, 1971.

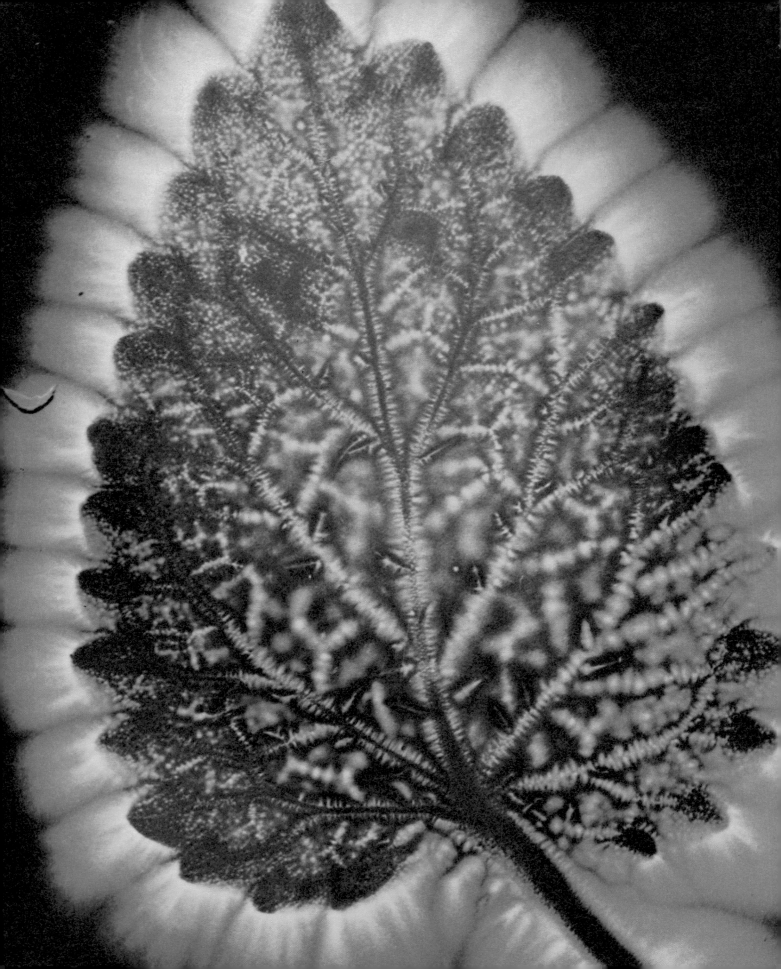

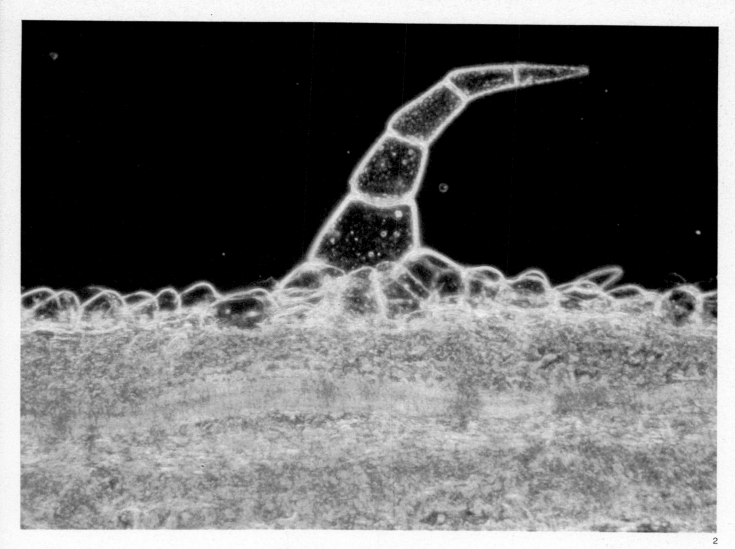

2

1. Kirlian photograph of an oak leaf taken by Viktor Adamenko, a leading Russian pioneer of electro-photography.

Pro-Kirlians believe that the technique makes visible a hitherto unknown form of organic energy. Kirlian photographs seem to show the presence of an "aura" common to all living things. This effect has been known to persist even when part of the object is removed before exposure – in one famous experiment, called the "phantom leaf," a leaf is sliced in half. After exposure, the finished electrograph shows the *whole* leaf.

V. G. ADAMENKO, MOSCOW, USSR. COURTESY OF JAMES C. HICKMAN, 3101 WASHINGTON STR., SAN FRANCISCO, CALIF. 94115. AS ORIGINALLY PUBLISHED IN *ELECTROPHOTOGRAPHY* BY E. LANE. AND/OR PRESS, BERKELEY, CALIFORNIA.

2. Light microscope cross-section through a hair on the leaf of a coleus, one of the most common of household plants.

BIOPHOTO ASSOCIATES.

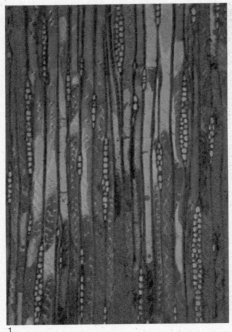

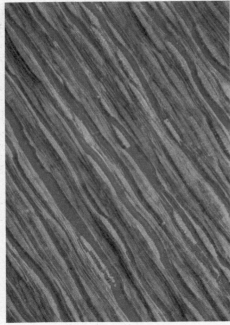

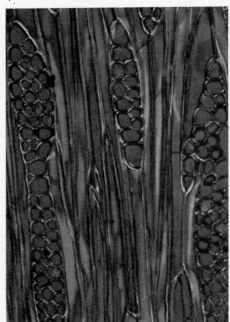

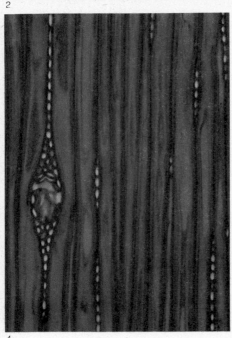

Although they have no "heart," trees, like humans, possess a circulatory system.

The trunk of a tree has three layers: an outer coating of bark, a core of pith, and a cylindrical middle of wood—the xylem.

Embedded within the xylem are lines of specialised cells, ferrying water and essential nutrients from root to leaf. In the photographs (cross-sections through the wood), these cells have been cut vertically, as if they were split hairs. The top-to-bottom dark lines delineate cell walls. Other cell groups, transporting water and nutrients across the trunk from xylem to bark and vice-versa, appear as spindle-shaped structures. The tiny circular or oval objects inside the spindles are cells cut "end on," analogous to salami slices.

1. *Sequoia semperverens*, more commonly known as the Coast Redwood. Redwoods flourished in many parts of the world before the great Ice Ages, but changes in climate and geology have since driven them to their present refuge, the coastal fog belt of California. Coast Redwoods boast the world's tallest tree, the 362 feet high "Howard Libbey Tree."

JAMES M. BELL

2. The carpet-like fibres of Pear Tree wood. Pear trees have been cultivated at least since Roman times. By the Renaissance, 232 varieties of edible pear were known, and it is said that Cosimo III, the Medici Duke of Tuscany, had no fewer than 209 varieties served at his table during a single season.

JAMES M. BELL.

3. Sassafras wood. The Sassafras, an aromatic-leaved tree of the laurel family, is no stranger to North Americans. Extracts of Sassafras bark and root are used to flavour root beer and perfumes, home-made medicines and tea.

MORTIMER ABRAMOWITZ. SUPERINTENDENT OF SCHOOLS. GREAT NECK, NEW YORK.

4. Wood of a species of Pine. The pine family includes the world's oldest tree, a bristlecone pine which probably began its growth on a Nevadan hillside in 2926 BC—4,900 years ago.

GENE COX. MICROCOLOUR LTD.

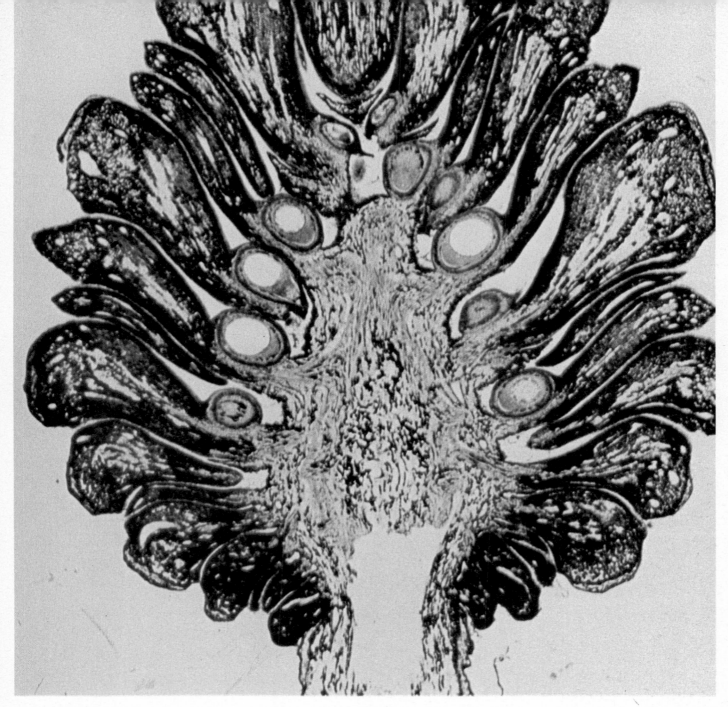

The complicated reproductive cycle of the pine tree lasts two years and involves both sexual and asexual phases.

During the asexual stage, pines bear both male (small and stunted) and female (large and woody) cones on the same tree. The cones in turn contain pairs of "microspores" of the same gender as the cone.

The microspores are the first cells of the sexual stage, which again takes a year to complete. During autumn, the female microspores develop into ovules in the female cones. In the spring of the next year, the ovules are ready for pollination. The female cone spreads her scales apart, allowing pollen grains containing the paired male microspores to sift among them. If fertilisation is successful, two nuclei are produced—the first cells of the new asexual generation—and the cycle begins again.

The photomicrograph shows a female pine cone in cross-section. The ovules, egg-like in appearance, are visible at the roots of the cone's scales.

GENE COX. MICROCOLOUR LTD.

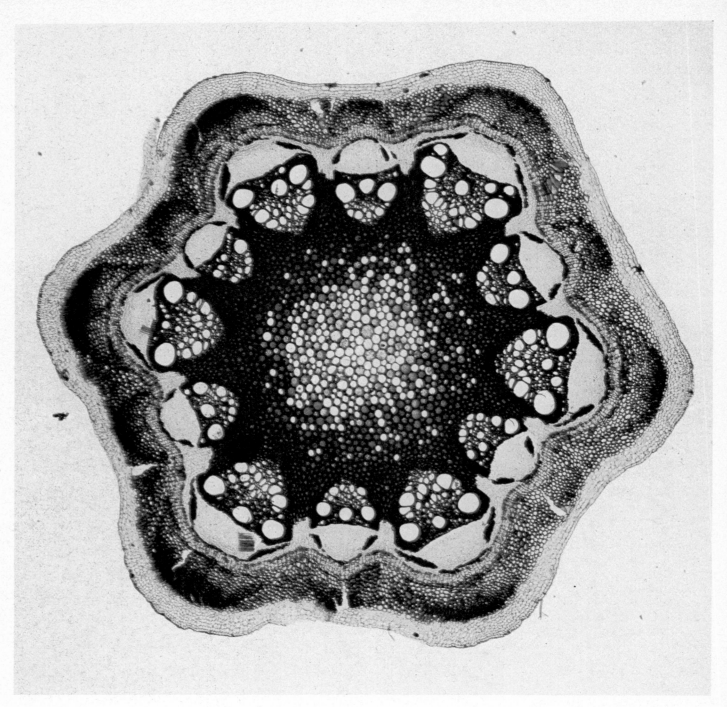

Light microscope cross-section through the stem of Old Man's Beard, *Clematis vitalba*.

Clematis is a climbing plant, native to Europe and North Africa, with several relatives in North America. It lives, in effect, as a parasite on other plants: its leaf stalks twine around the host's branches, thus gaining support. Although the stem is a mere inch across, clematis can attain heights of up to 40 feet.

They are everywhere, but we are rarely aware of their presence. They are neither plant nor animal, but they are among the most successful of all terrestrial organisms. They have been on Earth since the Precambrian Era, more than 570 million years ago.

They are the fungi, a class of perhaps 100,000 different organisms ranging from the common mushroom to bread mould. Fungi are essential to many household and industrial processes, including the making of bread, beer, wine, antibiotics, vitamins and organic acids. Yet they are parasites, living off plants and sometimes animals. They also feed off decaying organic material, and some of them are deadly. One species of fungus was responsible for the great Irish potato famine of the 1840's, others have ruined entire crops of tobacco and grapes, and a third type acts as a "fifth column" in the human body itself.

Most primitive fungi reproduce asexually: a multiplying device designed to produce hundreds of individuals identical with the parent organism. The young fungi spores develop inside a membrane, the *sporangium*, which initially contains a single mass of protoplasm. The mass develops dividing walls, the individual spores are formed, and then the sporangium bursts open and the spores are shot out, accomplishing the rapid and widespread dissemination of the species. One species, *Pilobolus*, shoots entire sporangia several feet by a unique explosive mechanism.

After release from the sporangium, each spore—now termed a "zoospore"—travels under its own power until it finally comes to rest. After germination, the zoospore forms a complete individual.

In this series of micrographs, spores of *Thraustochytrium kinnei*—an aquatic fungus—are seen developing in the sporangium. Eventually, it breaks open, and the zoospores are released to make their own way in the world.

H.-H. HEUNERT. FROM "MICROTECHNIQUE FOR THE OBSERVATION OF LIVING MICROORGANISMS," ZEISS INFORMATION NO. 81. WITH PERMISSION OF CARL ZEISS.

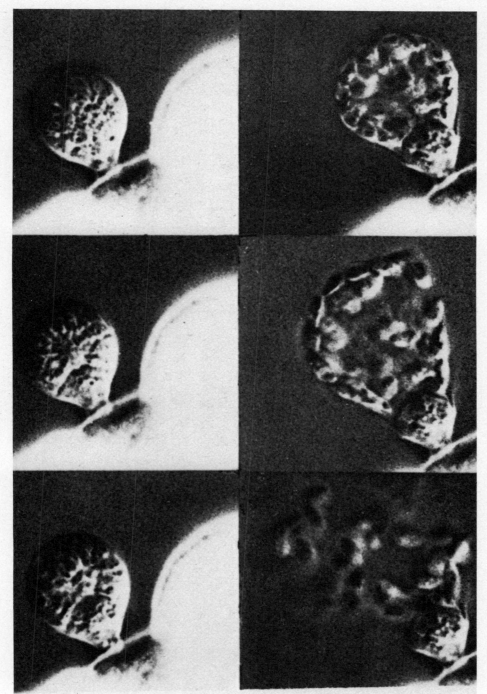

Pollen grains, containing the male components of plants, are an essential part of their reproductive process. To maximise a species' chances of survival, plants and trees will produce vast amounts of pollen: a single flowering shoot of Austrian pine may scatter 22,500,000 grains in a single season.

Pollen grains are tiny – the largest are only one quarter of a millimetre across – but their size belies their sturdiness. The outermost layer of a pollen grain, exine, is one of the most extraordinarily resistant organic materials known, and will even withstand laboratory attacks from powerful acids heated to 300°C.

Pollen grains can be carried by wind, animal or insect for hundreds of miles – they have been found 400 miles off the Atlantic coast – and have shapes designed to ensure their widespread diffusion.

Most grains, in fact, fail to find a suitable plant target. Those which land in lakes or bogs are often preserved in sediment, and their fossilised remains can be dated as far back as the Paleozoic Era.

1. Grains of a species of pine, equipped with twin bladders of spongy tissue. These sacs reduce the grain's air density and give it added lift.

DR. L. M. BEIDLER, FLORIDA STATE UNIVERSITY.

2. Pollen of Giant Ragweed. Each year, the Ragweed's turban-like flowers launch millions of such grains. It's a process many of us have cause to regret, for Ragweed pollen, spread by the wind, is a major cause of hay fever. As sufferers know, proteins triggered from the grain on contact with nasal tissue in turn release histamines, to which the unhappy allergic reacts with runny eyes and dripping nose.

DR PATRICK ECHLIN, DEPARTMENT OF BOTANY. UNIVERSITY OF CAMBRIDGE.

3. Grains of Horse Chestnut, which is pollinated by insects rather than the wind. As an added enticement to its pollinator, the bumblebee, the Horse Chestnut provides "landing lights" in the form of coloured patterns on its flowers. These indicate the location of sweet-smelling nectar glands.

DR PATRICK ECHLIN, DEPARTMENT OF BOTANY. UNIVERSITY OF CAMBRIDGE.

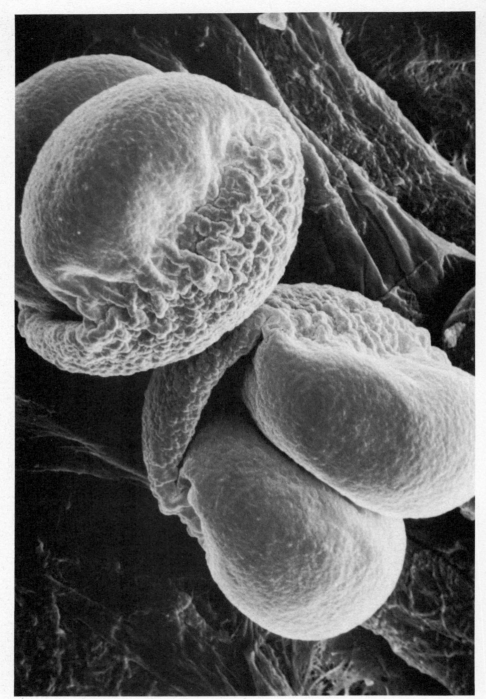

1

4. Pollen of Globe Flower, which extends its survival prospects by equipping each flower with up to 15 hidden nectar glands, thus making itself irresistible to insects.

DR PATRICK ECHLIN, DEPARTMENT OF BOTANY. UNIVERSITY OF CAMBRIDGE.

5. The receptor for incoming pollen grains—the stigma of a polyanthus flower.

SCANNING ELECTRON MICROGRAPH REPRODUCED BY COURTESY OF THE LONG ASHTON RESEARCH STATION, UNIVERSITY OF BRISTOL.

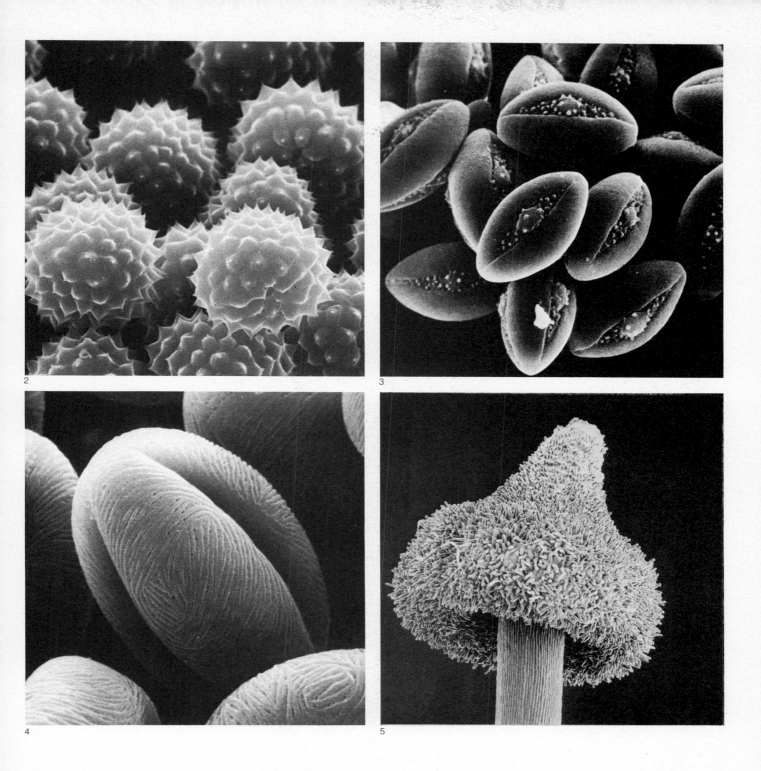

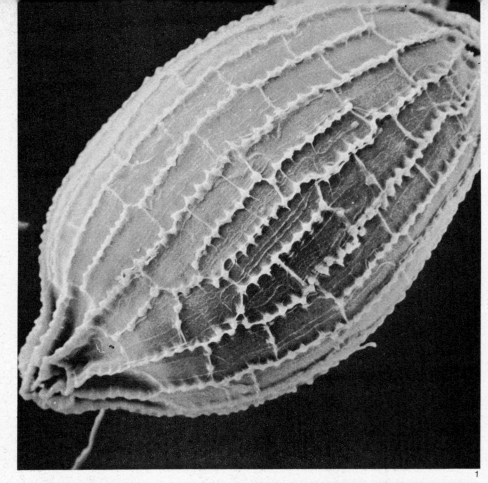

Successful pollination results in the formation of a seed, which carries within it the embryo of a new plant or tree. The seed will be dispersed, like the pollen before it, by insect, animal, wind or water to make its own way in the world.

1. Seed of Yellow-eyed Grass, a swamp plant which grows in tropical and sub-tropical areas. The seed is swollen with air, probably so that it can float on the swamp's surface.

2. Seed of a British species of Blinks. Blinks is also a denizen of wet places, and its seed is again constructed so that it can float.

The cell is life's lowest structural denominator. Higher life forms are complex arrangements of millions of cells, most of which are so specialised that they cannot exist outside the organism. But in other organisms, a single cell makes up the entire individual.

They are the protozoans, the "first animals." An ancient group of organisms, some of them straddle the dividing line between plant and animal, combining the plant's ability to photosynthesise – to convert sunlight into chemical energy – with the animal characteristic of movement.

We know of at least 80,000 distinct species of protozoans, some living freely in soil and water, others as parasites. Whereas the "free livers" must tolerate harsh environmental conditions, parasitic protozoans live a relatively sheltered life within the host body. However, survival of the parasite depends on that of its host. When a host dies, finding a new one is a risky business. To compensate for the low odds, parasite protozoans reproduce frantically.

Euglena spirogyra, the classic plant/animal. In sunlight, Euglena grows as a plant; by night, as an animal. The creature's shape is defined by the pellicle, a helical "winding sheet" of protein strips. Inside the cell are two storage granules containing food reserves. This particular free-living protozoan has been squashed to enhance visibility – part of the creature's insides are emerging bottom left.

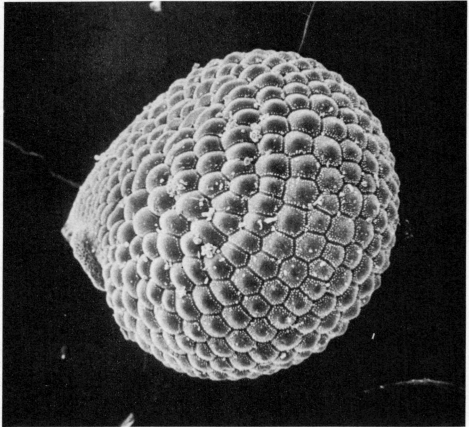

1

2

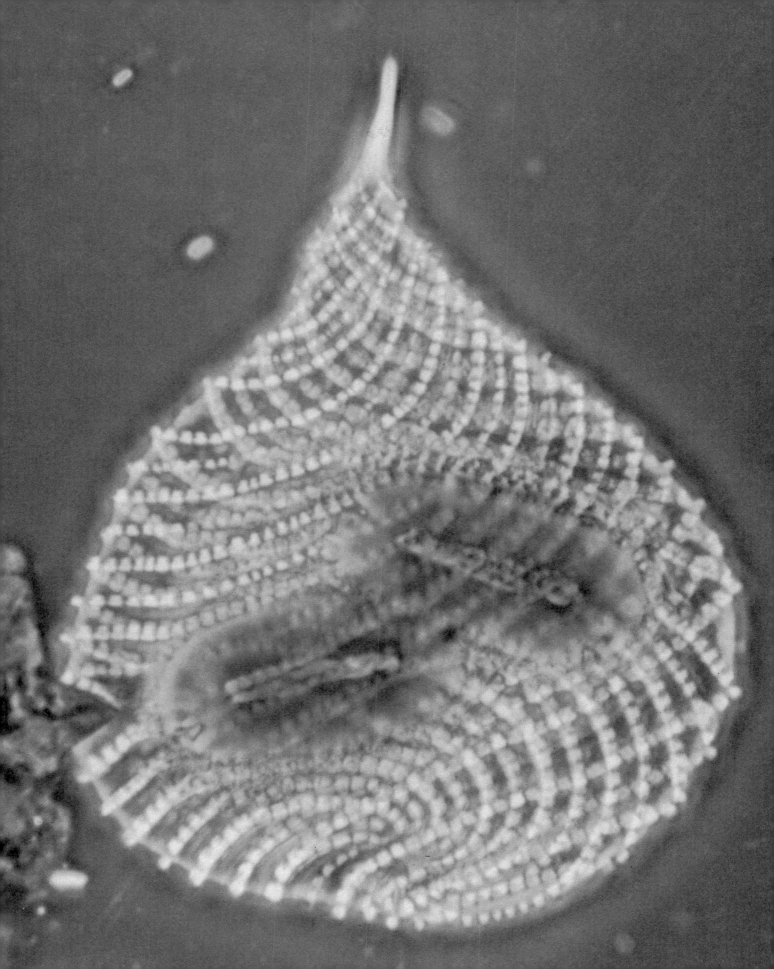

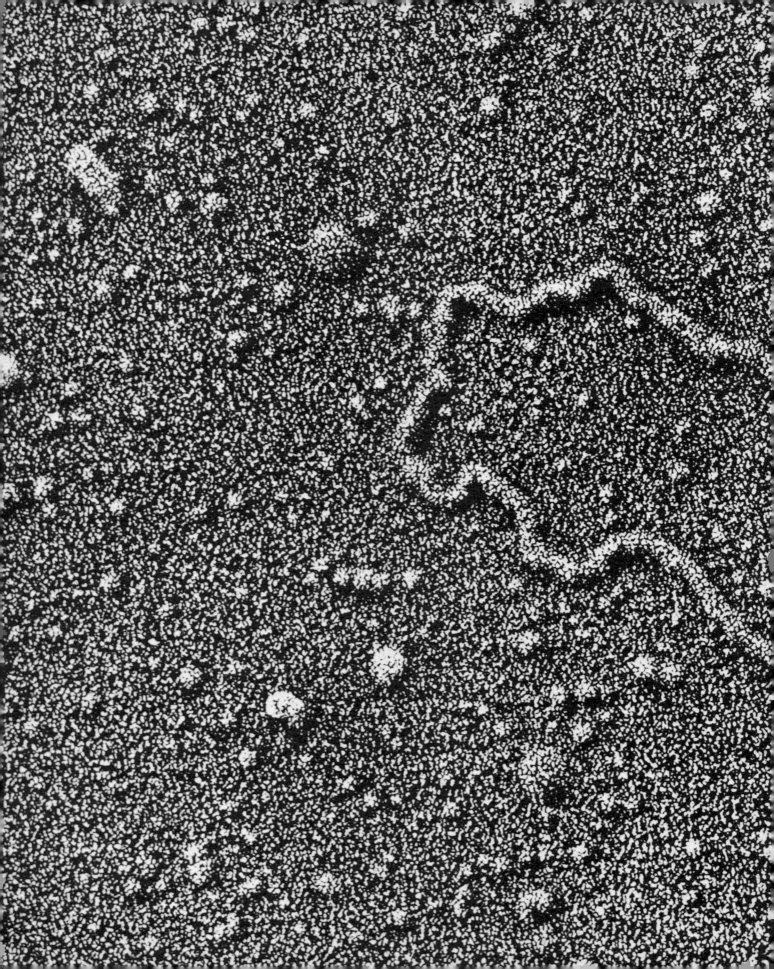

Genesis

It is not often that the real turning points of history are photographed, but this could be one of them. It is the actual molecule of DNA used in the first successful experiment in "genetic engineering."

This innocent loop, enlarged some 250,000 times, is a *plasmid*—a freelance piece of DNA which replicates itself and can be used as a carrier of genetic information from one cell to another. It is part of the coding for a benevolent bacteria which is found in our intestines, *Eschericia coli*, and was used in the first of three historic experiments carried out in 1973 by Stanley N. Cohen and colleagues at Stanford University.

The experiment consisted in cutting up two E. coli plasmids, making a composite genetic code out of the fragments, and putting it back into a living cell. In a later experiment, DNA from an unrelated bacteria was added to an E. coli plasmid, giving it an entirely new characteristic—resistance to penicillin. Shortly afterwards, a cross-species transplant was carried out when genetic information from a toad was grafted to bacterial DNA.

These techniques, especially the chemical cutting and gluing agents, only became available in the early 1970's, but the threats and promises of genetic engineering are already awesome. It might enable us to eradicate hereditary diseases, even to control our own evolution. But the slightest mistake could be catastrophic. For instance, E. coli might one day be "armed," purely as an experiment, with the DNA for cholera. The bacteria, essential to human life, would then be as dangerous as a nuclear missile. Should it escape from the laboratory to breed in the outside world, there could be a virtually unstoppable epidemic, more devastating than the Black Death.

PROFESSOR STANLEY N. COHEN. REPRODUCED FROM "THE MANIPULATION OF GENES," COHEN, S. N., *SCIENTIFIC AMERICAN*, JULY 1975.

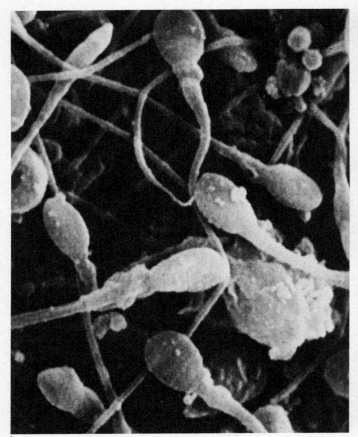

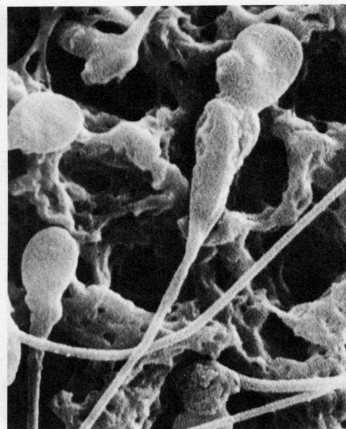

1. The problem of infertility has affected much of human history from private tragedies to the succession of kings. One reason for it is graphically illustrated in these scanning electron micrographs of human sperm. The first picture is a sample of the 500 million or so healthy sperm from a single ejaculation. At their microscopic scale they are fast, agile organisms which can travel at up to one-tenth of an inch a minute.

2. Crippled sperm, unable to make the marathon swim to the uterus, probably because of the gross distortion of their necks. The background is dried seminal fluid.

BIOPHOTO ASSOCIATES. X 3175.

1. The sperm of a bull, legendary symbol of sexual potency. But the myth is inappropriate, and reflects human preoccupations rather than reality. Compared by body-weight, man has the largest penis of all the primates. And woman, alone among female animals, is capable of an orgasm.

2. The sperm of a snail swoop and dive in unison. The snail's sex life is unbelievably complicated. To start with, they are hermaphrodites, each possessing a vagina and two penises. Mating can take up to twelve hours, which is understandable, and the foreplay involves firing solid (and often lethal) darts into each others' bodies.

T. E. THOMPSON, ZOOLOGY DEPARTMENT, UNIVERSITY OF BRISTOL.

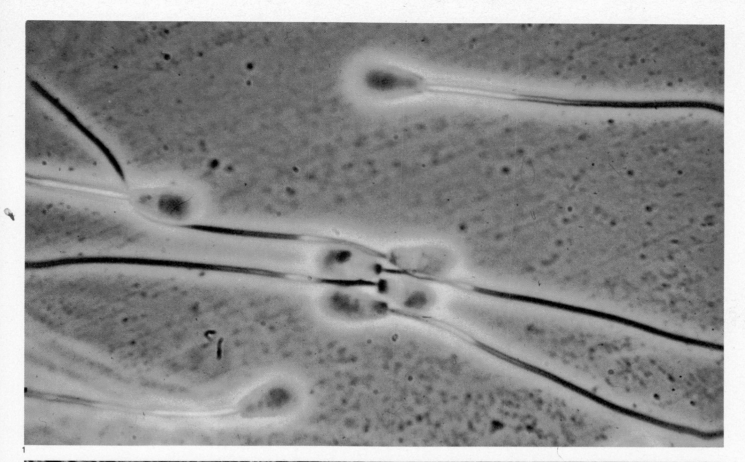

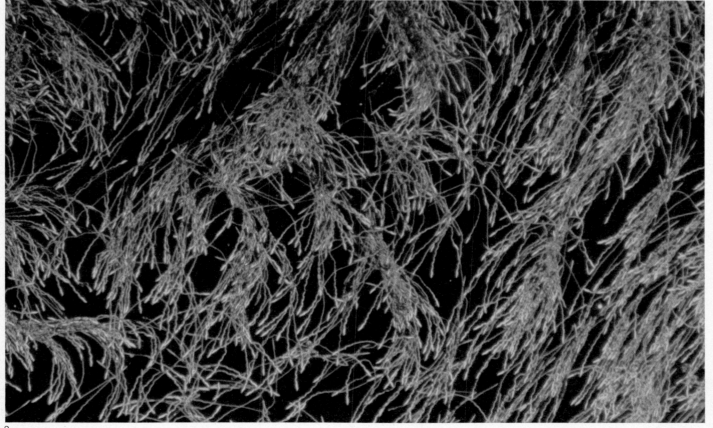

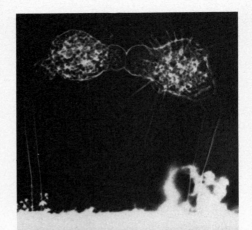

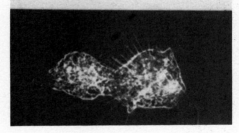

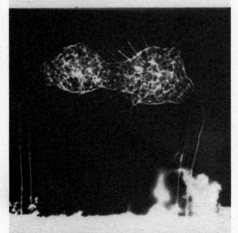

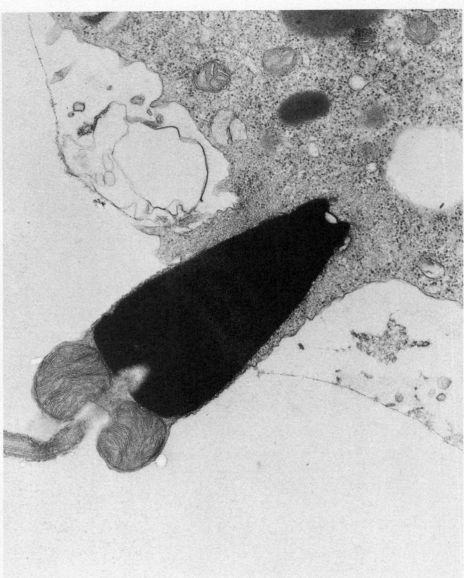

The strange conjugation of suctoria, as one leans towards the other and tears off its head.

Although they are only single cells, suctoria are complicated and self-sufficient creatures which live in ponds, attaching themselves to stationary pieces of weed, and living off other small organisms floating in the water. They paralyse them with their spines and then suck them into the cell in a way that is not fully understood.

They actually reproduce by forming buds at the base of the cell. The buds then break loose and swim off on their own.

H.-H. HEUNERT. FROM "MICROTECHNIQUES FOR THE OBSERVATION OF LIVING ORGANISMS," *ZEISS INFORMATION* NO. 81, BY PERMISSION OF CARL ZEISS.

The precise moment of reproduction as a sperm penetrates the membrane of a sea-urchin's egg. The dark wedge is the head of the sperm, which contains the genetic code. The grey shape behind it is the energy cell that provides power for the tail.

The sperm has digested the egg's surface coating of sugary protein and entered. Now the egg's internal fluid welds itself to the skin of the sperm, and draws it in to complete the mating. In some unknown way, the entry of one sperm prevents any others getting in, probably because of rapid changes in the egg's surface coating.

PROFESSOR EVERETT ANDERSON. FROM "SPERM-EGG FUSION IN THE SEA URCHIN," E. ANDERSON, *JOURNAL OF CELLULAR BIOLOGY*, 37:514-539, BY COURTESY OF THE AUTHOR AND PERMISSION OF THE ROCKEFELLER UNIVERSITY PRESS.

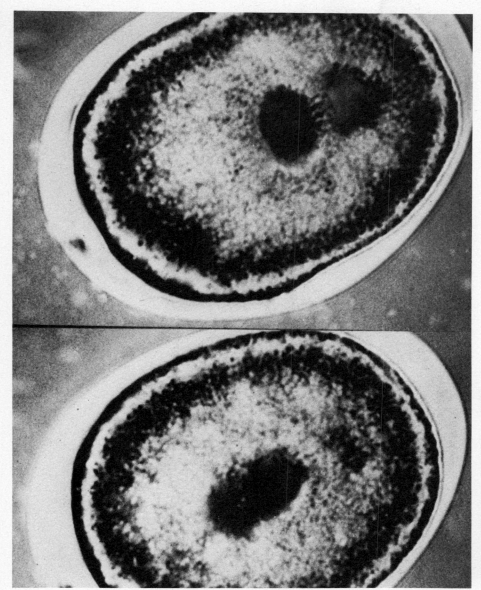

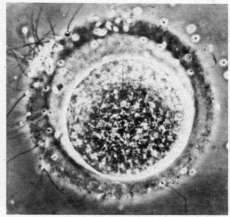

The act of fertilisation, as the warhead of the sperm finds its genetic target within the egg of a nematode worm.

Once inside the egg, the head of the sperm dissolves. Its load of DNA is released and drifts inexorably towards the egg's nucleus, and they combine.

H.-H. HEUNERT. FROM "MICROTECHNIQUES FOR THE OBSERVATION OF LIVING ORGANISMS," *ZEISS INFORMATION* NO. 81, BY PERMISSION OF CARL ZEISS.

Frustrated sperm continue to dance around a human egg after one of them has penetrated the outer skin. The shadow of the successful sperm can be seen as a dark line floating down towards the nucleus from the top of the ovum.

The genetic programme is now running. Within 36 hours the egg will divide for the first time and begin the slow process of building the 6,000,000,000,000 cells of an adult body.

DR LANDRUM B. SHETTLES. GIFFORD MEMORIAL HOSPITAL INC.. RANDOLPH. VERMONT.

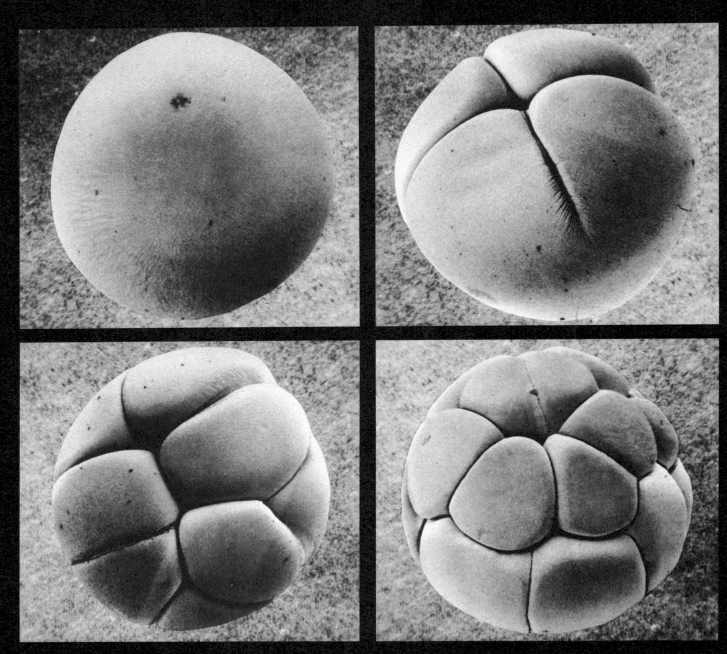

The cell divides. An egg crosses the boundary from haploid to diploid and takes the first steps to becoming a frog.

The embryo stays the same size for some time. The cells continue to divide until they form a hollow sphere, which then folds in on itself, layer upon layer, to form a complicated ball still not much larger than the original egg. Only then does it start to grow. The outer layers turn into skin and the nervous system, the middle ones become the internal organs, and those at the centre grow into bones and muscles.

These scanning electron micrographs show in turn the single-cell, four-celled, eight-celled and sixteen-celled stages of frog development. X 99.

DR L. M. BEIDLER. FLORIDA STATE UNIVERSITY.

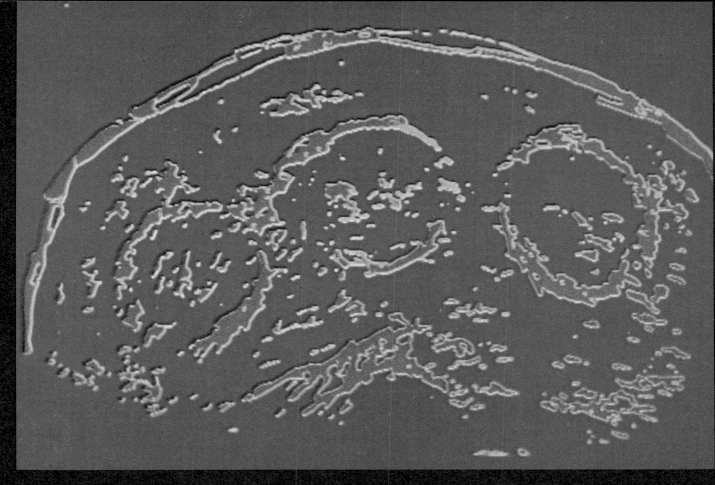

A "sound" picture of human triplets in the womb.

It seems appropriate that scientists should employ sonar, or "ultrasonography" as the medical version is known, to study our nine months of underwater existence. Sound waves are used because x-rays are potentially harmful and computers are able to reassemble the complex echoes into pictures from any angle. This, for instance, is a cross-section through the mother's body, looking down on the heads of the three children in her womb.

Multiple births are usually caused by more than one egg being fertilised. More rarely, as in the case of identical twins, it is the result of several sperm penetrating the same egg.

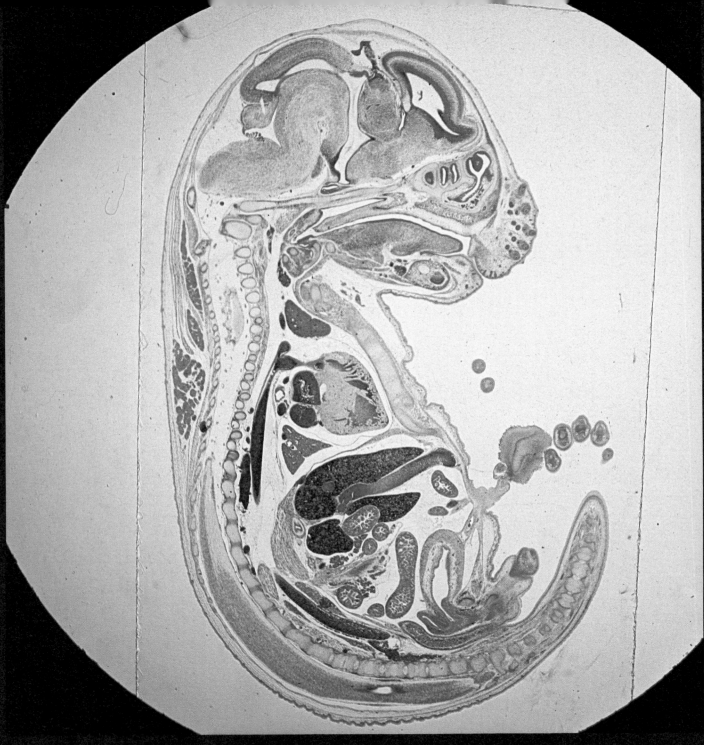

The embryo of a mouse.

A water flea gives birth to its young. It is commonly known that these fleas are fed to goldfish, but some of their other talents are less familiar. For instance, they are believed to eat by taking food in through their back passages; and they are as good a guide to the weather as dried seaweed, because they precisely regulate the number of their offspring according to environmental conditions.

Daphnia, like land fleas, lead a highly active life and have well developed escape reflexes. When attacked, some of them can perform a high speed abortion to give their young a chance of survival.

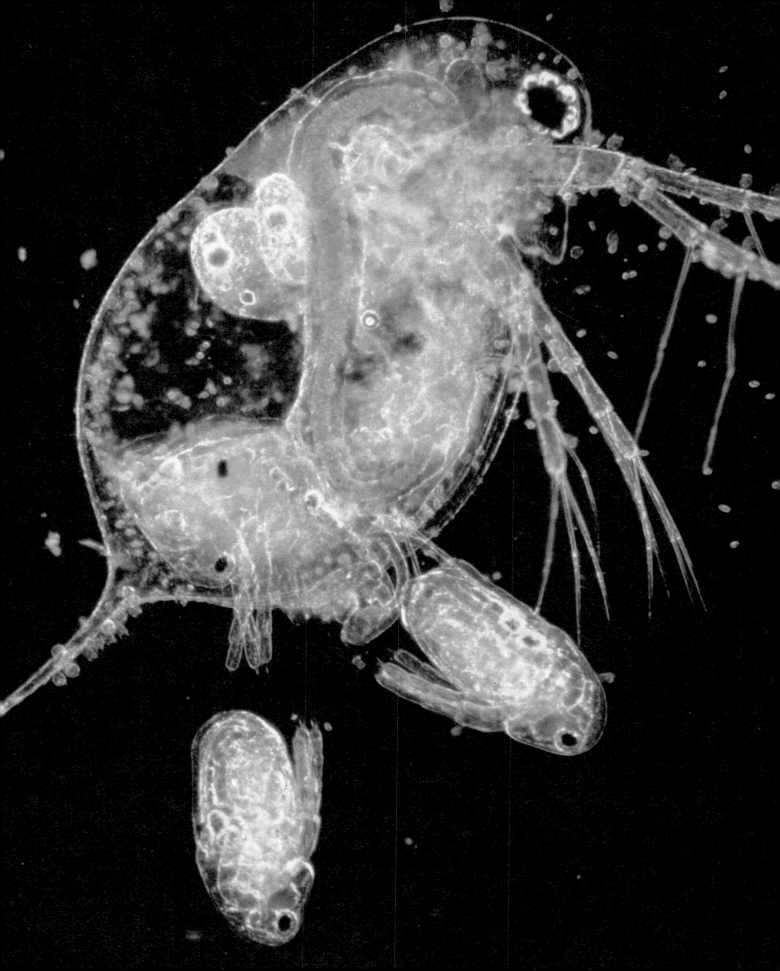

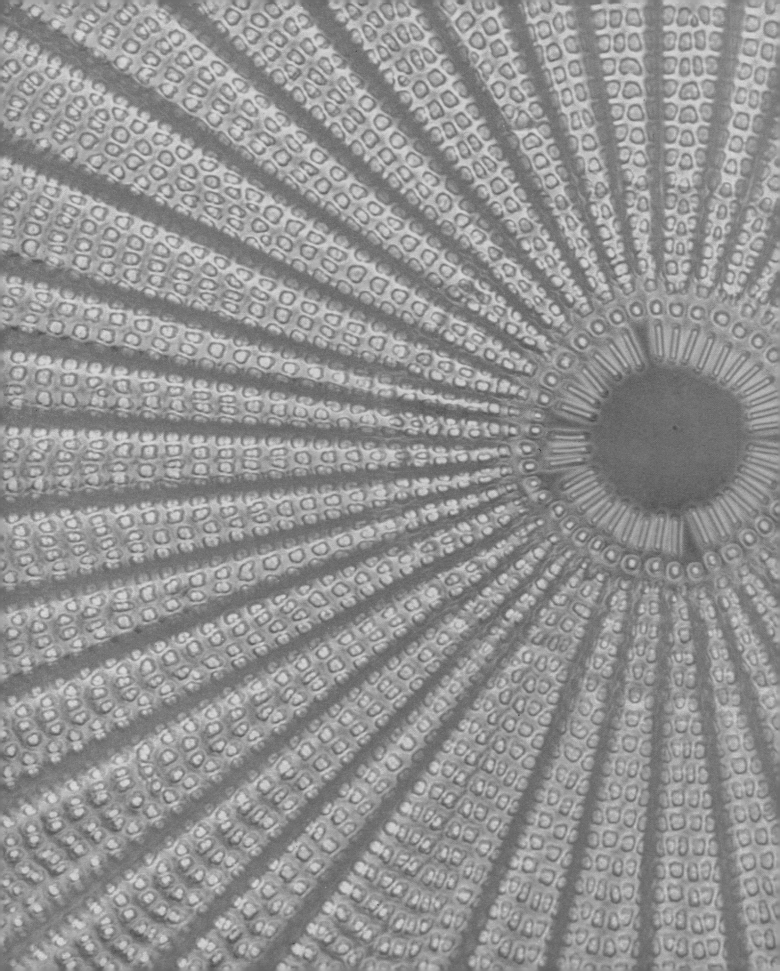

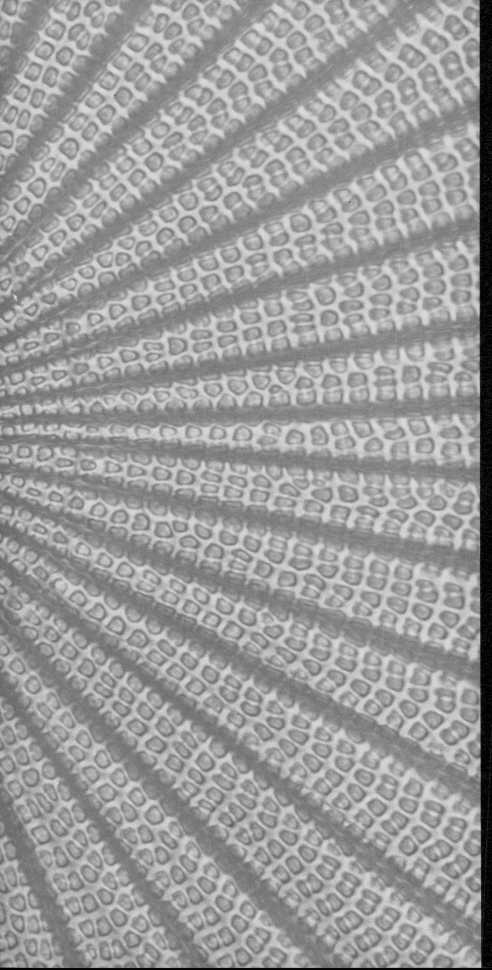

Water World

Plankton are among the oldest, arguably the most beautiful and probably the least known form of life on the planet. The whole pyramid of marine life depends on them, and they occur in such countless billions that they have made a major contribution to geology. Yet only recently has it been possible to look into their world of liquid engineering, where gravity has no meaning and space is defined by temperature. Some are next to invisible. Others are so small that a hundred or more could swim through the eye of a needle side by side.

Yet they have evolved an astonishing variety, from transparent flying snails to the opal skeletons of radiolaria. There are boggle-eyed larvae, foraminifera which construct their microscopic architecture from flakes of mica and sponge spicules, and the tiny mobile plants called diatoms.

Close-up of a diatom. Seen through a light microscope, it appears to be rainbow-coloured because the holes are fine enough to produce interference patterns.

MORTIMER ABRAMOWITZ. SUPERINTENDENT OF SCHOOLS. GREAT NECK. NEW YORK

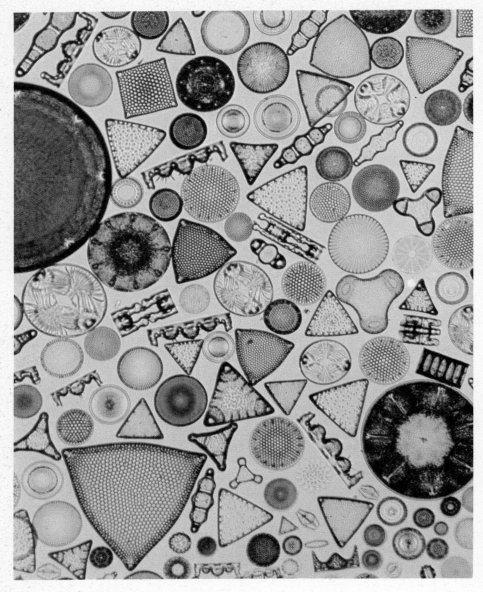

A collection of diatoms. Victorians amused themselves by arranging them into perfectly symmetrical patterns on microscope slides. Modern photographers prefer a less formal approach.

GENE COX, MICROCOLOUR LTD.

1. This intricate calcium architecture is the skeleton of a diatom, a few thousandths of an inch across – just one of the countless billions which make up the deposits of chalk, sand and diatomaceous earth around the world.

2. The geometry of diatoms is so precise that they are used to test microscopes. The pictures opposite, which are enlarged up to 1500 times, were taken by scanning electron microscope.

3. Diatoms reproduce when the "lid" of one "box" becomes the bottom of another, or vice-versa. If the lid reproduces, and then generates the box, the offspring is the same size; but if the box reproduces, and then forms a lid, each generation is smaller.

4. Unlike microorganisms such as forams and radiolaria, diatoms are plants and capable of photosynthesis. Most living things in the seven seas are directly dependent on their ability to harness sunlight.

5. This fossil of a foram is so small that five or six of them would fit on a single full-stop. The White Cliffs of Dover are largely composed of the remains of these tiny marine animals. Geologists use them to accurately date strata, and oil companies employ foram experts when they are prospecting for new deposits.

6. The skeleton of this radiolaria is made from a kind of animal "glass." When the animal was alive, only the silicon spines were visible, projecting from a ball of waving tendrils feeding on still smaller species of microorganism. But now, with its elegant skeleton exposed, it is just a wastebin for bits of organic debris.

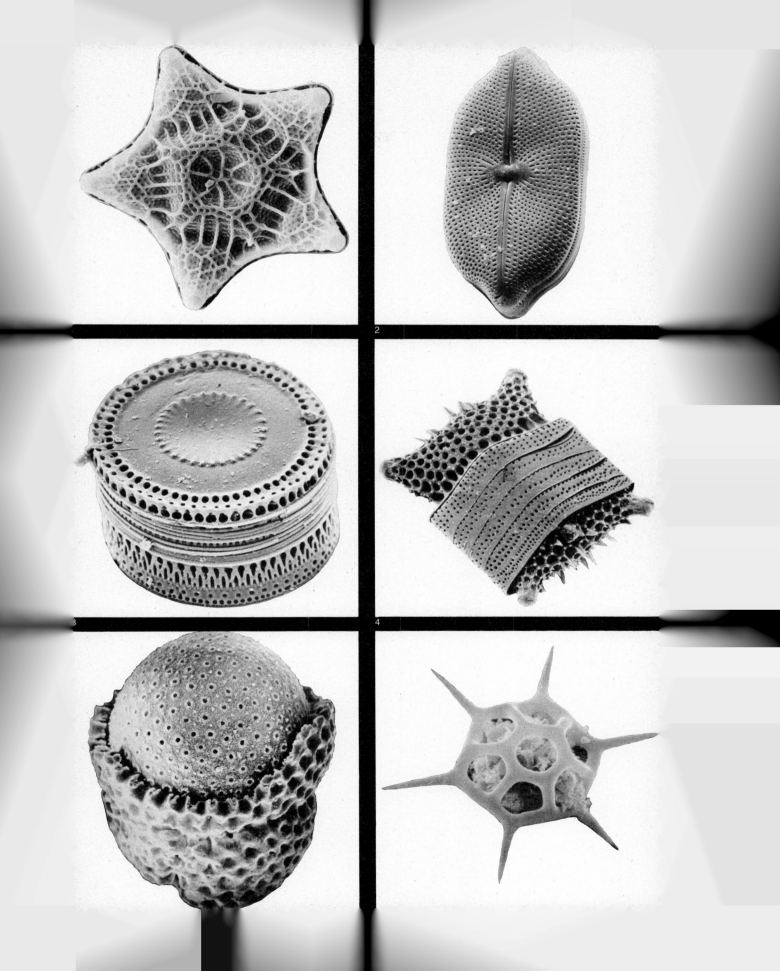

1. The larva of a mantid shrimp. One of the commonest forms of plankton are the larvae of larger animals living on the ocean floor. In this case it is the offspring of a tropical shrimp, rather like a praying mantis.

All that is visible in normal light are two apparently unrelated black dots. But using the technique of dark-field illumination, the whole structure appears, the dots become baleful eyes, and the bunches of muscles in the limbs produce a delicate blue interference colour.

2. A micro-snail in full flight. Water snails, which abound in coastal waters, are similar to their garden relatives except that they are far more active. They "fly" through the water on a wing-like foot equipped with flapping extensions which produce a crude but directional flight-path. But somehow the power ratio is all wrong. So strong are the beats that the snail's body appears to move up and down instead of its "wings."

3. A solitary, and nearly transparent, salp. These sea-squirts, about 3cm long, propel themselves about with a reciprocating water jet. They spend much of their lives attached nose-to-tail in chain-like colonies up to 30cm. long. The water jets allow the colonies to remain mobile.

The salps' main predator is an unpleasant creature, the female *phronima,* which swims up their blow-holes and eats them from the inside. It then uses their shell, open fore and aft, as a perambulator in which to carry about its young.

4. The larva of a "heart" urchin, a five-pointed creature like a starfish. The larva develops from an egg, and later undergoes a strange metamorphosis, when the entire adult form grows from its stomach. A piece of gut tissue detaches itself and settles down to become an urchin, while the rest of the body, still beating its ciliated arms, simply starves to death.

PHOTOS BY OXFORD SCIENTIFIC FILMS.

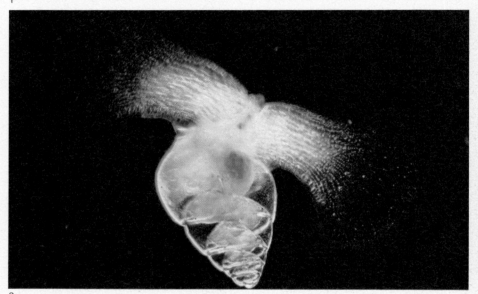

1

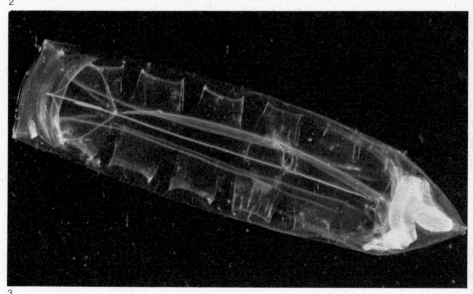

2

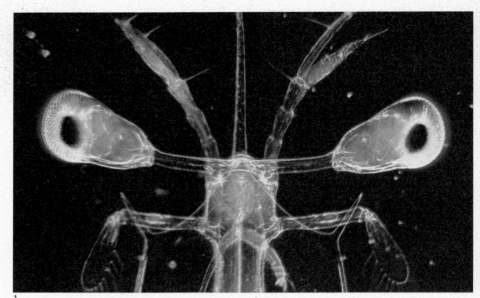

3

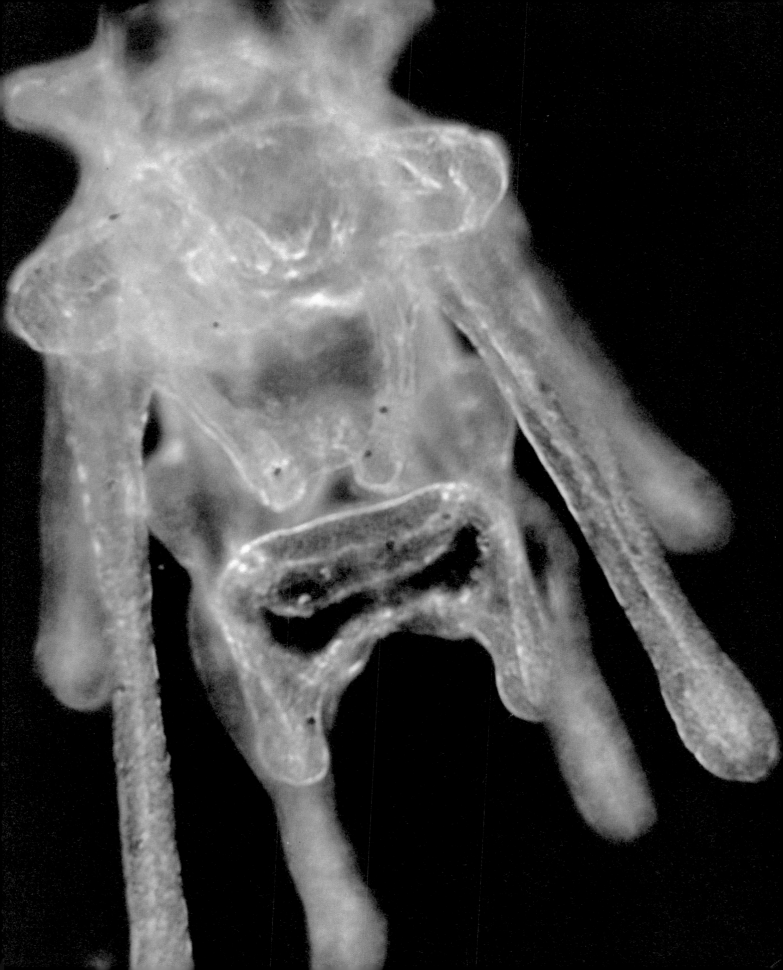

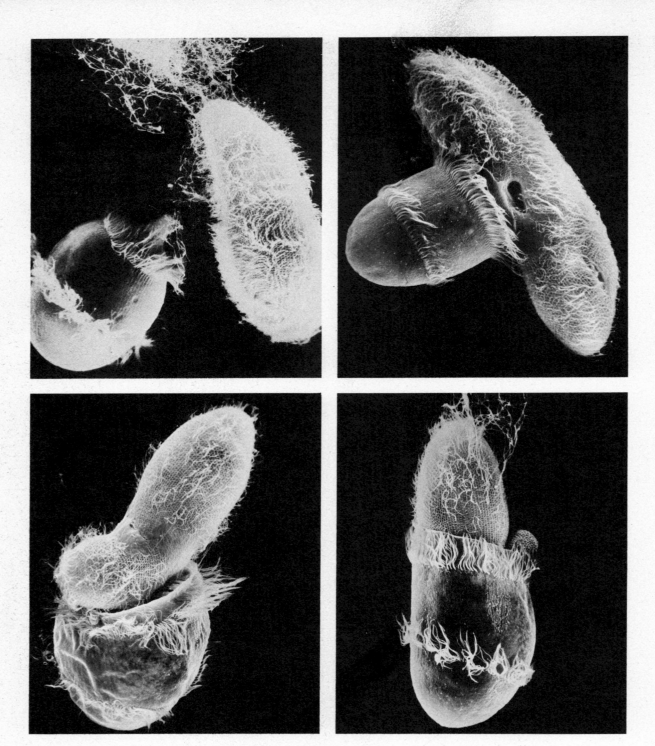

In this unusual series of pictures, the scanning electron microscope gives us an action replay from the ruthless world of microorganisms.

These two submarine creatures have met to do battle. On one side is the prey, the much-studied, slipper-shaped paramecium. On the other is the hunter, the globular didinium. The fringes of hair on each are cilia, pneumatically operated fronds with which they propel themselves through the water.

As the paramecium senses the didinium, it fires off its defence system—the cloud of tangled white threads at the top of the first picture. These threads are in fact hundreds of tiny harpoon-like spears, which current military jargon would describe as wire-guided missiles. The paramecium has fired too late, however, and misses.

The didinium seizes its prey, paralysing it with tiny darts of its own. Extending its mouth ever wider, it gradually folds the now passive paramecium until it can suck it into its own swelling body. Finally, the didinium swallows, and the unfortunate paramecium disappears completely.

BIOPHOTO ASSOCIATES.

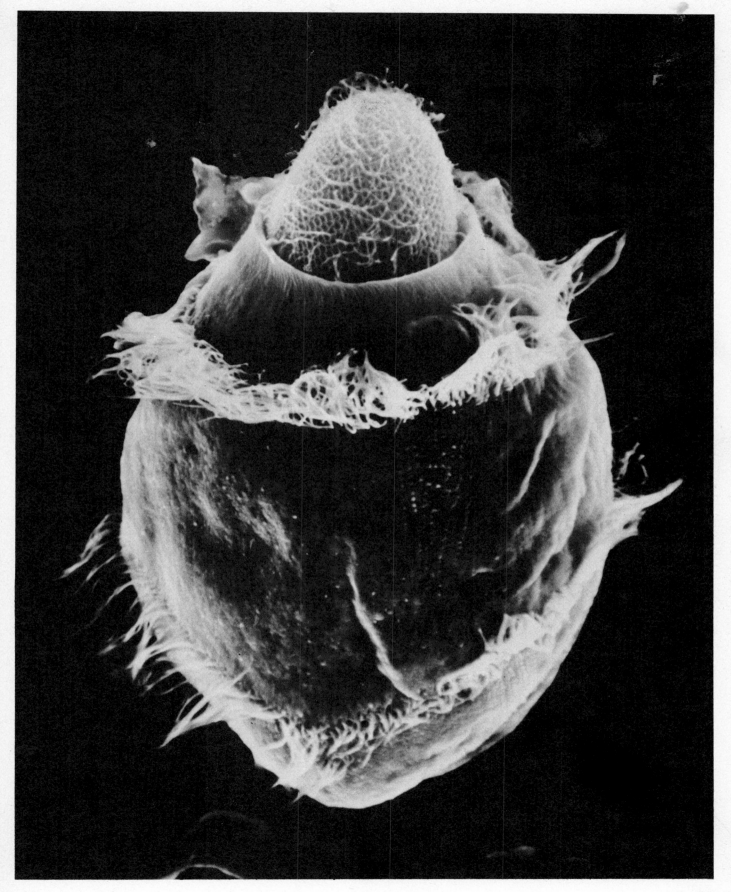

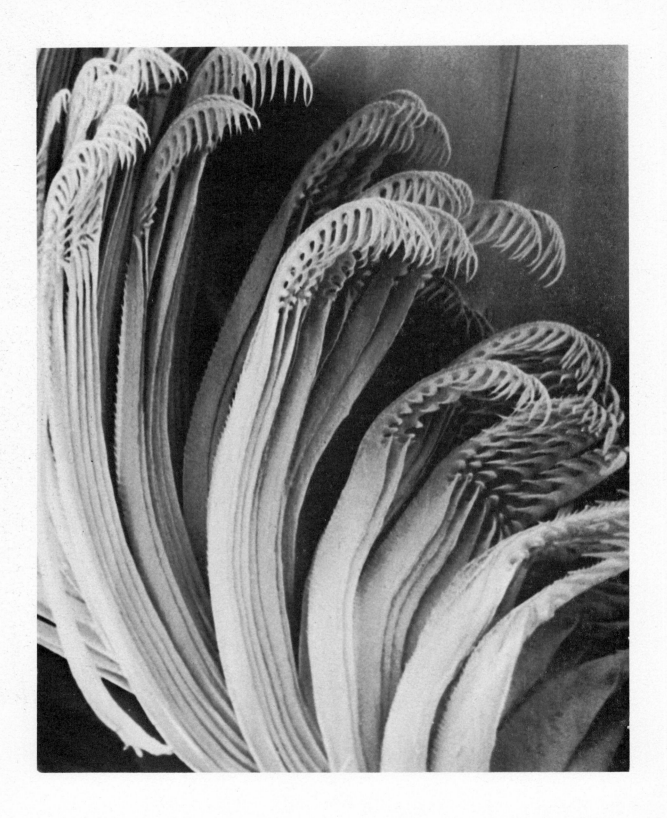

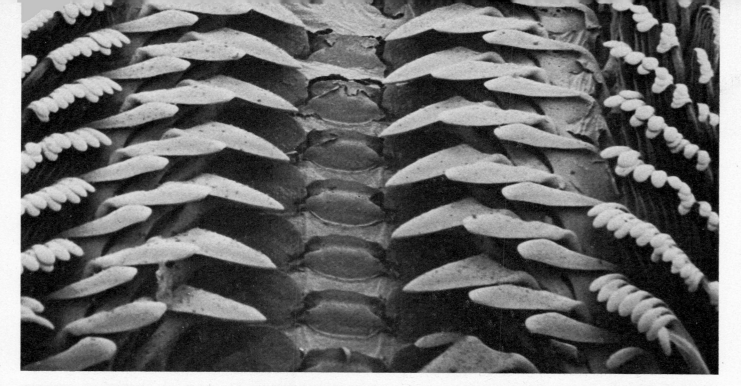

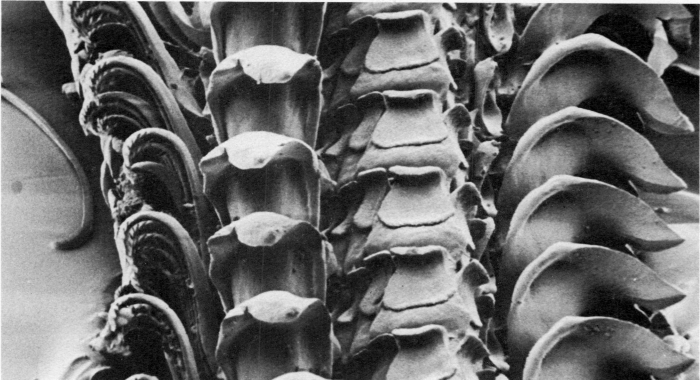

These baroque exuberances are the surfaces of mollusc tongues. Molluscs, such as snails and squids, have no jaws and, naturally enough, no teeth. So instead of chewing their food, they file it down with a rasping tongue called a "radula."

These scanning electron micrographs show some of the thousands of blades on the tongues of three molluscs—*Calliostoma ligatum* (left), *Haliotis ruber* (top), and *Emarginula reticulata* (bottom).

T. E. THOMPSON AND LONG ASHTON RESEARCH STATION. UNIVERSITY OF BRISTOL

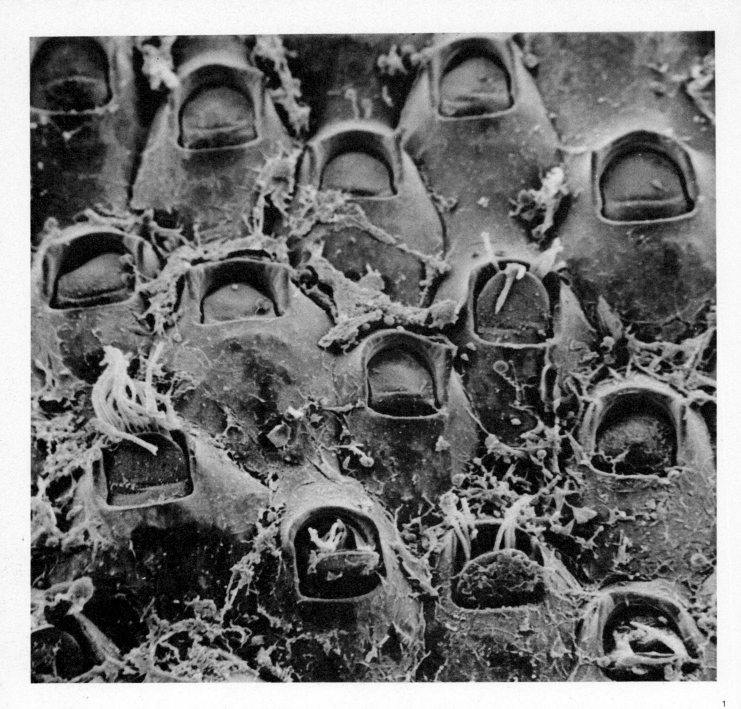

1. This tenement of trapdoors houses a colony of bryozoa. There are simple colonial animals like sponges, and complicated ones like barnacles, but the bryozoa are probably the most successful.

Each trapdoor hides a single animal, with its own nervous system and digestion. The tentacles waving hungrily from the doorways at the bottom of the photograph are covered with millions of tiny hairs beating in rhythm to push food into the mouth. When the trapdoor shuts, the animal pulls these tentacles inside out, like the fingers of a glove.

These bryozoa were magnified 130 times. They are attached to a strand of eelgrass, and the debris on the surface is a mass of single-cell animals, including diatoms, scavenging for food.

FROM *MICROBIAL SEASCAPES*. BY JOHN McN. SIEBURTH. UNIVERSITY PARK PRESS. BALTIMORE. 1975.

2. This 15cm periphyllid jellyfish comes from the dark waters about 1000 metres below the surface. It is thought to live off crustacea and lantern fish.

There seems to be no reason why some deep water creatures are so brightly coloured. Indeed there may be no reason. Whatever purpose such colouring once had, evolution would not have changed it unless it became a positive handicap.

OXFORD SCIENTIFIC FILMS.

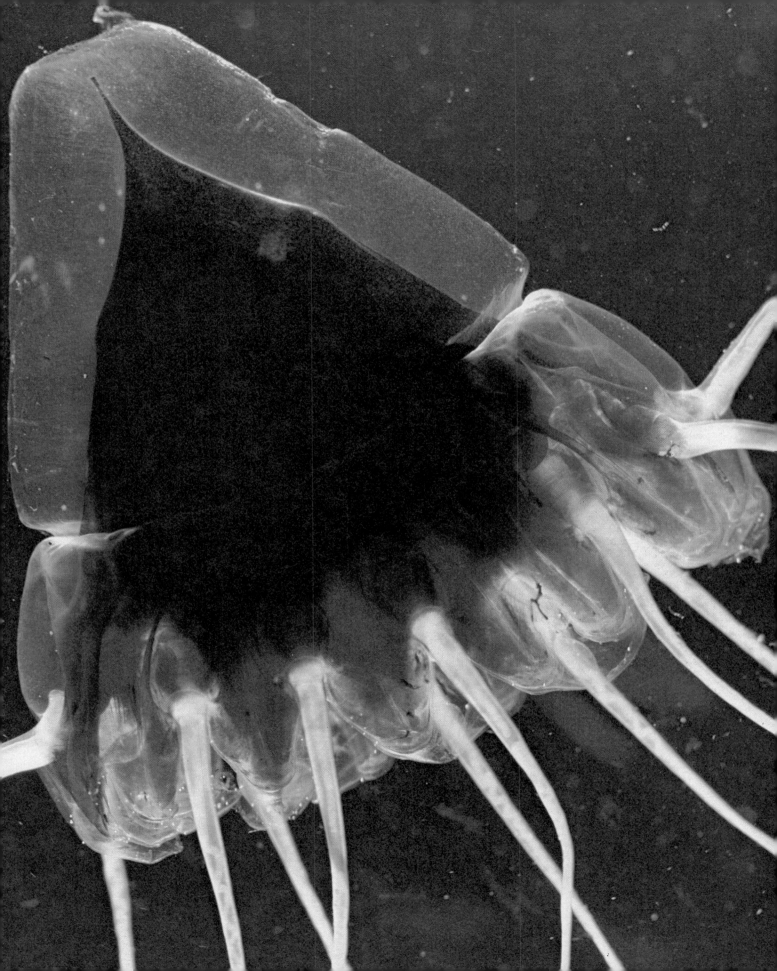

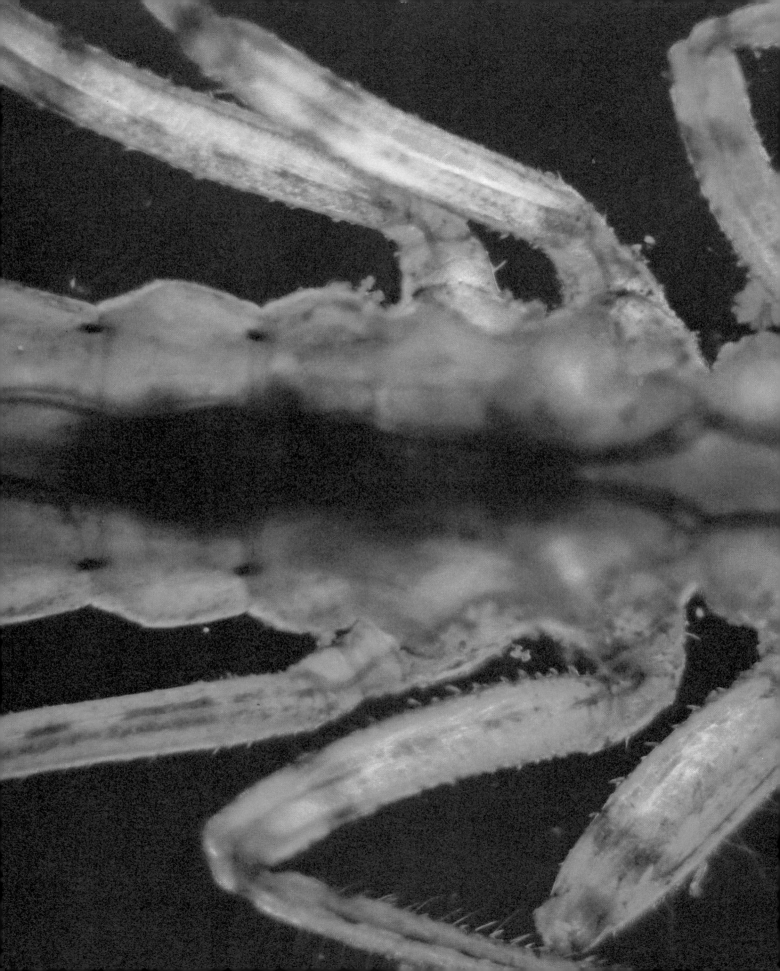

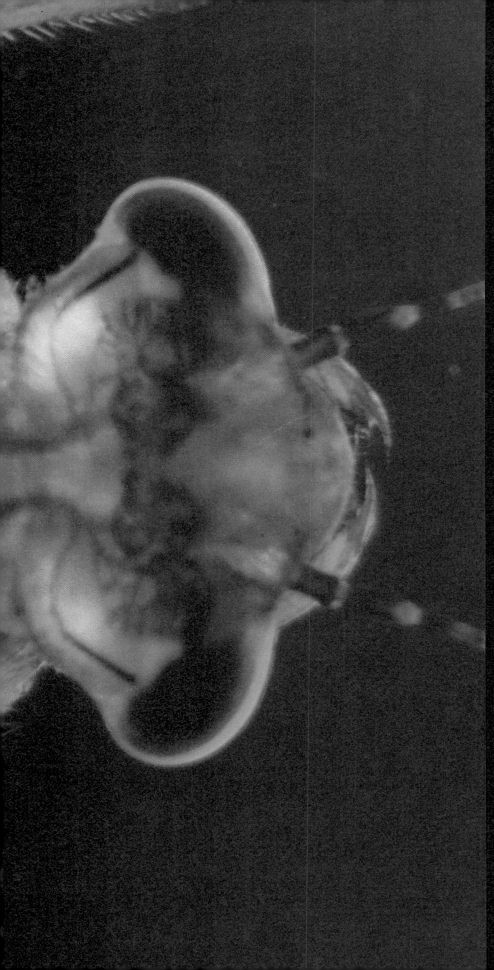

Microlife

In the universe of the microscopic, creatures we take for granted in our everyday lives are revealed in their true light. In every home and garden, on every body and household article, a subworld of mites and insects eat, reproduce, survive and die. They existed on Earth for millions of years before Homo Sapiens, and they will undoubtedly survive him.

This crawling rainbow is the larva of the damsel-fly. Larvae are unlovely things, as a rule, but interference patterns have turned this one into an iridescent illusion, worthy of its adult form.

The damsel-fly, like a small dragon-fly, is an insect-of-prey with a brilliant dark blue body. It is an accurate high-speed flier which hunts the overgrown banks of streams and rivers. Its eyesight is so sharp that it can spot its microscopic prey at 50 feet, and take it on the wing. One species, with a wingspan of up to 7½ inches, has an optical system as large as that of a mouse.

JAMES M. BELL

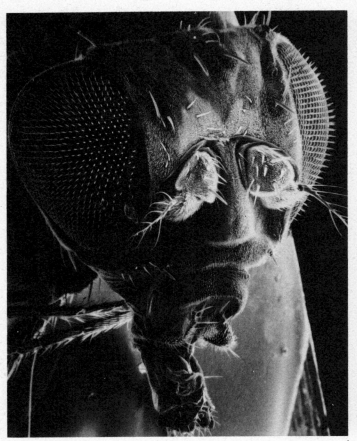

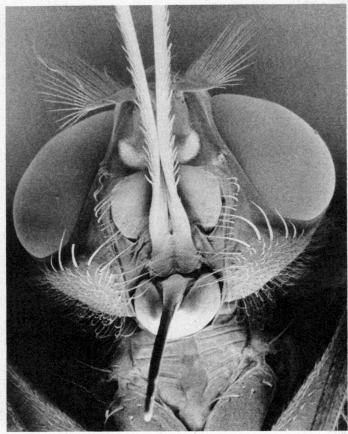

1

2

1. The most popular of all domestic animals, by a head count, would probably turn out to be a bacteria called E. coli and this fruit-fly. Because of their fast, neat breeding patterns fruit-flies have become a standard scientific tool and millions are being reared in laboratories around the world. They have led to many major discoveries, especially in genetics, and more is known about them than almost any other animal.

We know, for instance, that those huge eyes can only distinguish between 3 shades of grey (as compared to ours, which can make out 300 shades, plus about 17,000 mixed colours). But their sense of smell more than compensates for this. Although there are more than 2000 species of these *Drosophila,* they can sharply distinguish between each other by scent alone.

The regular rows of hairs on the eyes are wind-speed indicators. If they took off into a wind of more than 10 mph they would just be blown backwards.

DR L. M. BEIDLER, FLORIDA STATE UNIVERSITY.

2. The head of a tsetse fly. Fatal to cattle, dangerous to humans and apparently indestructible, the carrier of sleeping sickness is once again on the increase. "I can think of no other insect which has got man so tied down," Dr John Strangeways-Dixon of the Nairobi Centre for Insect Physiology and Research said recently. "The tsetse fly has taken over 25% of Africa."

Like the mosquito, it has a lethally accurate homing instinct. "The tsetse fly's behaviour is decisively influenced by temperature sensitivity. As long as the temperature is bearable, it instinctively seeks brightness; that is, it flies out of the bush onto the grasslands where its victims are grazing. But directly the thermometer rises above 86°F (30°C), when cows and antelope are looking for shade, the tsetse fly, which is short-sighted, switches over, now heading for anything that looks dark. It is thus bound to find its victims again."

Vitus B Droscher, *The Magic of the Senses*.

REPRODUCED BY KIND PERMISSION OF THE EASTMAN KODAK COMPANY AND KODAK LTD.

Ants may look the same, but all they really have in common are narrow waists and bent antennae. In close-up, under the scanning electron microscope, they are horrifyingly distinctive.

1. The bald head of *diocondyla.* The strange bump on the side, like a raspberry, is one of its remarkable eyes, which can locate the position of the sun through overcast cloud by analysing polarised light. The mouth parts are designed for biting and taking up liquid food. The hairs form a bristling sensory array with many functions, including the sense of balance and the detection of gravity.

DR L. M. BEIDLER, FLORIDA STATE UNIVERSITY.

2. With mandibles neatly folded over its mouth, this is the face of *cardiocondyla.* Drumming the mandibles together is an important part of its communication system. Ants have a language of smells and clicking noises so complicated that it is believed to have its own syntax.

REPRODUCED BY KIND PERMISSION OF THE EASTMAN KODAK COMPANY AND KODAK LTD.

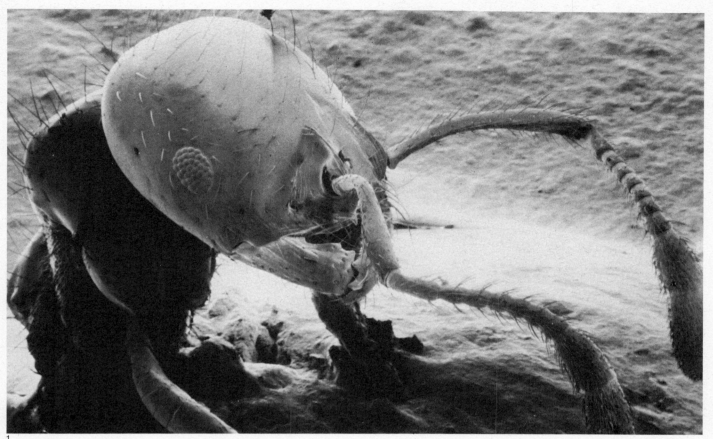

1

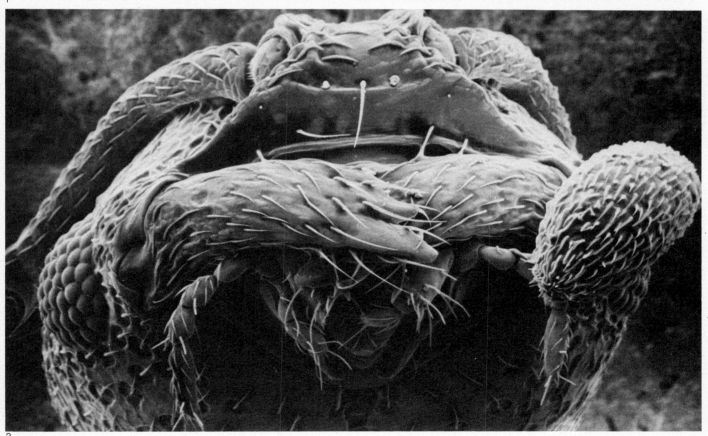

2

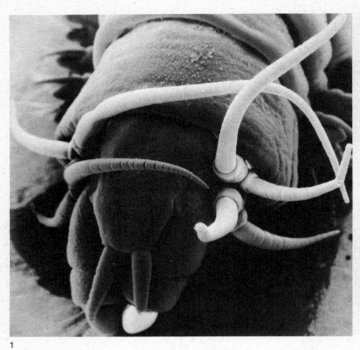

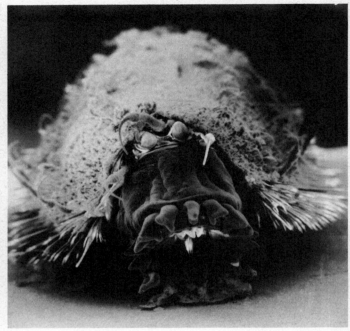

1

2

1. The nereid worm is often dug out of the foreshore by fishermen for use as bait. They call it the ragworm because of the flapping skirt of tissue (*parapodia*) down its side. The nereid has some remarkable adaptations including the ability to push its gut out through its mouth as a form of proboscis, for picking up food.

Just before it mates, the whole rear section of the worm undergoes metamorphosis, and the parapodia turn into paddles. It then swims away into the sea to perform an elaborate sperm dance.

2. The head of a scale worm, a relative of sea mice, which lives under stones, on rocky foreshores or even, like some of the more determined species, under the shells of limpets. It gets its name from the rounded scales which line its back.

FROM *MICROBIAL SEASCAPES*, BY JOHN McN. SIEBURTH, UNIVERSITY PARK PRESS, BALTIMORE, 1975.

3. The head of a tapeworm, showing the hooks and suckers which firmly attach it to the intestines of its host. The tapeworm has no digestive system of its own and absorbs food directly through the skin. Without eyes or mouth, and bathed in its own warm pre-digested food, its body is little more than the envelope for a reproductive system.

Because they do so little harm, tapeworms have a long life (at least, as long as their hosts) and can grow to great lengths. A worm more than 100 feet long was removed from a whale captured off Santa Catalina Island, California, in 1957. This particular tapeworm lived in a dog.

PICTUREPOINT LTD.

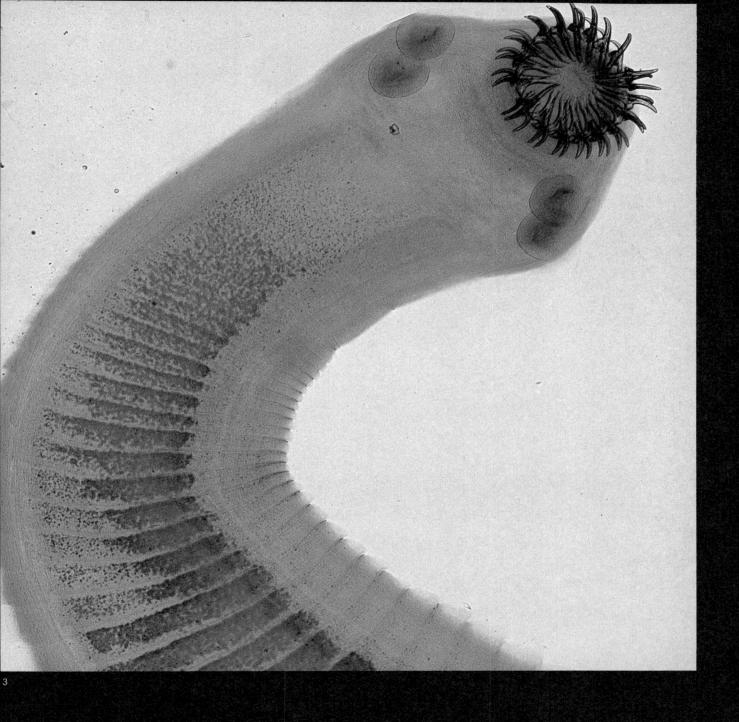

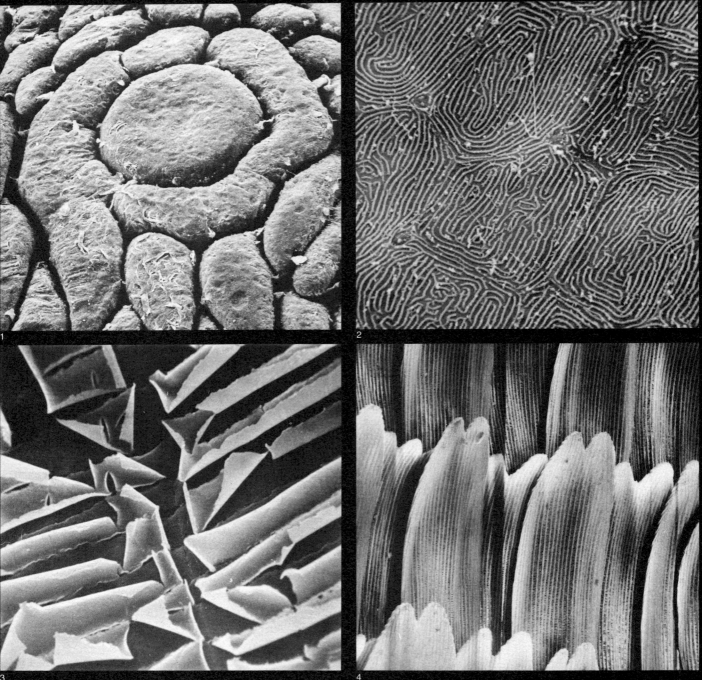

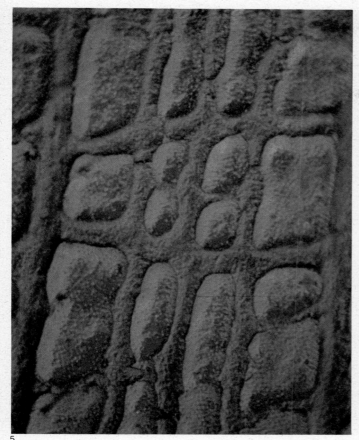

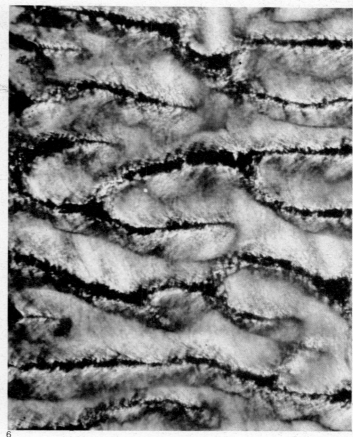

5   6

We think of skin as "rough" or "smooth," but the scanning electron micrographs (left) and light microscope pictures (above) show some of the complex and beautiful structures we are missing.

1. The tongue of a three-week old puppy, magnified 80 times. The taste cells are buried within the crevasses.

Taste, in both humans and animals, is a blunted sense, a clumsy reflex system which decides how much saliva is produced and prevents us eating poisons. Smell is not only a completely separate system, but far more sophisticated. For instance, it takes 25,000 times as many molecules on the tongue to produce a taste as it takes molecules up the nose to produce a scent.

DR L. M. BEIDLER, FLORIDA STATE UNIVERSITY.

2. The patterned skin on the tail of a salmon.

One would imagine that the skin of a fish would be waterproof, but it isn't. In salt water, fish lose body moisture to the sea and have to drink large amounts to make it up. Conversely, fresh water fish are in danger of flooding and urinate constantly. The salmon, to complicate matters, is both a salt and fresh water fish. Its sensitivity to types of water, coupled with an acute sense of smell, enables it to perform extraordinary feats of navigation. Swimming in from the open sea to its spawning grounds, it can identify the water of a particular estuary, then the river, then the tributary, the stream and, finally, the pool where it was reared, years before.

FROM *MICROBIAL SEASCAPES*, BY JOHN McN. SIEBURTH, UNIVERSITY PARK PRESS, BALTIMORE, 1975.

3. The cracked and peeling skin of a lizard. It is common knowledge that lizards shed their skin, but so do most other animals including human beings. The skin is our largest organ and we change it entirely once every six months or so, as the dead cells flake off and new ones grow beneath.

COURTESY OF CAMBRIDGE SCIENTIFIC INSTRUMENTS.

4. Minute petals on the surface of a butterfly wing, magnified 680 times.

Considering their fragility, some butterflies make extraordinarily long flights. It is now known that they can travel up to 2000 miles. For instance, the American Monarch butterfly makes the journey from Mexico to Hudson Bay, *and back*, each year; and the noisiest of them all, the squeaking Hawkmoth from tropical Africa, has turned up in Finland and Iceland.

DR L. M. BEIDLER, FLORIDA STATE UNIVERSITY.

5. A micrographic close-up of the wing of a cockroach.

Cockroaches are among the most maligned animals. There is no evidence that they transmit serious disease or damage us in any way. In fact, they should be welcomed in households as useful scavengers.

This one came from Ecuador.

JAMES M. BELL.

6. A section of ox horn. The horn material is laid down in thin wafers which buckle under one another, according to different rates of growth, to produce the final shape. Parallel layers, and parallel molecules within the layers, produce this effect of "birefringence" under polarised light.

BIOPHOTO ASSOCIATES.

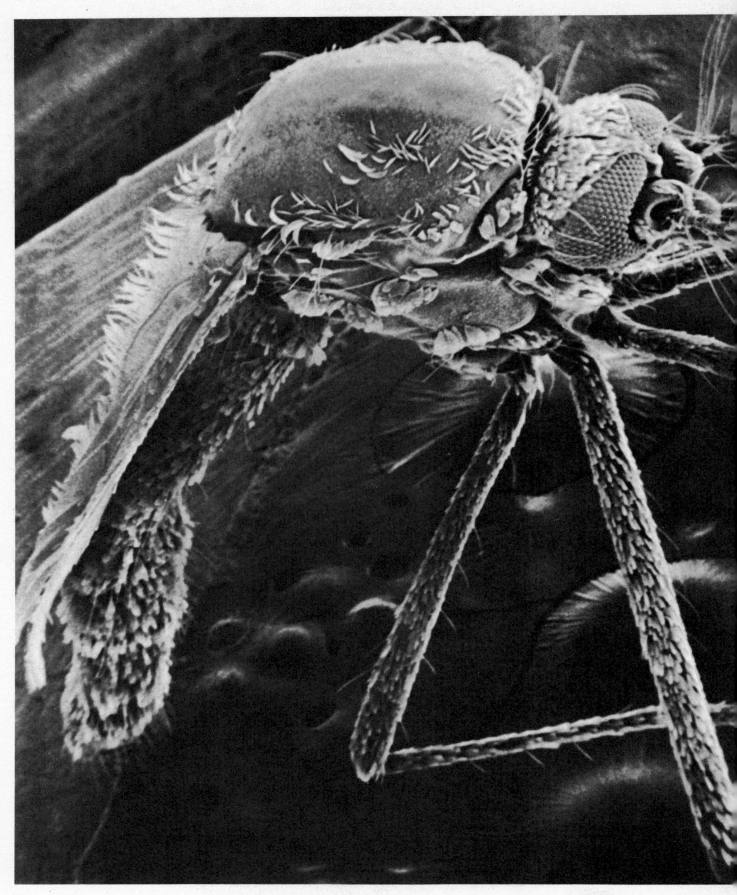

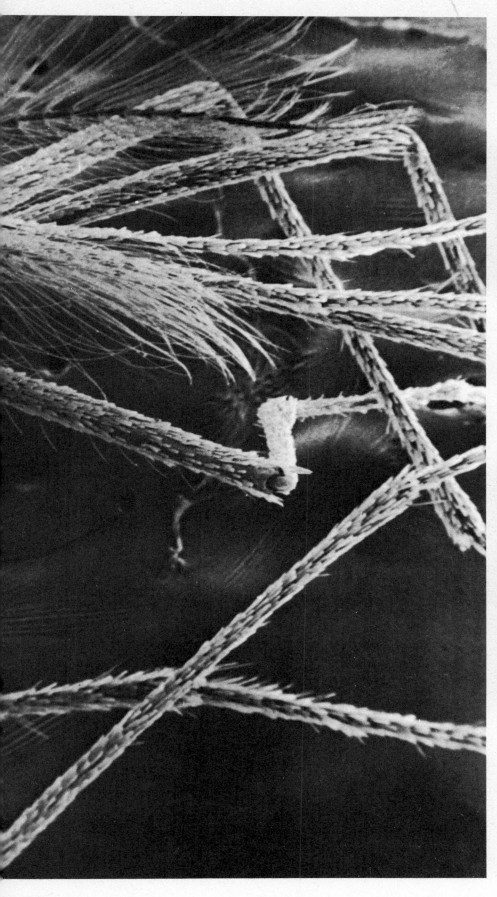

1. A mosquito, carrier of malaria and directly responsible for the deaths of over a million people every year. In spite of worldwide campaigns to wipe it out, the mosquito is still flourishing with a kill record that can only be compared to a major war.

DR TONY BRAIN.

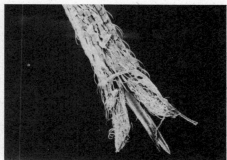

2. The mosquito's hypodermic needle pierces the skin and sucks up a meal of blood, while the matted structure around it ejects a fluid which prevents the blood from clotting. When it has finished feeding, the hairs will reabsorb most of the anticoagulant.

REPRODUCED BY KIND PERMISSION OF THE EASTMAN KODAK COMPANY AND KODAK LTD.

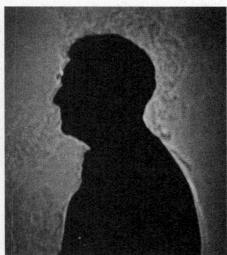

3. This could be a mosquito's eye view of its victim, except that the attraction is neither sight nor smell, but humidity. The insect is first aroused by a rise in the level of carbon dioxide in the neighbourhood, and then zeros in on the warm moist air currents (shown here by schlieren photography).

BRITISH COLUMBIA RESEARCH COUNCIL. REPRODUCED WITH PERMISSION FROM *SCIENTIFIC AMERICAN*, JULY 1975.

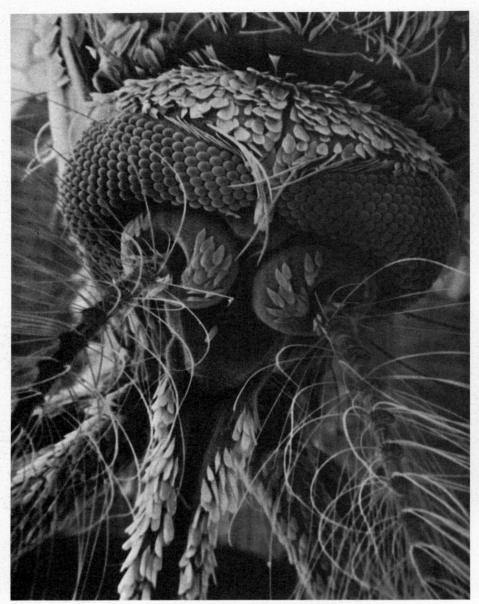

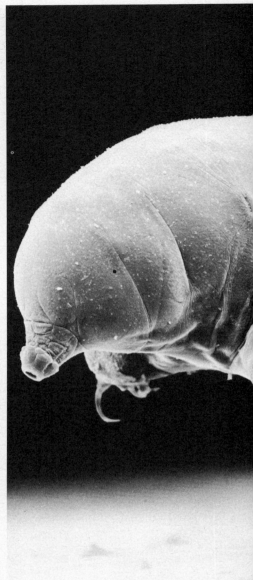

The head of a mosquito, bristling with automatic sensors. Insects are equipped to register minute changes of air pressure, record the impact of individual molecules, analyse their composition and even their electrical charge. The mosquito's antennae are so sensitive they can detect temperature changes of just 1/500th of a degree Centigrade.

The almond-like flakes still puzzle scientists, but they are similar structures to the petals on butterfly wings. They may be a device, common among insects, for confusing predators in flight by "blurring" their sonic echo.

DR TONY BRAIN.

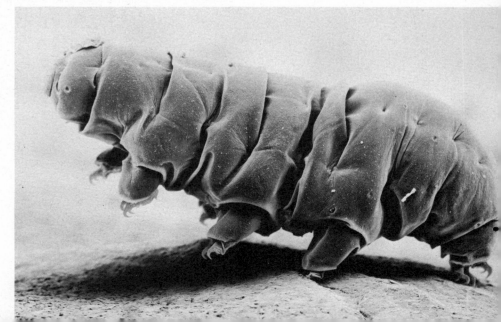

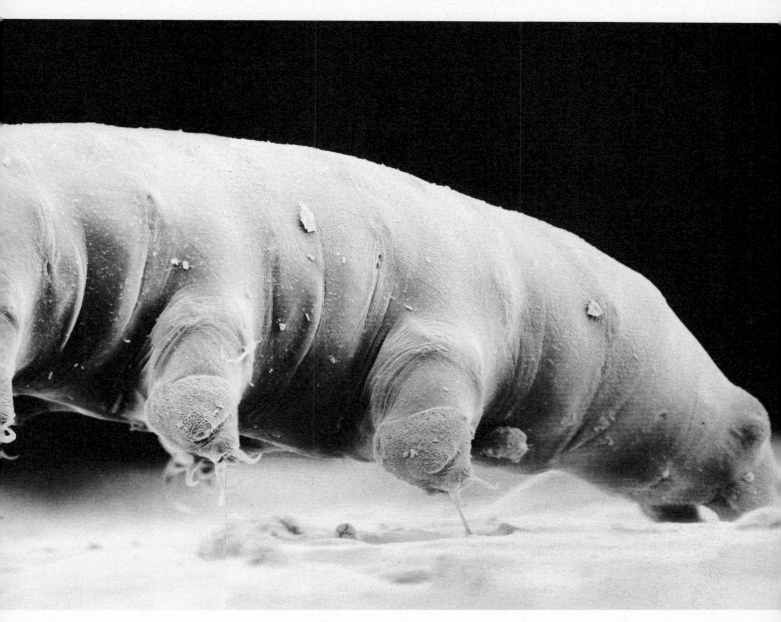

As well as the portraits of familiar insects, the scanning electron microscope has revealed a number of eccentric little beasts, among whom the tardigrade *(above and left) is surely one of the oddest and most endearing.*

The tardigrade has a strange life style, because it is capable of suspended animation. Like some microorganisms and the spores of fungus, it can survive hostile conditions by voluntarily "dying."

The tardigrade normally lives in damp mud, but if its surroundings become dehydrated it simply turns off all its systems. Its body, which is 85% water, dries out and it virtually ceases to be a living organism. It can be heated to over 150°C, far above the boiling point of water, or frozen to minus 200°C for days on end without being damaged. Yet it only needs the correct amount of moisture in its surroundings to come bouncing back to life again.

The tardigrade only has about twelve months of active life, but by switching off and on in this way, it can survive as long as sixty years. There are even examples of tardigrades which were found in museum specimens of dried moss and briefly revived after 120 years.

ROBERT O. SCHUSTER, UNIVERSITY OF CALIFORNIA, DAVIS.

Overleaf: A tick, at home on its familiar landscape of human skin.

Mites and ticks are among the least welcome of the many creatures that inhabit us. In the past they even proved to be fatal. Herod Antiochus, King Philip II and Pope Clement VIII all died of a mite disease *(acariasis subcutaneae)* related to scabies, the final symptoms of which were so repulsive that the corpses had to be sewn into leather shrouds before burial.

This is the argasid tick which carries a common disease of North Africa and the Middle East called relapsing fever.

OXFORD SCIENTIFIC FILMS.

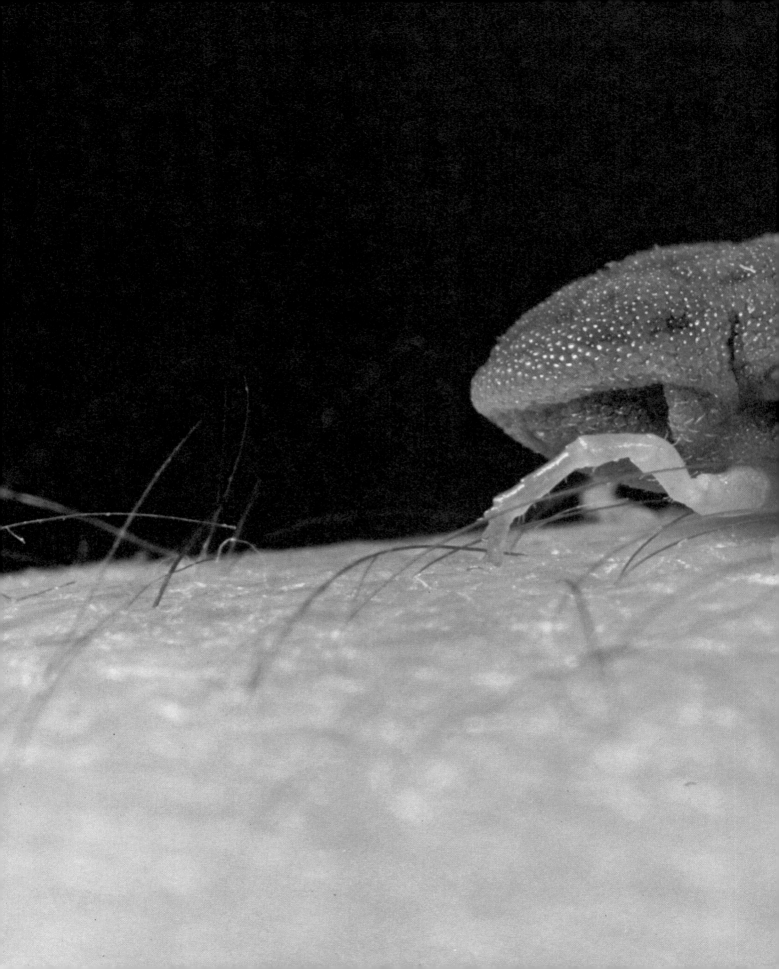

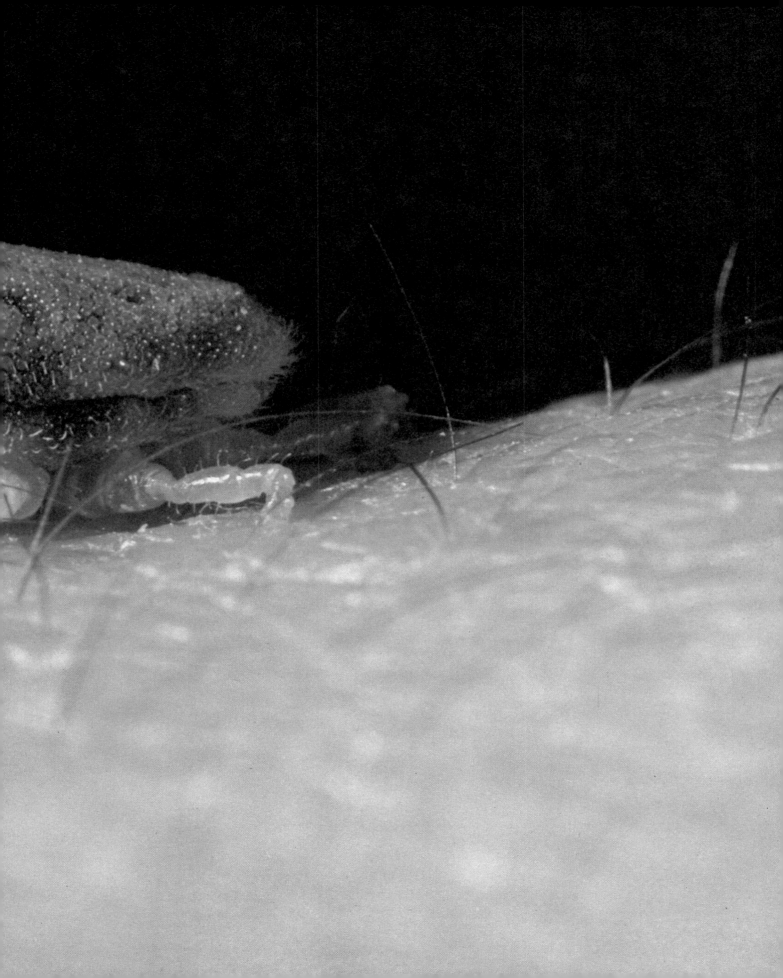

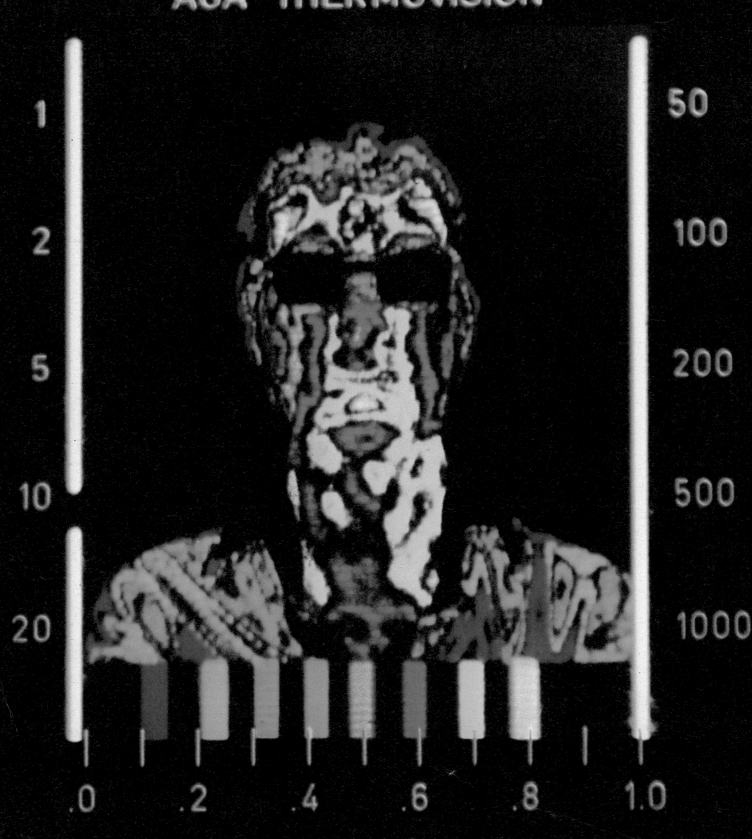

The Human Landscape

*"Know then thyself, presume not
  god to scan,
The proper study of mankind is
  man."*
Alexander Pope.

*Beyond the range of our senses,
electronics is giving us a new
image of ourselves – from
computer-generated portraits of
radiation to action photos of our
internal geography and
echo-location maps of the womb.
Electron microscopes and fibre
optics reveal the organs (and
organisms) of our bodies as teeming
colonies. Automatic factories over
which we have no control. A
landscape we can neither feel nor
experience. But there is nothing
artificial about these shapes and
structures. They are there, within us.*

*Now that we can see them for the
first time, maybe we can begin to
understand ourselves better. By
giving the lie to our arrogant
preconceptions about "uniqueness"
and "individuality," we might even
regain a sense of wonder.*

This alien man-scan is a
thermograph, showing the heat
structure of a human face.

The infrared radiation from the
head is scanned from side to side by
an electronic camera, transforming it
into a TV-like signal. A computer
codes the different temperatures in
terms of colours and feeds the
picture to a video screen.

White and yellow are the hottest
colours, green and blue the coolest.
The heat of the breath shows up in
white, but the other main "hot spot,"
between the eyes, is obscured by
dark glasses.

MICHAEL FREEMAN. DAILY TELEGRAPH COLOUR
LIBRARY

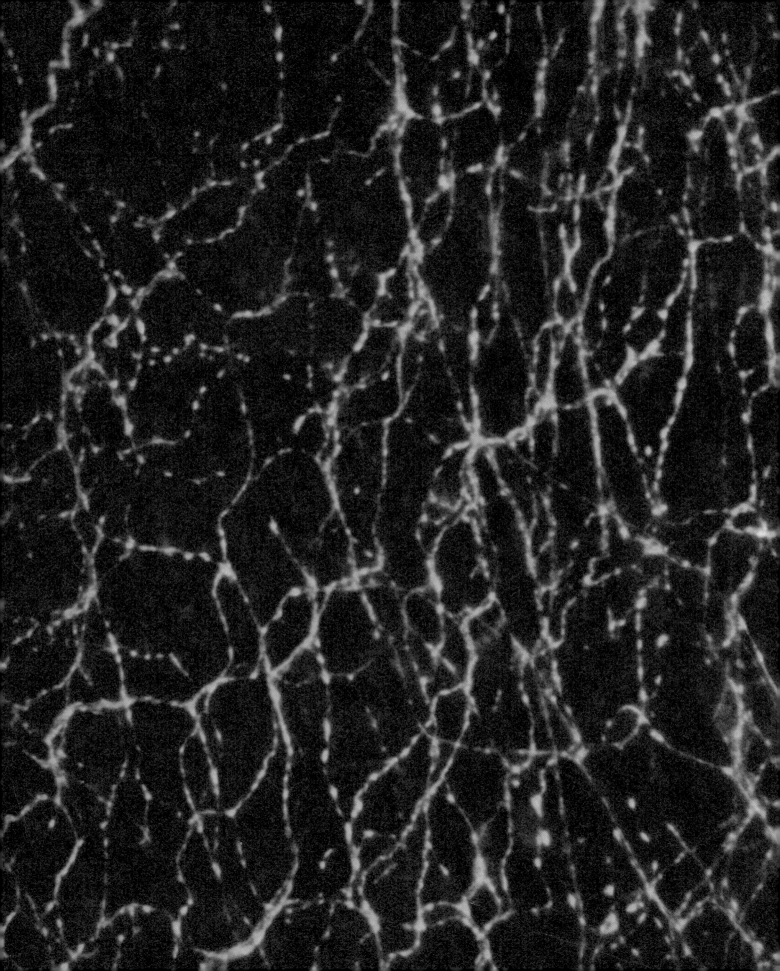

1. A fluorescent tangle of nerve endings. The green glow results from treatment with formaldehyde and reveals the presence of the chemical "messenger," *noradrenalin*, which the nerves use to transmit their signals. Each tiny glittering bead can produce a flash-flood of noradrenalin into the surrounding cells, reacting with other nerves or muscle cells and triggering chemical changes.

The balance of these "messengers" affects our moods and emotions, and a wide range of drugs are used to control it, from anti-depressants and tranquillisers to stimulants like amphetamines, and even LSD. Parkinson's Disease was cured by the introduction of an artificial "messenger" called L-dopa, and there is even hope for a chemical cure of schizophrenia using a similar drug.

These nerves come from the iris of a rat's eye, but are not dissimilar to the human equivalent. X 2400.

DR. DAVID M. JACOBOWITZ, NATIONAL INSTITUTE OF MENTAL HEALTH.

2. X-ray of a human lung, showing the complex blood vessels which serve it. This branching pattern – whether nerves, tree-roots or blood vessels – is nature's basic solution to covering the maximum area. The internal surface of our lungs is enormous. If it was unfolded it would cover about 100 square metres, or 50 times the area of the skin on our bodies, yet these blood vessels reach every part of it. The heart does the rest. Pumping at the rate of 75 gallons an hour, it ensures that our total blood volume washes through this network once every thirteen seconds of our lives.

DR JULIUS H. COMROE JR. REPRODUCED WITH PERMISSION FROM "THE LUNG," JULIUS H. COMROE, *SCIENTIFIC AMERICAN*, FEBRUARY 1966.

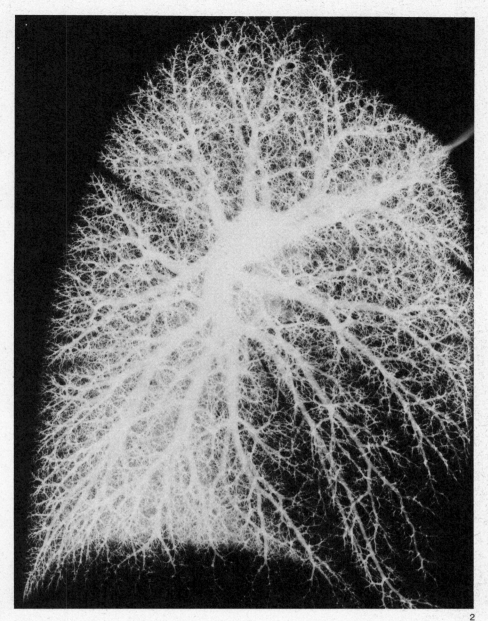

2

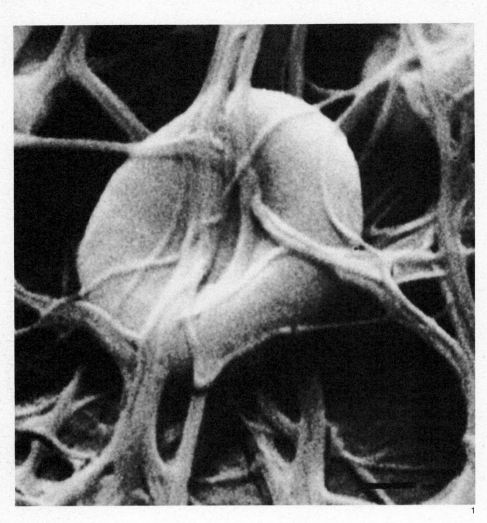

1

1. Scanning electron micrograph of a red cell being slowly woven into a blood clot.

Without this unique function of the blood, even a scratch could be fatal. The first line of defence when a vessel is damaged are particules much smaller than this cell, which stick to each other and the site of the injury to plug the breach. Unfortunately, these *platelets* also tend to form clots on the roughened surface of old arteries and block the blood supply.

But the main defence against wounds is shown in this micrograph. A protein dissolved in the blood suddenly changes into long strands of a material called *fibrin.* The threads enmesh blood cells to form a semi-solid mass, then slowly contract, squeezing out a clear yellow serum, to form a firm dry clot.

DR EMIL BERNSTEIN AND EILA KAIRINEN, GILLETTE RESEARCH INSTITUTE

2. A field of blood, at the depth of a single cell across a microscope slide – part of the gallon or so of this liquid tissue contained in our bodies.

The reason why it is red is an accident of evolution. The colour, which actually varies from crimson through rust to black, comes from the metal content of blood cells, which are designed to absorb and release oxygen. Vertebrates chose an iron pigment *(haemoglobin)* for the task, but spiders and molluscs use a copper pigment and certain worms have violet, and even green, blood – all of which functions in much the same way.

These red cells cannot reproduce (they lose their nucleus when they take on the haemoglobin) and each one only lasts about four months, but we produce them in such number that a pint of blood contains roughly 4,000,000,000,000.

DR ROSALIND KING, ROYAL FREE HOSPITAL, LONDON

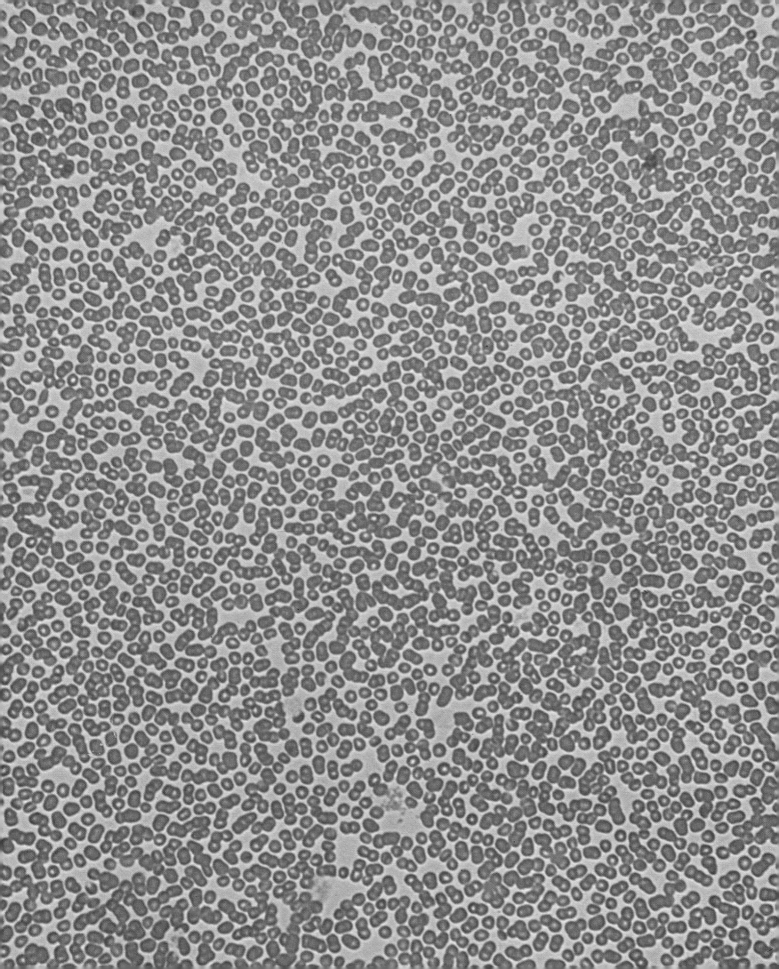

1. The human body is a vast colony of apparently independent creatures, such as these elegantly ruffled *macrophages,* at work clearing the debris from our lungs. They move around on their own – the elongated one is probably in pursuit of the particle on the left – and they will "eat" bacteria, dust, pollen and even certain components of tobacco smoke.

However, they are vulnerable to some of the toxic pollution we inhale and their destruction can give rise to pulmonary diseases.

A. R. BRODY AND L. L. HAHN. REPRODUCED FROM BRODY, A.R., AND CRAIGHEAD, J.E. *AMERICAN REVIEW OF RESPIRATORY DISEASES,* 112: 645, 1975, WITH PERMISSION OF THE PUBLISHER.

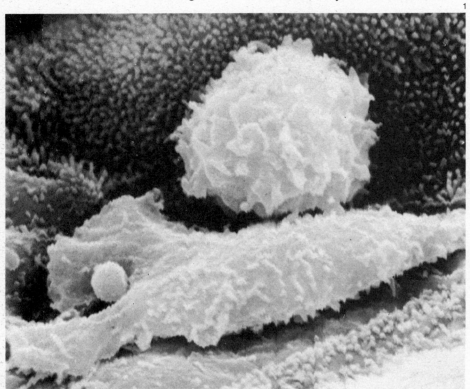

2. Inside the kidney, the coils of a *glomerulus* sprout like a flower amid a litter of stray blood cells and humps of folded tissue.

There are three main waste products of the food we eat: the carbohydrates produce gas (which is easily disposed of), fats produce water (which is a valuable acquisition), but proteins produce ammonia, a dangerous poison that must be got rid of as soon as possible. This is where the glomerulus comes in.

There are thousands of these tiny filtration plants in each kidney. They consist of a coil of porous blood vessels which first strain out the liquids, and then reabsorb everything the body can use, such as water and salts. All that is left is a strong solution of urea that gets passed in the urine. The normal (and healthy) frequency for this is every fifteen minutes or so, though social convention usually intervenes.

It is beautiful machinery – and one of the most efficient drainage systems in nature. Simpler creatures lose most of their body liquids in the process. Frogs have to pass 25% of their total body weight, and earthworms up to 60%, each day, whereas we only discharge 2% of ours.

BIOPHOTO ASSOCIATES

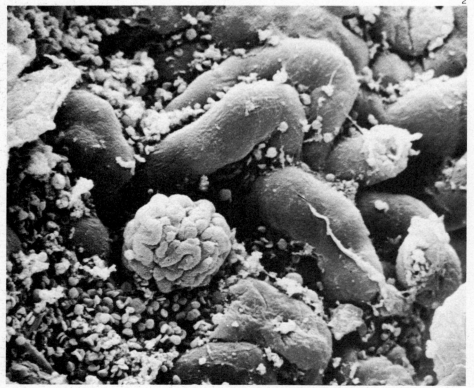

3. Colour-coded x-ray of a tooth. The layers of dentine underneath, and the enamel coating on the surface, are both crystalline in structure and show the flaws typical of crystals. Enamel, incidentally, is the hardest form of animal matter known. The core of the tooth is a soft pulp of nerves and blood vessels, though only a small part of it is visible here through the central opening.

Saliva tends to deposit an additional layer in the form of a chalky precipitate called tartar or calculus.

PAT MORRIS, DAILY TELEGRAPH COLOUR LIBRARY.

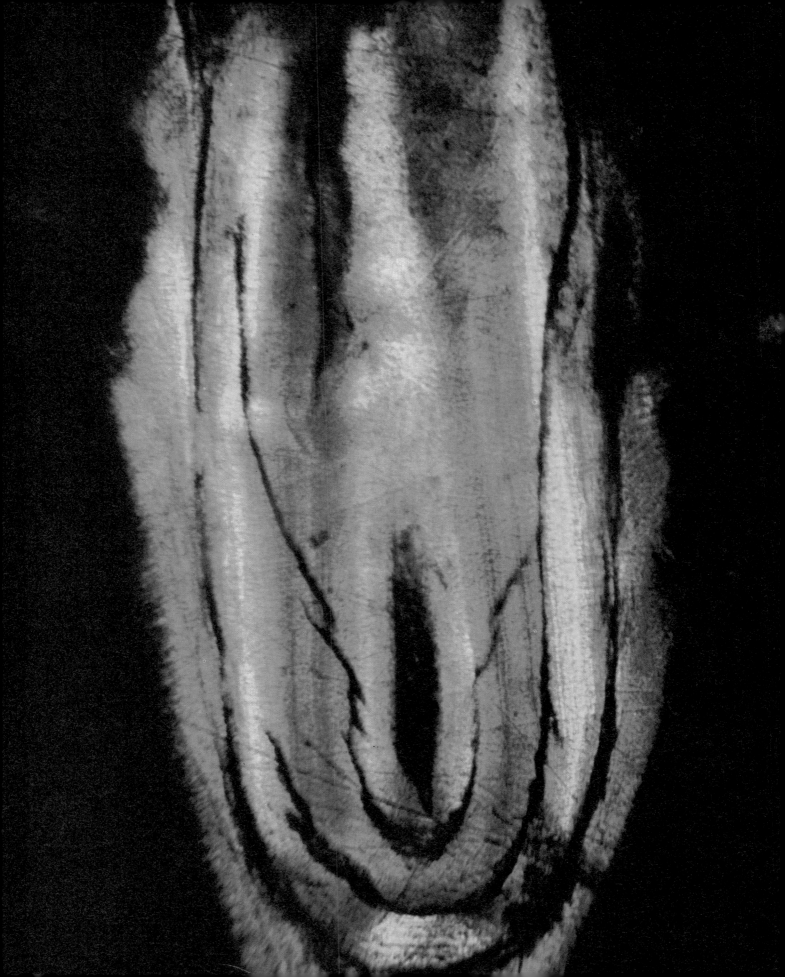

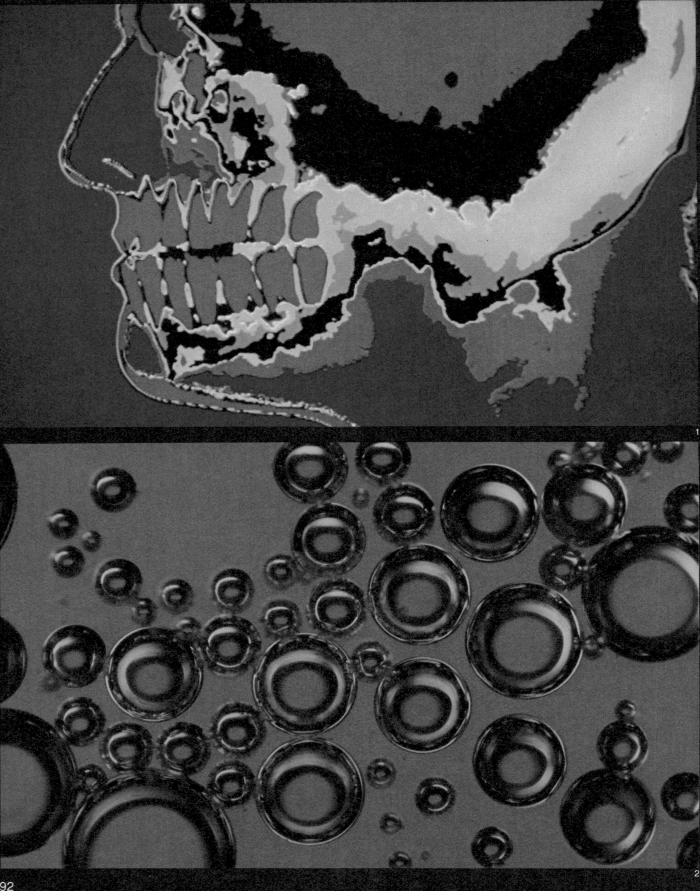

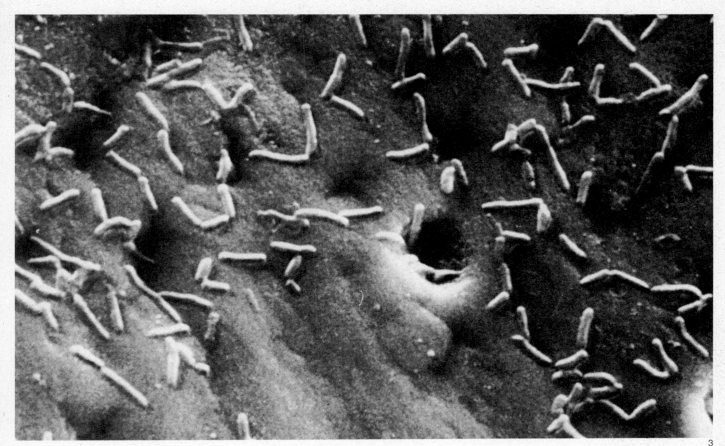

3

1. A sonograph, or sound picture, of the jaw and skull with positive echoes from a full set of teeth.

The human jaw has been rapidly shrinking during our recent evolution, which explains our instinctive attractions to other flat-faced creatures such as koalas and teddy-bears. But it has also given us the most crowded and ill-fitting teeth in the animal kingdom. With thirty-two of them crammed into less than a foot of jaw-line, it is hardly surprising that we suffer from so much dental trouble.

Nowadays our teeth are more or less the same size, but we once had large canines (third from front) for seizing and shaking prey. When we learned to use our hands for this, the canines shrank and our jaws started to recede. We lost the heavy neck muscles that were needed for the task, together with the thick ridges on the skull to which they were attached. Later on we developed enormous molars (rear three teeth) because the food we had started grubbing from the ground was abrasive and difficult to chew; but these, in turn, grew smaller as we

adopted a more civilised diet.

If we allow ourselves time to evolve much further, the process will probably continue and one day we may dispense with teeth altogether.

© HOWARD SOCHUREK, FROM THE JOHN HILLELSON AGENCY.

2. A light microscope slide showing droplets of saliva, the mildly alkaline cocktail of chemicals which floods the mouth from a dozen different glands. One of the mouth-watering ingredients, an enzyme called *amylase,* starts the digestion process by breaking starch down into sugar – which is why bread tastes sweeter the longer it is chewed.

Dentists have studied saliva in the search for an unidentified ingredient which would explain why certain people seem to be naturally immune to tooth decay. So far, the results are inconclusive.

JAMES M. BELL

3. A micrograph of bacteria on the surface of a tooth. Our mouths are full of bacteria, some of them

necessary and most of them harmless. They only become actively dangerous when they are kept away from oxygen, so the secret of good dental care (and the reason for brushing teeth) is simply to expose as much of the mouth as possible to air. Food lodged between the teeth, tartar, and plaque all provide hiding places for bacteria. Tooth decay is started by certain bacteria (*lactobacilli*) which convert sugar to acid. This eats through the enamel and creates cavities where bacteria can really get to work.

Fluoride helps produce stronger teeth, but the single most important factor, which no tooth-paste advertisement is likely to mention, is a properly balanced diet.

DR EMIL BERNSTEIN AND EILA KAIRINEN, GILLETTE RESEARCH INSTITUTE

1. Look deep into someone's eyes, and this is what you will see—the inside surface of an eyeball.

These words are being focused on a similar surface within your own eyes right now. The blood vessels and nerves run together, and leave the eyeball through the "blind spot" on the left. The darker circle on the right is the centre of focus, presently being pulled along this line in a series of jerks (eyes cannot "pan" like a camera).

But how does this apparently opaque tissue actually "see" anything at all? It is only in cross-section that the secret of the retina is revealed.

COURTESY OF CARL ZEISS

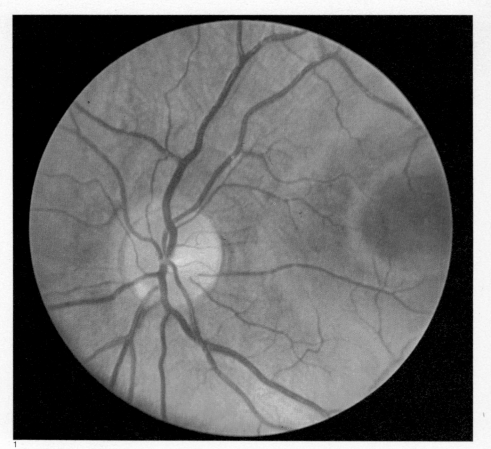

2. Cross-section through the retina. The light has to shine right through the dense surface layer of nerves and blood vessels, and then on through at least another nine layers of tangled nerves and cells before it reaches the light-sensitive equipment at the very back of the retina. This is composed of elongated cells, the *rods,* which operate in dim light and are colour-blind (which is why "all cats are grey at night"), and the *cones,* which operate in bright light and come in the same three primary colours as the dots on a colour TV screen. The whole complex network acts as a mini-computer, processing much of the information before it starts its journey to the brain.

Note: 8% of men are colour-blind, compared to only 0.4% of women.

MICROCOLOUR LTD.

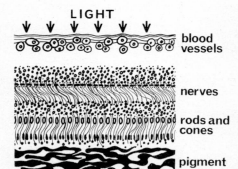

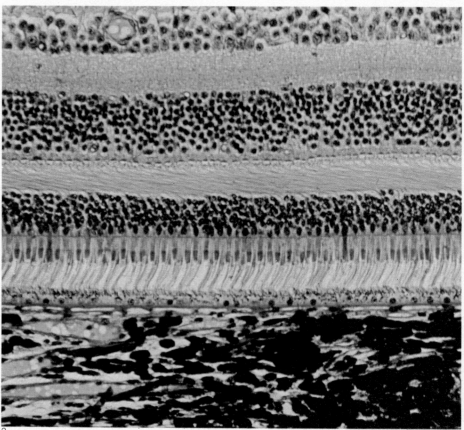

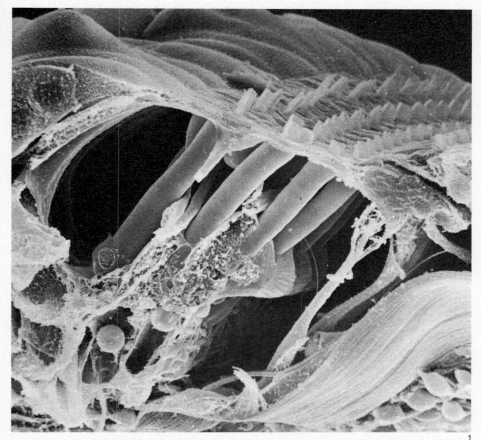

This is one of the smallest and most intricate organs in the body – the inner ear, where our sense of sound and balance originate.

The sound vibrations on the ear drum are transmitted, by a set of small hinged bones, to a tiny membrane set in the side of the inner ear.

The organ itself is filled with liquid because, paradoxically, the auditory nerves cannot respond in a "soft" medium like air. Some of the fluid runs along doughnut-shaped loops to tell us which way up we are, and the rest is sealed into a coiled tube like a snail's shell. These micrographs show the astonishing details of what happens inside the coil.

Running down its length, and dividing it in two, is an ultra-sensitive membrane, rather like an interior-sprung mattress. It is inside this double-sided "mattress" that the listening devices are arranged. The "springs" joining the top and bottom of the "mattress" are bundles of delicate hairs which respond to the slightest pressure (1). The hairs project through the top of the "mattress" into the upper canal (2), while a separate nerve ending is attached to the base of each bundle or "spring."

As the membrane is compressed and vibrations run through the fluid, the hairs which receive the strongest signal trigger their particular nerve (the other signals are filtered out), and their position in the tube as it narrows towards the centre gives us the pitch of the sound.

Loud noise is known to damage the hair cells and there is recent evidence that it upsets the body's hormone system with long term effects on sexual activity, muscles, heart palpitations and even the incidence of diabetes.

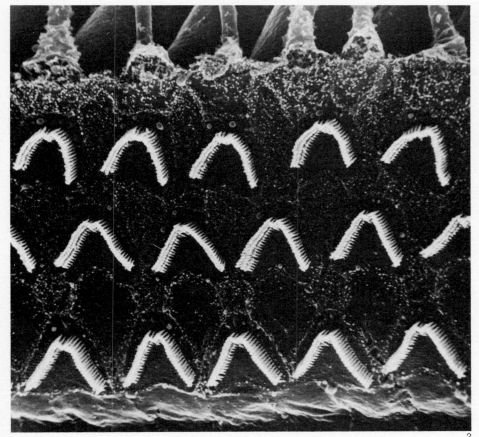

1. A cross-section through the ultra-sensitive membrane running through the coil of the inner ear. The top and bottom surfaces are joined by bundles of pressure-sensitive hairs.

2. The top surface of the membrane dividing the inner ear, showing the fine hairs projecting into the fluid.

DR GORAN BREDBERG, UNIVERSITY HOSPITAL, UPPSALA, SWEDEN

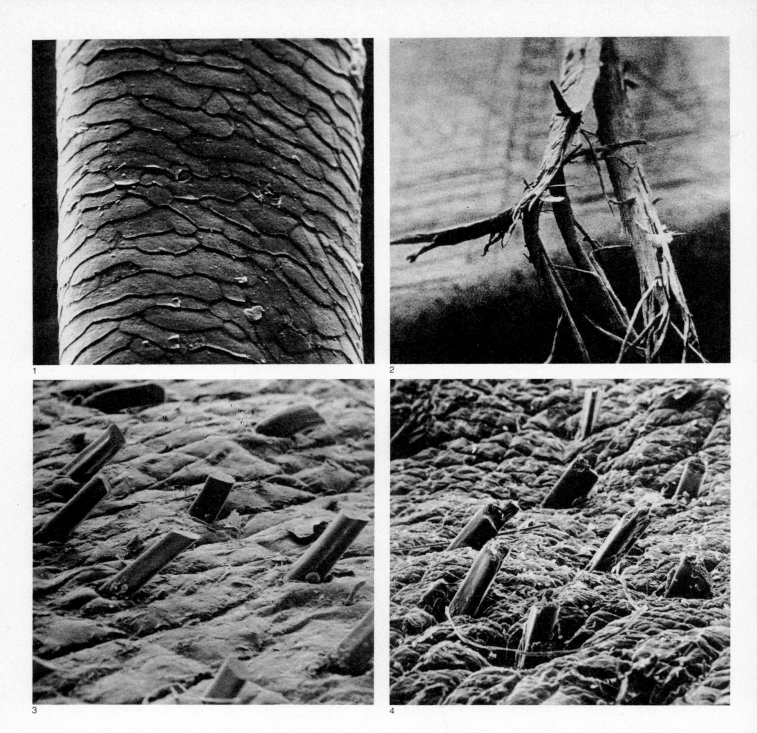

1

2

3

4

In almost every society, from head-hunters to hippies, hair has been a cultural obsession. Yet human beings are one of the few mammal species steadily evolving towards baldness. This does not mean that we have fewer hairs, but smaller ones. In fact our bodies, both men and women, still have a follicle-count comparable to gorillas. It is just that most of them are minute. Babies are visibly hairier than adults, and a young foetus actually has fine dense hair all over its face, which it loses as it grows older.

But when we talk of hair, we usually refer to the tubes of protein oozing from our scalps at a third of a millimetre a day—the "crowning glory" we spend so much effort and money re-shaping, distorting and generally mutilating in the name of social convention.

Hair that is round in cross-section grows naturally straight, a mixture of round and oval is wavy, and ribbon-like sections are kinky. Contrary to popular opinion, hair does not go white from shock (though some of the finer, darker strands may fall out, leaving paler hair behind). Shaving does not make hair coarser, nor does it grow after death (it is the skin which shrinks). On the other hand, hair does stand

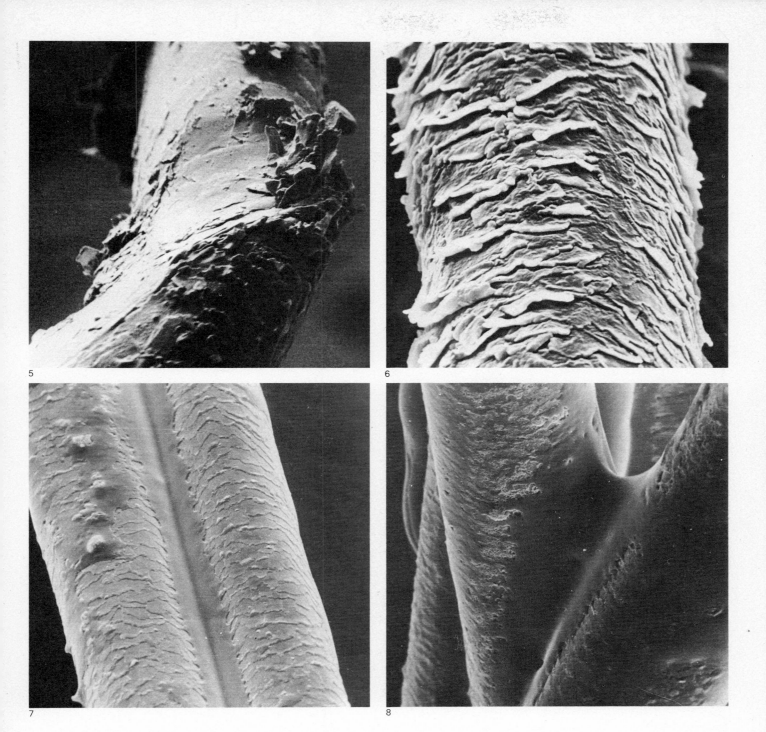

5

6

7

8

on end when fright hormones contract the skin muscles, and there is a connection between baldness and "virility." The male hormone (androgen) which causes hair growth is also, paradoxically, responsible under some circumstances for baldness. Aristotle once remarked that eunuchs seldom lost their hair. He was quite correct and, needless to say, was himself bald.

These scanning electron micrographs show some of the realities behind the cosmetics.

1. The neatly layered scales of protein on healthy, normal hair.

2. A "split end" in disastrous close-up.

3. Cleanly sliced beard hair after shaving with a wet razor.

4. The ragged results of using an electric razor on the beard.

5. "Back-combing" strips the protein scales off the hair's surface.

6. The effect of bleaching and then "perming."

7 & 8. Hair sprays hold the hairs in place by "welding" them together. One example shows a "seam weld", the other a "spot weld."

PHOTOS COURTESY OF A MULTINATIONAL CORPORATION.

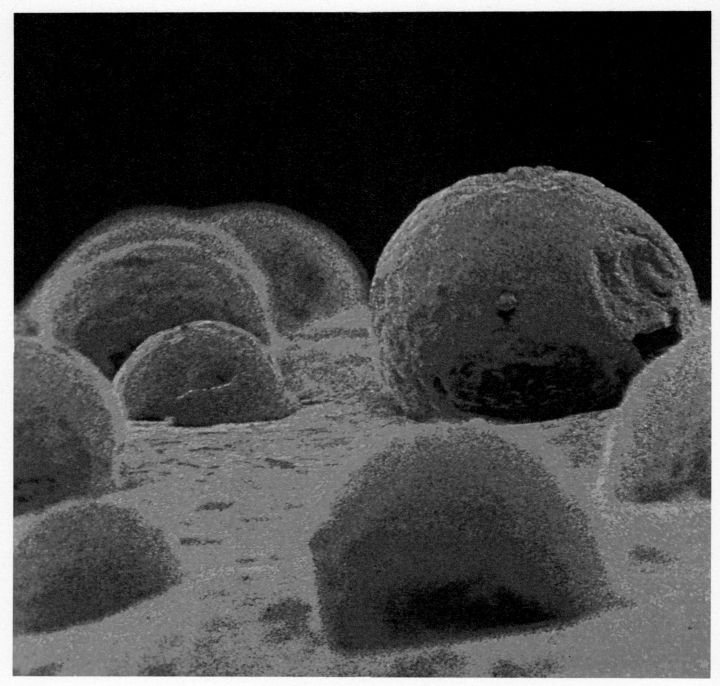

False-colour micrograph of beads of sweat on a human thumb.

Two distinctive features of the human animal are its rapidly evolving baldness and the amount it sweats. There are many kinds of sweat, from the sticky milk common to most mammals, which oozes from around hair follicles and gives us our natural body odour, to the recently evolved system, unique to humans, which cools our skin by dowsing it with water. But there is a third type—the "cold sweat" of fear or excitement—which lubricates our hands and feet, improving our grip and increasing our sensitivity to touch.

Since objects viewed under a scanning electron microscope must be covered with a coating of metal, this picture of beads of sweat represented an extraordinary problem. It was solved by making a cast of the droplets from silicone rubber, moulding a positive replica in epoxy resin, and then coating it with a layer of carbon and silver.

PHOTO COURTESY OF A MULTINATIONAL CORPORATION.

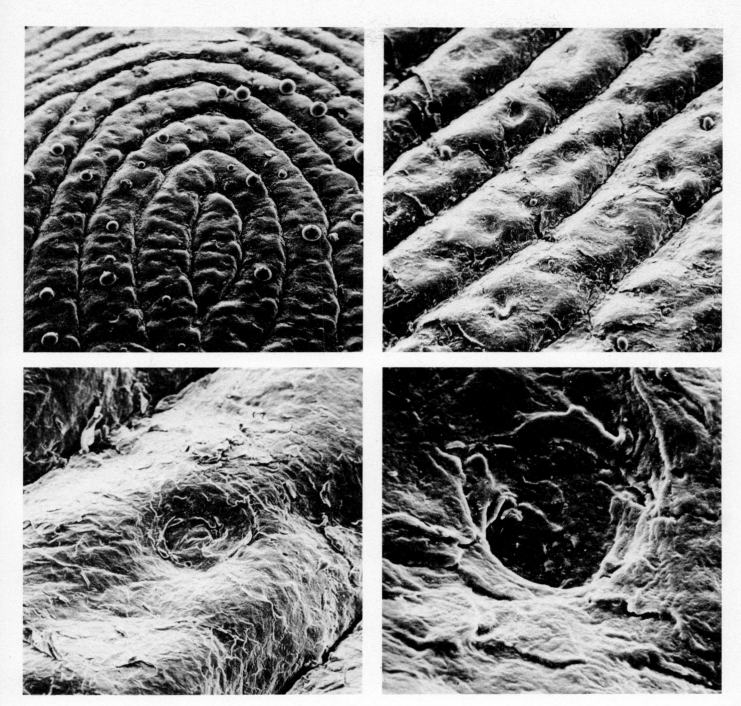

In increasing close-up, an electron microscope explores a sweat gland in the fingertip. If the final picture were life size, the gland itself would be about four or five feet deep:

The sweat on the opposite page was produced from an *eccrine* gland like this. There are up to five million on our bodies, and those which respond to psychological stress are concentrated in the fingers of our hands and soles of our feet. They are one of the first glands to develop, being formed during the third month of pregnancy. Because of this, scientists believe they are an ancient evolutionary heritage. Monkeys have them on their knuckles, for instance, and cats and dogs on their paws.

PHOTOS COURTESY OF A MULTINATIONAL CORPORATION

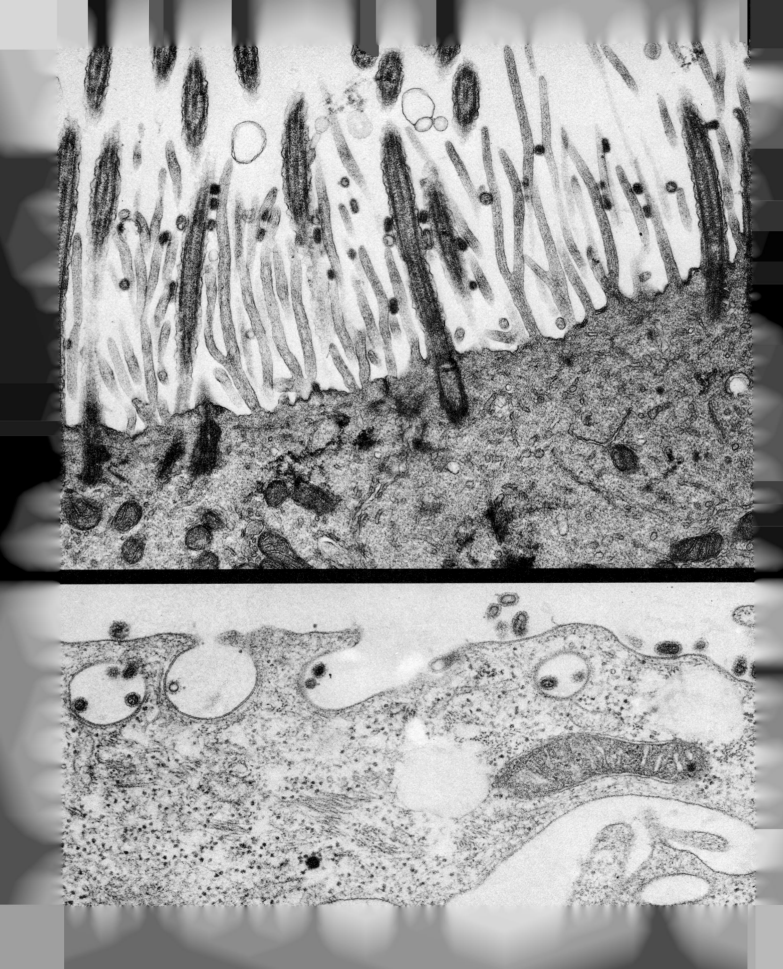

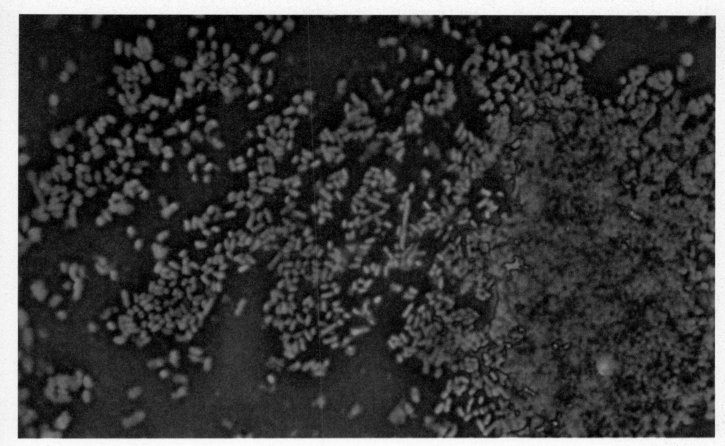

The short deadly shapes of cholera bacteria. This is a one-symptom disease which ultimately kills its host by fusing the electrical systems of his body. Instead of reabsorbing the water and salts used in digestion, the victim discharges them at such a rate that a quarter of total body-weight can be lost in 24 hours. The loss of these salts interferes with the conduction of electricity, especially in the heart muscles, and the patient dies of seizures.

For thousands of years the disease was confined almost entirely to India, but during the 19th century it followed the Imperial trade routes into the industrial slums of Europe. It was spread through contaminated drinking water and accounted, in part, for the Victorian obsession with the technology of sanitation. Pasteur's great rival, Robert Koch, isolated the bacteria in Egypt in 1883, and by the turn of the century it seemed to be under control. But no victory is ever final when it comes to bacteria.

In 1905 an almost identical, but apparently harmless bacteria was detected among Islamic pilgrims from Mecca. It caused no disease, so no action was taken against it. But somehow, during the next fifty years, it acquired the same lethal characteristics as its relative, and since 1961 it has been spreading wave after wave of cholera epidemics throughout the Middle East.

BIOPHOTO ASSOCIATES

Influenza in action. Antibiotics transformed influenza from a lethal plague into the sniffling, but minor, misery most of us are familiar with. But only recently has it been possible to see the evil little virus in action.

1. This strange scene is in fact a cross-section through the surface of the windpipe, with the waving fronds of internal hairs *(cilia)* which constantly sweep it clean. This section, magnified 35,000 times, is sliced so thin that not all the cilia can be seen to join the surface. The smaller branched fronds, called *microvilli*, were unknown before the advent of the electron microscope. The flu viruses are the small dark blobs drifting into this submicroscopic jungle. They attach themselves to the fronds like burrs, sticking them together, so that others can infiltrate between them to the surface.

2. When the prickly balls of flu virus reach the surface, they stick to the membrane of a cell. The membrane reacts by forming pockets, in an effort to swallow the intruders. But once inside, the virus easily works its way into the cell itself, where it multiplies and eventually causes the cell to die.

TRANSMISSION ELECTRON MICROGRAPHS BY COURTESY OF DR R. DOURMASHKIN

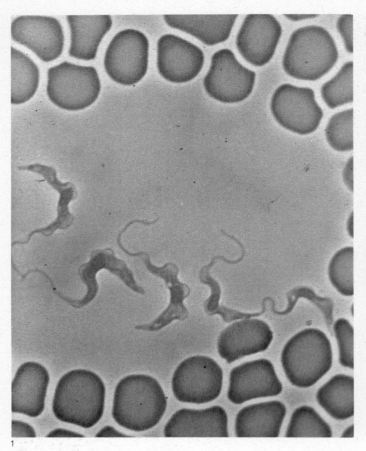

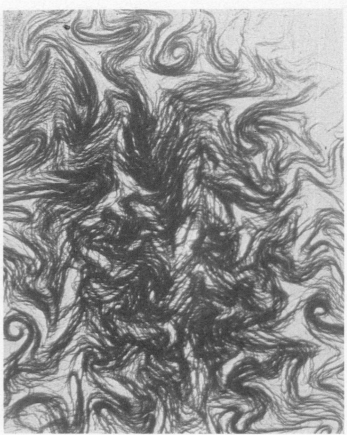

1. These wispy microbes, *trypanosoma brucei*, seen here surrounded by red blood cells, are responsible for one of the oldest diseases of all—sleeping sickness. They evolved alongside our ancestral apes in central Africa, and have lived with us, and in us, ever since. By a strange irony, they were even responsible for the discovery of evolution.

A young Victorian biologist became infected with them while on a research trip to South America, and caught a wasting illness, similar to sleeping sickness, called Chagas Disease. He was forced to retire from field work and, because of the trypanosoma circulating in his bloodstream, he spent the rest of his life in enforced inactivity, working on theoretical papers. His name was Charles Darwin and the work became *The Origin of the Species*.

2. The first bacterium to be identified, in 1849, was this anthrax bacillus. It was a common disease among farm animals, and could be transmitted to human beings as a virulent form of pneumonia. The mill workers of the Industrial Revolution called it "woolpickers' disease," and it was usually fatal.

First serum, then antibiotics, largely wiped it out, but during World War II intensive research went into reviving it as a weapon of biological warfare. Full-scale field trials were carried out off the west coast of Scotland, and an ominous memorial to them remains there today. Gruinard Island is uninhabitable. It is still a lethal no-go area thirty years after those original tests, and will be for years to come.

1. Viewed through a remarkable telescope, deep in the chest, the windpipe branches in two to supply the lungs.

In order to get pictures of this quality a fixed lens system must be used, so the patient goes under a general anaesthetic and a rigid tube is pushed down his throat. The telescope is then passed through the tube. Light is supplied along a bundle of glass fibres running down beside the telescope.

A recent development is the use of fibre optics to carry the image as well as the light. The technique requires the light fibres to be arranged in exactly the same pattern at either end of the tube, which produces a picture made up of rows of dots. This means that the bronchoscope can be flexible and can reach even less accessible parts of the body, but the resulting image is very small and not sufficiently sharp for high-quality photography.

2. The smaller the tube, the more surface area it has in proportion to its volume—and so the windpipe divides into narrower and narrower passageways. The trachea branches into the main bronchi; these in turn divide into smaller bronchi, then into twig-like bronchioles and finally into thousands of tiny air-sacs called alveoli rich in minute blood vessels where O^2 can be exchanged.

The bands of cartilage around the passageways are incomplete rings, like bicycle clips, with the open ends joined by muscles. These expand or contract to alter the diameter of the tube.

3. One irritating sign of bronchitis is the excess mucus usually produced by tissues inflamed by smoke particles. It blankets the cilia, which normally sweep the bronchi clean by brushing inhaled foreign particles back into the trachea, where they can only be removed by coughing. But it is difficult to remove all the mucus, and any that remains is liable to become infected with bacteria and so perpetuate a chronic form of the disease, which is often fatal.

4. The ominous swelling of a cancer has almost entirely constricted the air passages of the patient.

Both bronchitis and lung cancer

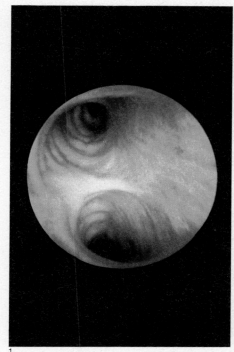

1

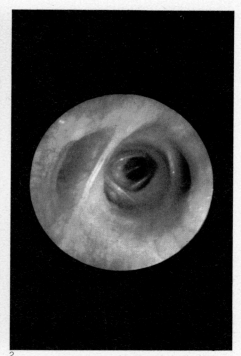

2

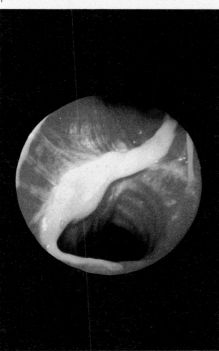

3

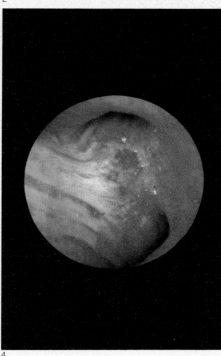

4

are distinctly modern phenomena. The air pollution and cigarette smoking of the past few generations have turned rare diseases into very common ones. Air pollution is now coming under control, but cigarettes are still a profitable source of revenue, not least to the governments who licence the sale of this lethal drug.

Cancer is a parasite formed of our own tissue. It is a colony of cells which have become alienated from their neighbours and no longer respond to the normal control systems of the body. Thus, with nothing to stop them, they simply reproduce as often as they can.

DR PETER STRADLING, DIVISION OF RESPIRATORY MEDICINE, ROYAL POSTGRADUATE MEDICAL SCHOOL, HAMMERSMITH HOSPITAL, LONDON.

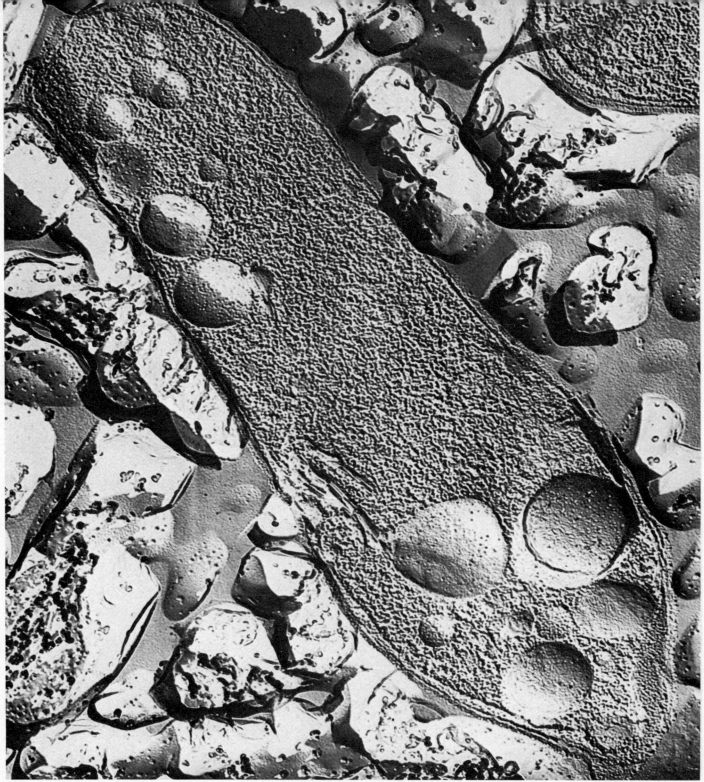

A single bacterium, split open by freeze-fracturing to reveal its contents. The spherical shapes are food-storage elements. The multiple layers of the membrane, one of the most complex parts of the cell, also show up clearly. The surrounding material is the solution of glycerol and water in which the specimen was frozen to −150°C before going under the scanning electron microscope.

These bacteria were found in the soil adjacent to a Japanese factory making mercury compounds and originally came under scrutiny for their unique resistance to the poisonous chemical. They have not yet been positively identified, though they are probably a single-tailed variety called *pseudomonas*. Unfortunately, the tail or flagellum seldom survives the freeze-fracture process.

DR TONY BRAIN REPRODUCED WITH PERMISSION FROM AN ENTRY IN THE ROYAL MICROSCOPICAL SOCIETY'S ANNUAL MICROGRAPH COMPETITION

The life and death of the smallest organisms on earth.
The world of bacteria and viruses are the soft jungles and oceans within our bodies. In this environment. at a sub-microscopic scale, they carry out a ruthless struggle for existence between themselves.

1.   A platoon of viruses attacks a bacterium. The bacterium (an E.coli) is certainly a living organism, but by most definitions the viruses are not. They consist solely of a genetic code – a simple piece of DNA or RNA – in a casing. They need to hijack the bacterium in order to get at its reproductive mechanisms. Once inside, they force the unfortunate cell to reproduce their code instead of its own, until it is filled with viruses and bursts.

   But are these offspring alive? Since they are incapable of independent movement or growth or any other "living" function, and can even be crystallised like common salt, scientists now classify them as interesting, though frequently dangerous, biochemicals.

DR THOMAS F. ANDERSON AND DR LEE D. SIMON

2.   A male bacterium (on the left) conjugating with two females. As befits the smallest organism, its sexual activities are classically simple. Like warships refuelling at sea, the DNA is pumped across, through fine tubes, from one to the other. But even the smallest organism has its predators. The little dots which line the tubes are still more viruses persistently trying to get in on the act.

DR LUCIEN CARO, GENEVA UNIVERSITY. REPRODUCED FROM CURTISS ET AL, *JOURNAL OF BACTERIOLOGY*, 100: 1091-1104, 1969, WITH PERMISSION OF THE PUBLISHER

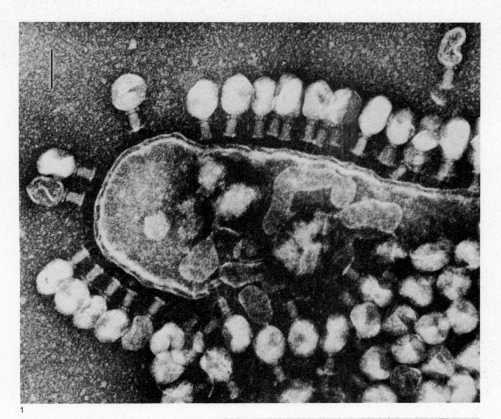

1

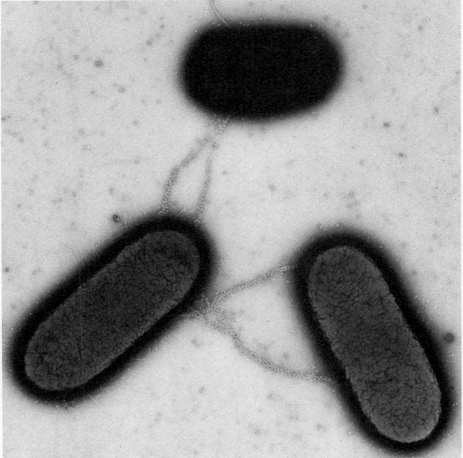

2

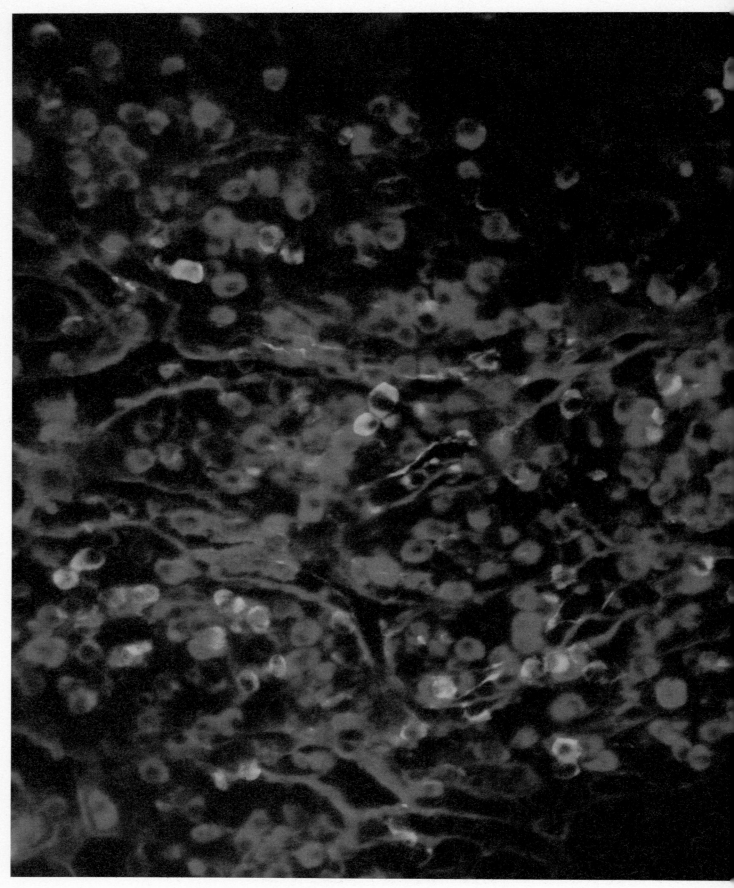

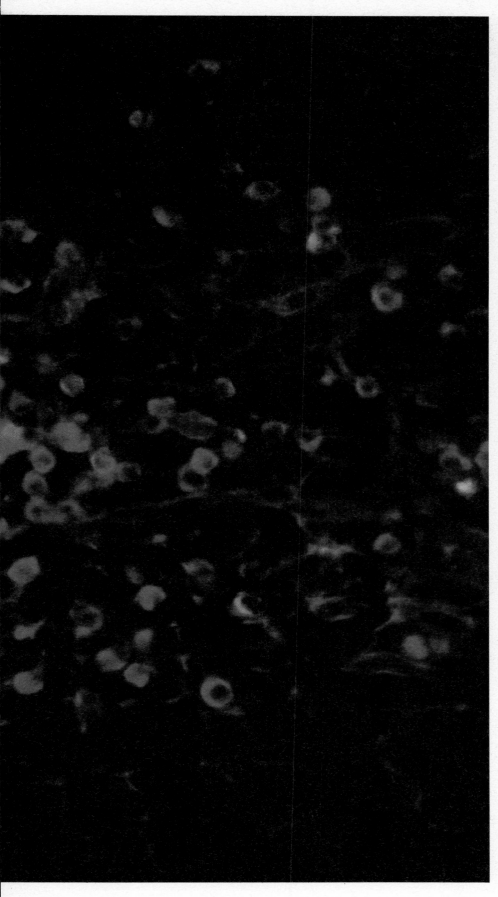

In response to an alarm signal, the body's defence system swings into action and plasma cells release a flood of antibodies into the blood stream. The two types, coloured with red and green fluorescent dyes, can be designed to attack quite different intruders.

Antibodies are not living cells but molecules of protein designed to smother an intruder by attaching themselves to its surface in large numbers. To do this they need to fit as accurately as a piece of a jigsaw puzzle and since there are millions of possible combinations, they need the exact shape and measurements before they can start production. This information is provided by extraordinary organisms called *lymphocytes* which prowl through the body like police patrols, swimming the lymph ducts, hitching a ride in the blood stream and even moving through tissue, in a constant search for intruders. When they find one, say a bacterium which has found its way into a scratch, they report back to their headquarters—the lymph nodes at strategic points around the body—with a full description. The nodes then make the specialised plasma cells which can pump out the precise antibody for the job. If necessary they can also send out specialised hunter-killer lymphocytes to join in the attack.

While this is happening, the body's other defence system is already in operation. Within seconds of the bacterium making its appearance, the first white blood cells are on the scene, devouring the enemy and holding back the invasion until the antibodies come washing around the blood stream to reinforce them.

PROFESSOR ALEXANDER R. LAWTON, UNIVERSITY OF ALABAMA IN BIRMINGHAM.

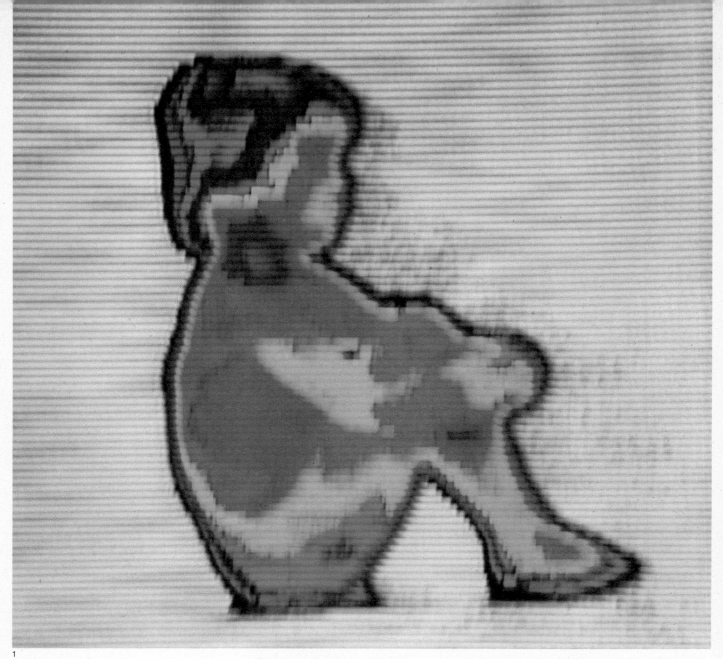

1

New electronic scanning techniques, originally borrowed from space technology, have revolutionised medical diagnosis in the past few years. Though the images on the next few pages may look similar, they carry very different types of information—sound waves bounced off the body's interior, shadows cast by x-rays, heat patterns on our skin, and even the radioactivity of chemicals injected into the patient and recorded by a kind of "visual" Geiger counter.

1. Thermographs give a new perspective on everyday life. Infared home movies, for instance, might demonstrate the minor hazards of family life, such as the cold bottom this four-year old has acquired from sitting on the floor. They also show the importance of protecting one's head on a cold day (there is considerable heat loss from the head and neck), and have proved the old theory that a hot drink is the best way to cool down on a summer's day (because the body's thermostat only responds to your *internal* temperature).

© HOWARD SOCHUREK, FROM THE JOHN HILLELSON AGENCY.

2. This full-length view of a mildly radioactive human being, from the front (left) and the back (right), illustrates a new technique which may soon replace traditional x-rays.

Like a thermograph, it is a picture of body radiation. But instead of heat, it records the invisible glow of gamma rays from a radioactive isotope which has been swallowed or injected. The isotopes collect in certain sites or organs – in this case the backbone, pelvis and ribs (brown and orange)—and an electronic eye then scans to and fro across the body, recording an outline of them.

COURTESY OF ELSCINT (G.B.) LTD.

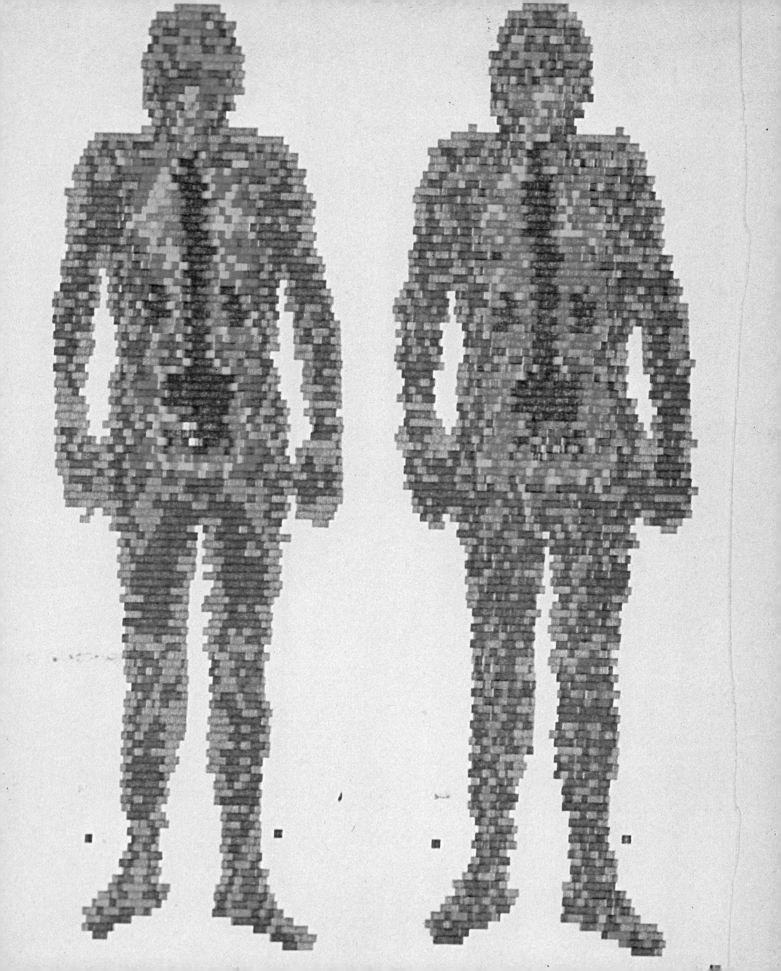

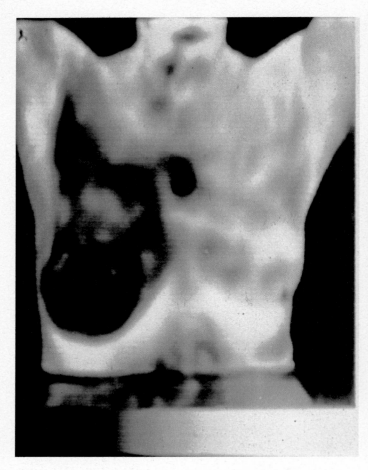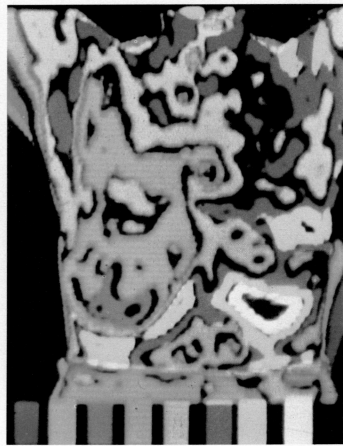

A heat picture reveals the cancer in
a woman's breast. Statistics show
that one in every twenty girls born
will develop breast cancer, so new
methods of treatment or detection
are welcome.

The doctors have a choice of
video pictures—a graded monochrome
image similar to a normal photograph
(left), or a colour-coded version
(right), which gives accurate contour
lines for each temperature and enables
the exact area of the tumour to be
measured. The colour code runs from
dark blue (cold) to yellow and white
(hot). The cancer growth is cooler
than the surrounding tissue and, in
this instance, is so extensive as to
be virtually inoperable.

Thermographs also have many
other medical uses, from showing
when a transplant has "taken" to
detecting vascular diseases and
measuring the severity of burns.

COURTESY OF AGA INFRARED SYSTEMS

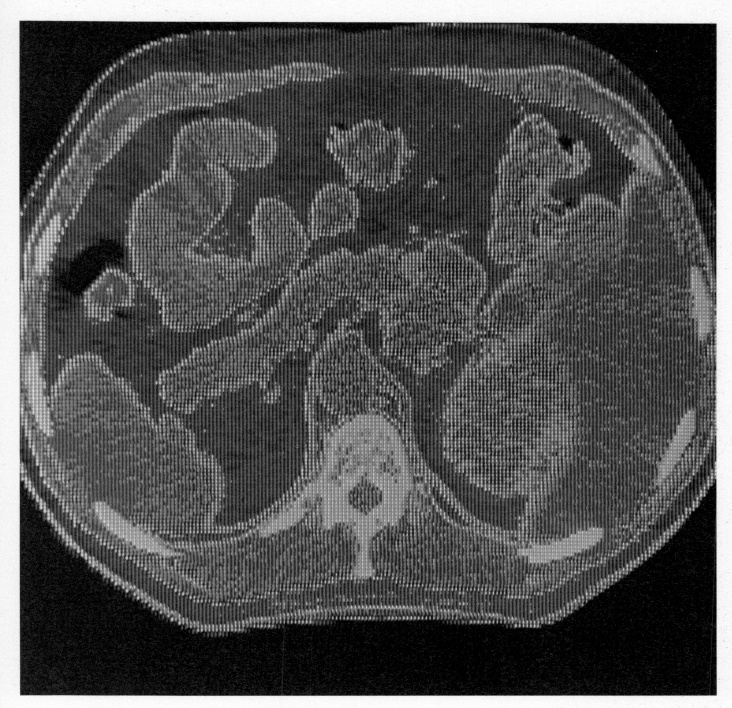

A cross-section through a living person, in this case a "slice" through the mid-abdomen looking down into the body.

The backbone is at the bottom of the picture with the aorta, the body's main blood supply, running down immediately in front of it. The blue lagoons on either side are the spleen (left) and the kidney (right). But a doctor's attention would focus on the green area just off the kidney, which is the clear outline of a renal cyst.

The technique involved, called cross-sectional x-ray, has been described as the biggest advance in medical technology since Wilhelm Roentgen discovered x-rays themselves. A flat, thin beam of the rays is projected through a patient's body. Then, by taking scores of pictures in a circle around it, and using computers to combine the results, it is possible to look into the body from any angle. The shades of grey in the x-ray are then given different colours: bones are yellow, the muscle tissue blue-green, and fats and fluids red-brown. The doctor can then discover the exact area of the cyst at the touch of a button.

COURTESY OF OHIO-NUCLEAR INC.

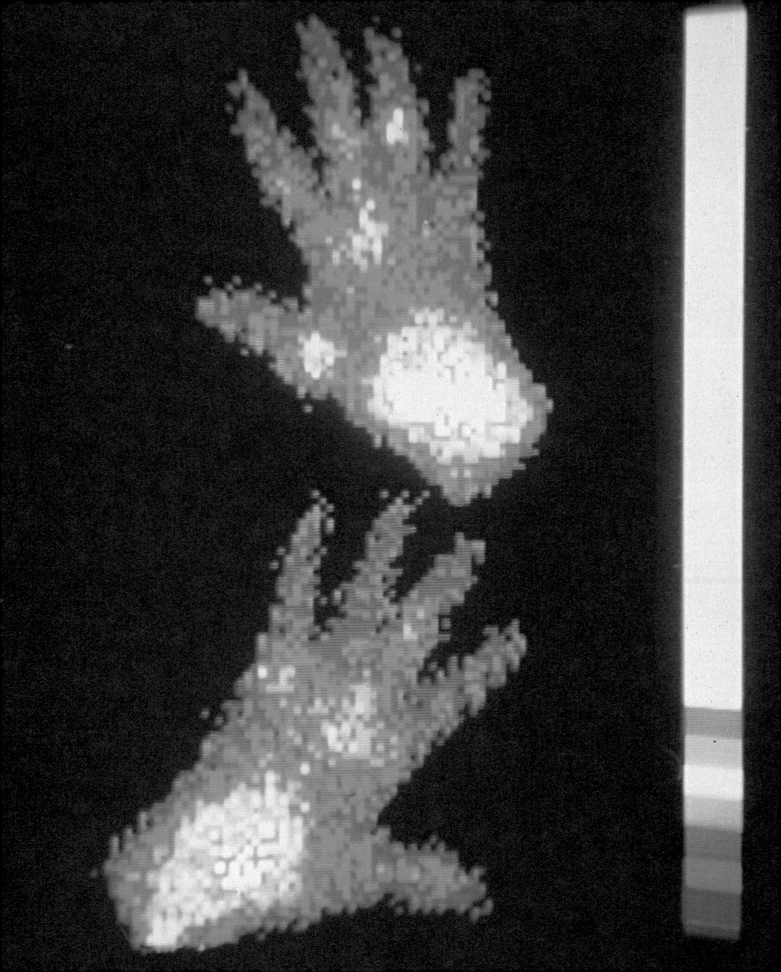

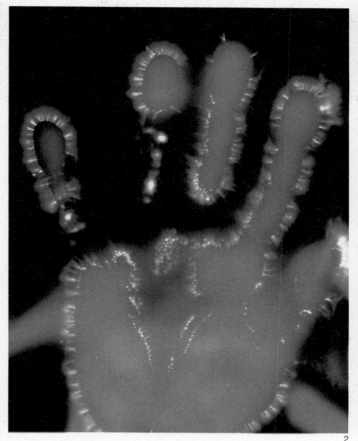

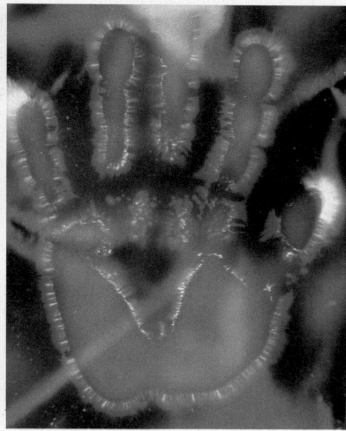

2

3

1. A radioactive trace maps the contours of pain in hands crippled with arthritis. The isotope (white, brown and yellow on the scale) is concentrated in the inflamed tissue around the knuckles and wrist, the most common site for rheumatoid arthritis. In severe cases of this complaint, which affect at least one person in twenty, the adjacent muscles contract as a defensive reaction, deforming or even dislocating the damaged joint.

Doctors have little idea of the causes, but they probably involve a fault in the immune system which makes it attack its own body. Nor is there any clear idea of how the remedies, which range from aspirin and hormone steroids to compounds of gold, actually work. As so often with medicine, one can only alleviate the symptoms and let nature do its work. But when the threat comes from the body's own repair system, there is not much hope of a cure.

COURTESY OF ELSCINT (G.B.) LTD.

2/3. Kirlian photos of the hand of a spiritual healer, Olga Worrel, in its normal state (left) and during a healing session (right). They show what many believe to be the radiant "aura" of all living things. When live tissue, a finger or a leaf, is placed in an electrical field oscillating at high frequency, an extraordinary flaring corona appears around it. This varies with the frequency and with the health, and even the state of mind, of the subject.

DR THELMA MOSS, UNIVERSITY OF CALIFORNIA, LOS ANGELES

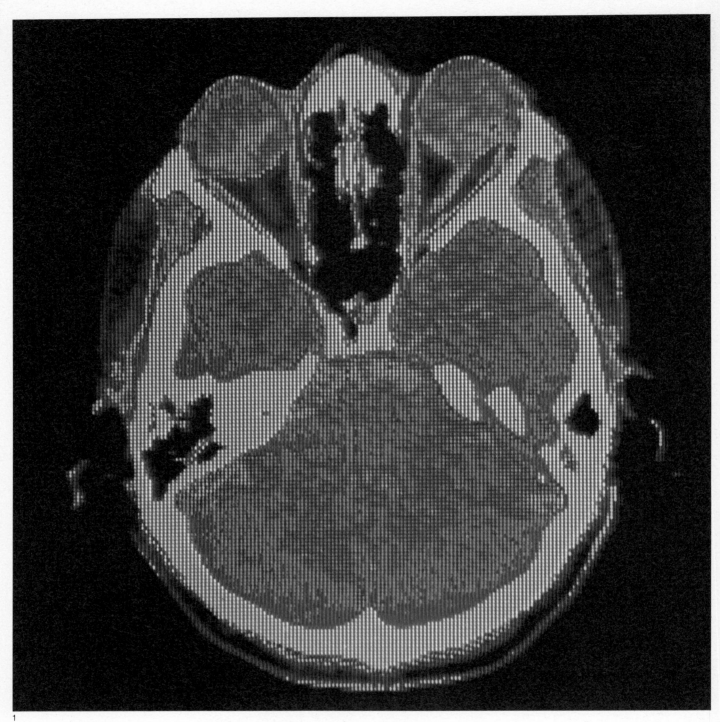

1

The brain consists of about 3lbs of the most complex matter we know of in the universe, and its soft vulnerable tissue almost defies analysis. In order to discover the extent of tumours and other damage, surgeons once had to probe deep inside the skull. Now they can sit at a computer terminal and read the information off a monitor screen.

1. A cross-sectional x-ray (colour coded according to density) through the skull, showing the lower part of the brain at eye-level. The ear and nose cavities are clearly visible and the picture shows the surprising amount of space taken up by the eyeballs with their complex muscles and nerves stretching back into the head.

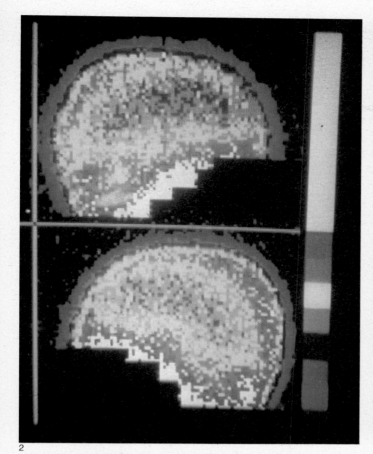

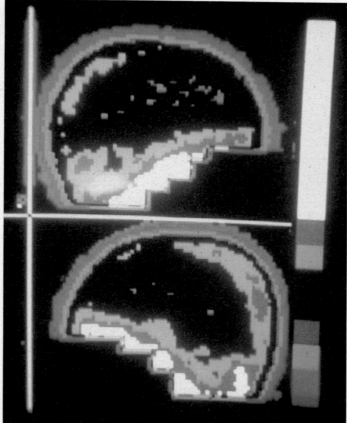

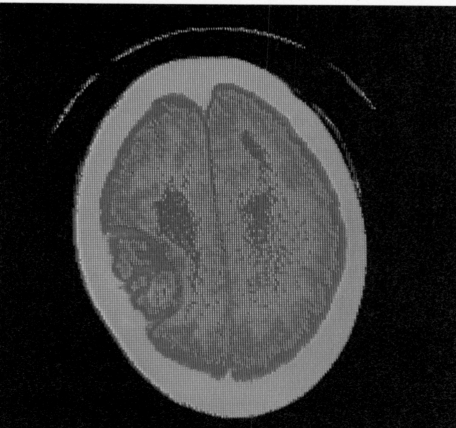

2/3. Radioactive isotopes are also used to map the inside of the skull. Electronic scans of either side of the head (left) show that they have concentrated at the base of the brain. The colour code ranges from red for maximum concentration, to blue for minimum. When the computer has "cleaned up" the picture and provided an accurate isotope-count (right), the diagnosis is confirmed as an *angioma*: a type of tumour which is usually benign.

COURTESY OF ELSCINT (G.B.) LTD.

4. Another cross-sectional x-ray, this time through the top of the brain, showing the two hemispheres which control each side of the body and act as semi-independent computers. The left half controls speech and functions such as mathematics, while the right is concerned with our appreciation of space.

This patient is suffering from a swollen lymph gland (on the left) surrounded by engorged blood vessels applying dangerous pressure on the brain.

COURTESY OF OHIO-NUCLEAR INC.

2

3

4

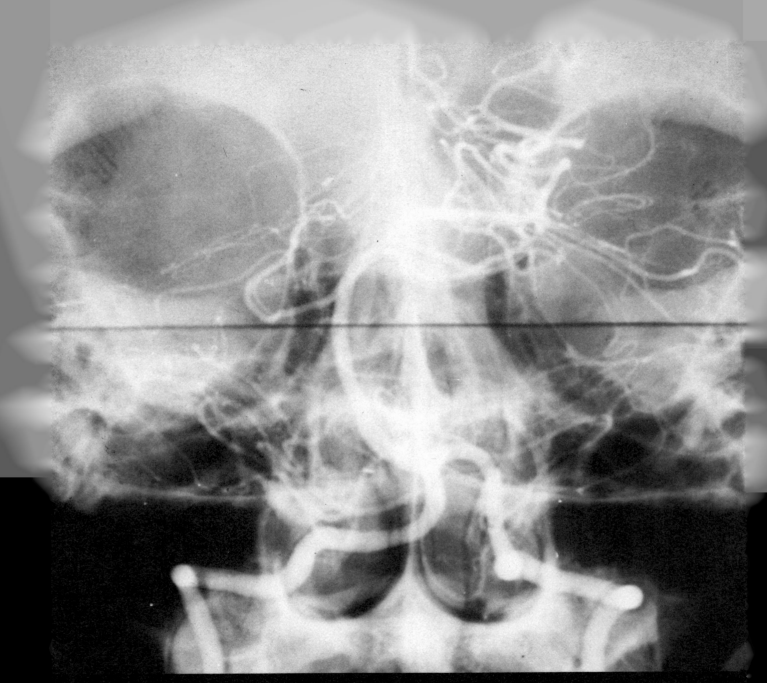

1. Face-on x-ray view of a human head clearly picks out the main arteries supplying blood to the rear part of the brain.

In order to make the blood vessels visible, narrow tubes or *catheters* are inserted into the arteries in the patient's legs, and pushed all the way up until they reach his head. Then a water-soluble contrast agent that is opaque to x-rays is passed through the tubes.

The two *vertebral* arteries can be seen as the heavy white lines twisting their way upwards at the bottom of the picture. They join up behind the nose to form the *basilar* artery. The *carotid* arteries, which supply the front part of the brain, do not appear in the picture.

This x-ray technique is useful in spotting diseases of the arteries or displacements of them caused by tumours. The insertion of the catheters is not excessively uncomfortable, though a general anaesthetic is usually used.

COURTESY OF THE LYSHOLM RADIOLOGICAL DEPARTMENT, THE NATIONAL HOSPITAL, QUEEN SQUARE, LONDON.

2. X-ray portrait of a healthy young woman wearing a necklace.

The "density slicing" is not electronic in this case. The colours were produced by a new kind of photographic paper. A normal x-ray, similar to the previous picture, was printed on a special emulsion, using several exposures of different lengths, and gradually building up the various colours according to the shades of grey in the original negative.

COURTESY OF AGFA-GEVAERT.

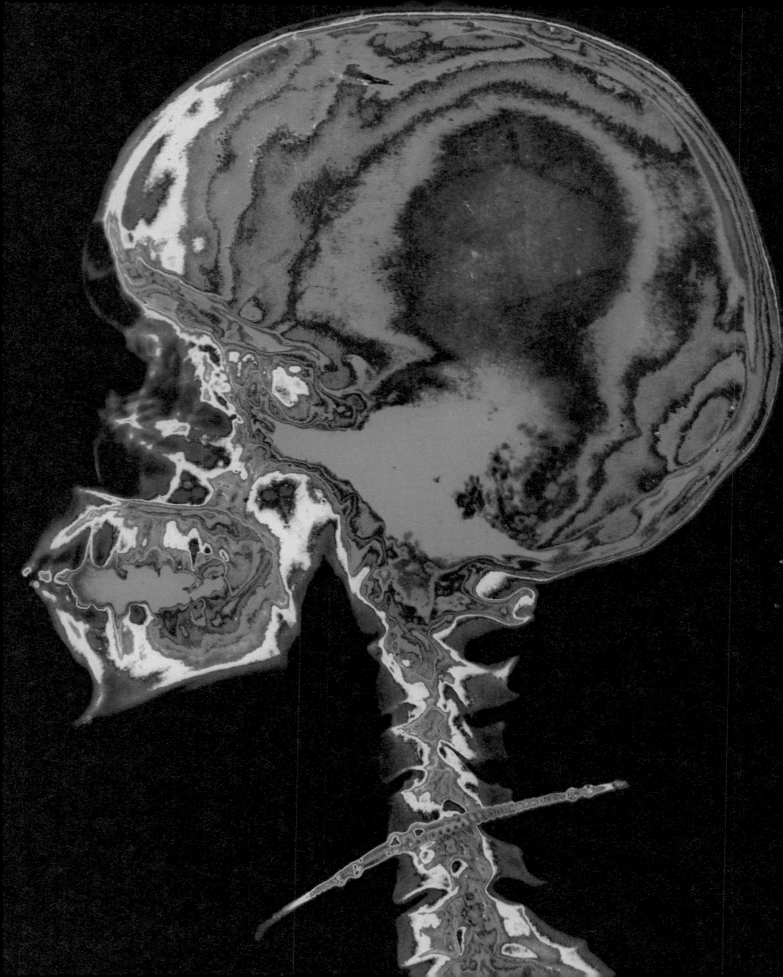

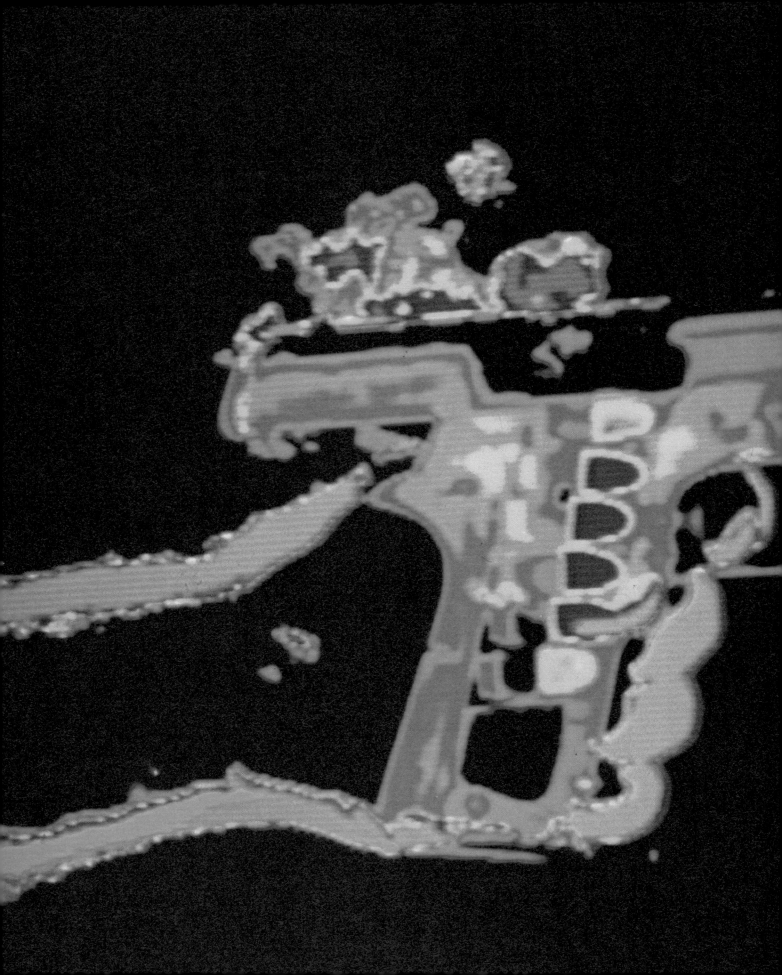

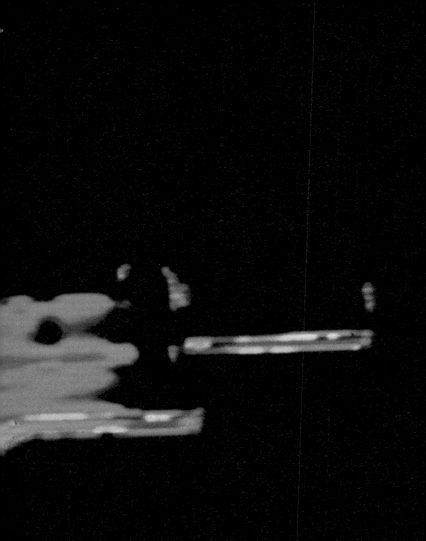

World About Us

When electronic techniques are focused on our familiar world, it suddenly seems very unfamiliar. The food we eat, the machines we use, the watches, needles and telephones, the automobiles and buildings we take for granted, are changed. They shimmer with radiation or develop startling detail. But the images and patterns have always been there. It is just our senses that are too slow or clumsy to perceive them. We can only experience averages—the effects and illusions of our reality.

High-speed x-ray of an automatic weapon turns the trademark of macho violence inside out—and the gun becomes a bouquet of candy.

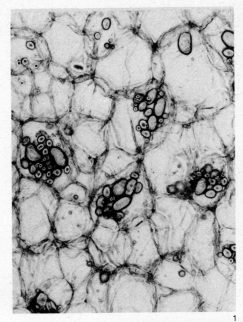

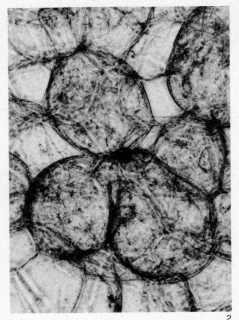

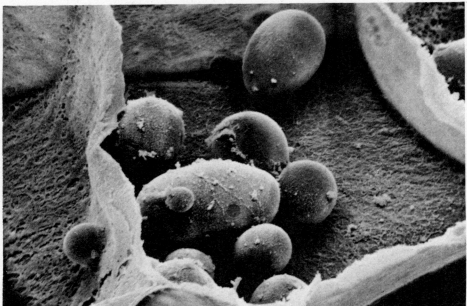

1. Microscope slide of a potato before cooking. The small dark objects are grains of starch which have accumulated in some of the cells. X 80.

BIOPHOTO ASSOCIATES.

2. Microscope slide of potato after cooking. The starch grains have burst under the internal pressure of steam and their cells have ballooned out, crushing the surrounding tissues. X 80.

BIOPHOTO ASSOCIATES.

3. A scanning electron micrograph reveals what the starch grains actually look like in the box-like compartment of a potato cell.

If our bodies could digest cellulose, we could solve our food problems by simply eating grass. But starch—a long untidy chain of glucose molecules—is the closest thing to cellulose that we can digest. It has no special fattening properties. Potatoes and bread are usually omitted from a diet simply in order to cut down the overall intake of food. X 750.

DR L. M. BEIDLER, FLORIDA STATE UNIVERSITY.

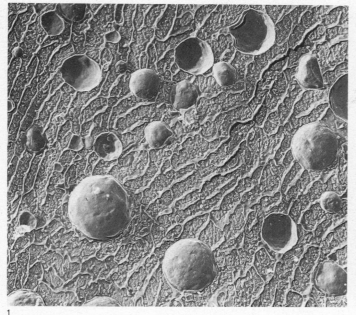

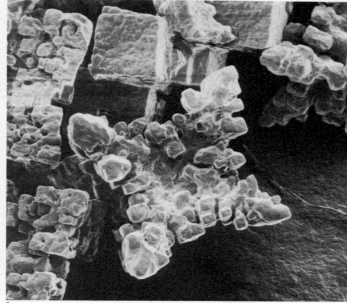

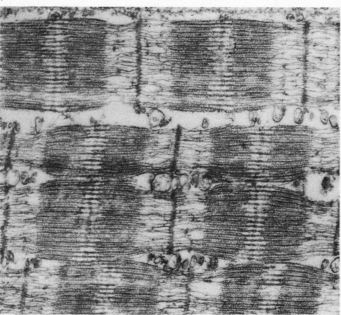

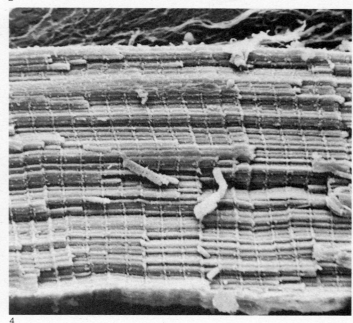

1

2

3

4

1. A slice of milk . The technique used to split open bacteria on page 108 also produced this freeze-fractured section of creamy milk. The spheres are globules of fat, floating in the whey.

BIOPHOTO ASSOCIATES.

2. Grains of common table salt, enlarged 600 times under an electron microscope, become a mosaic construction-kit of crystals.

COURTESY OF ICI LTD., MOND DIVISION.

3. A microscope slide of human muscle tissue. Raw meat, in other words.

The muscles of humans and animals contain two nourishing proteins, *actin* and *myosin,* in long thin bundles of cells. When they are alive, they contract by a chemical process. The proteins combine to produce *actomyosin,* the actin bundles are then drawn further into the myosin bundles, and the overall length is shortened.

The stripes across the bundles, about 1/1000th of an inch wide, are formed by the alternation of the two proteins. Most flesh (and meat) is composed of striped muscles, although there are other types in the body, such as the smooth muscles of the digestive tract and blood vessels.

DR H. E. HUXLEY, MRC LABORATORY OF MOLECULAR BIOLOGY, CAMBRIDGE.

4. Muscles (of beef in this case) are turned into steak by the application of thermal stress. This scanning electron micrograph, magnified 2500 times, shows how the heat breaks down the connecting tissues, liquifies fats and damages the cell membranes, so that stomach acids can get to work on the proteins more easily.

DR L. M. BEIDLER, FLORIDA STATE UNIVERSITY.

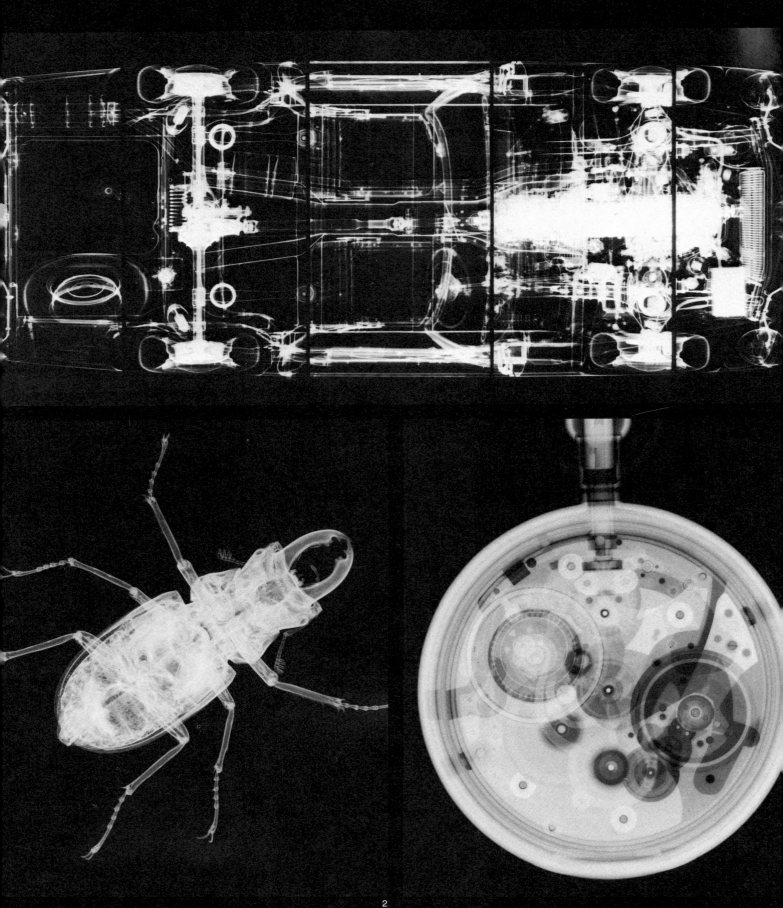

2

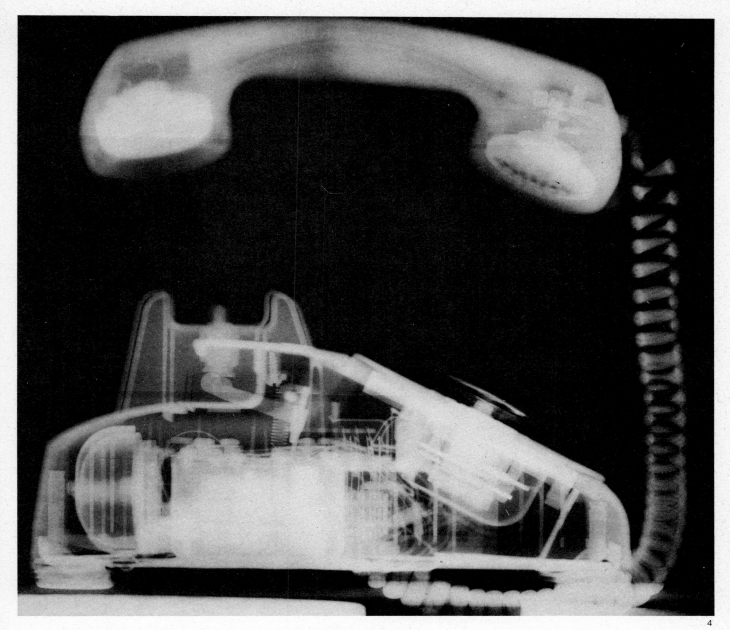

4

1. It required a lethal 50-hour exposure to radioactive cobalt to obtain this x-ray of a Mercedes sports car. The huge picture is made up from five strips of film, and among the features of interest are the "cross-sections" of the tyres and the opaque square of the lead-lined battery.

COURTESY OF AGFA-GEVAERT

2. X-rays have come a long way since Wilhelm Roentgen won the Nobel prize for discovering them in 1901. One new development is that they can be focussed and projected through an object, which allows magnified and stereoscopic pictures to be taken. The technique also provides extraordinarily sharp definition, as this view of a stag beetle demonstrates.

UNITED KINGDOM ATOMIC ENERGY AUTHORITY.

3. Even the most sophisticated x-ray devices have their limitations. Metals show up as sharp black shadows but most "soft" materials are blurred or invisible. However, a new technique called neutron radiography (which uses a stream of particles generated by a nuclear reactor) reveals the details of chalk and cheese, water and even gas. It can photograph a wax candle through four feet of solid lead or, as here, the insides of a stopwatch.

UNITED KINGDOM ATOMIC ENERGY AUTHORITY.

4. Neutron radiograph of a telephone.

COURTESY OF THE GENERAL ELECTRIC COMPANY OF THE USA.

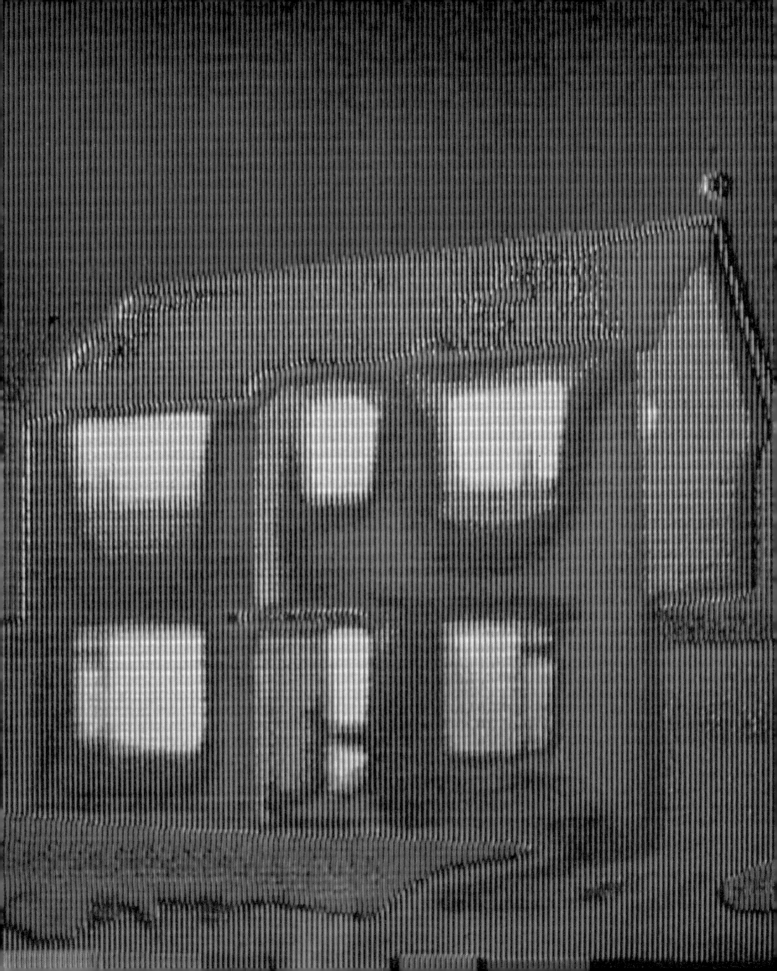

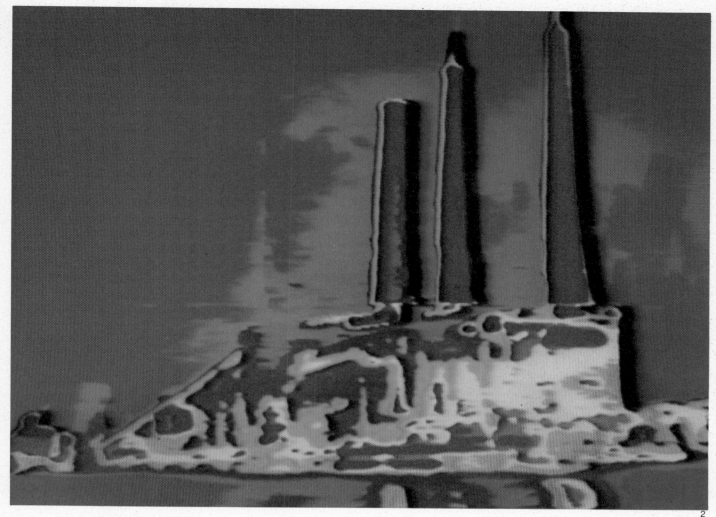

2

Heat cameras reveal the pathology of our environment as effectively as that of our bodies. They document the extraordinary wastage of energy in urban areas which creates a micro-climate over our cities up to 5° F warmer than the surrounding country.

1. Heat scan of a suburban house. The colour scale runs from white and yellow (hot) to green and blue (cold). It shows that although the roof is well insulated, the thin gable wall is costing the owner a small fortune in fuel bills, and the windows are almost as transparent to heat as they are to light.

Houses are difficult to insulate because small buildings, like small organisms, tend to cool more rapidly than large ones. Paradoxically, the more effective the insulation the more energy then has to be spent on cooling and ventilation. Massive buildings, shopping centres and office blocks have severe problems

getting rid of surplus heat from such innocent sources as light bulbs and people's bodies.
COURTESY OF AGA INFRARED SYSTEMS.

2. Thermograph of a power station, showing the heat of the smokestacks (red) due to flue gases flowing through them.

Power factories are among the worst examples of energy wastage. In most cases heat is used to create steam to drive the generators to make electricity. The heat is then either dumped into the environment, or recovered at considerable cost, using still more energy in the process.
INFRARED THERMOGRAM COURTESY OF BARNES ENGINEERING COMPANY.

Overleaf. The buildings of New York City, with the Empire State building in the centre, are red-hot. Around and above them a layer of warm yellow air rises and becomes dispersed in the cool green atmosphere above.

The thermogram was made to show the amount of heat produced by a big city like New York. Some of this heat comes from the solar energy absorbed by the ground and the walls of buildings during the day. But a larger part of it is output from the human consumption of energy—to light streets, heat buildings, operate machinery, and drive cars.

New York, in this frame of reference, is just a giant bonfire. And we keep feeding it with more and more fuel in the form of coal, gas, oil and electricity.
© HOWARD SOCHUREK, FROM THE JOHN HILLELSON AGENCY.

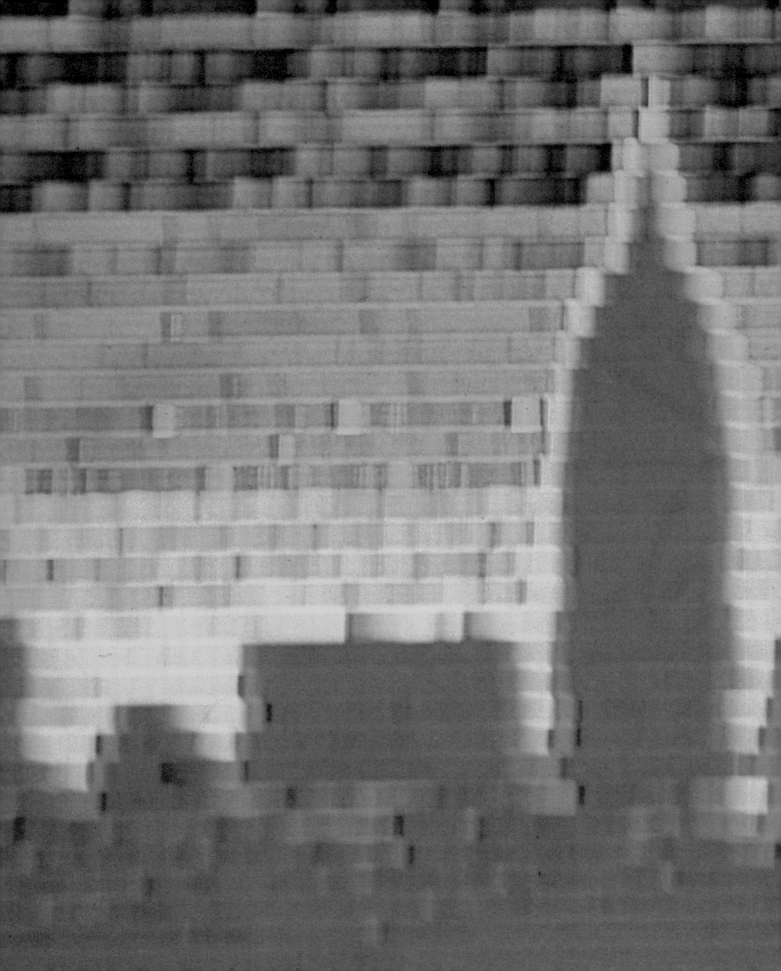

Scanning electron micrographs of an artificial fibre called Meterofil (right) and a spider's web (below).

The man-made fibres look like a smooth piece of engineering, but they do not compare with a spider's thread. The liquid protein that webs are spun from sets hard, in seconds, to the tensile strength of steel. Yet it can be swallowed and digested as easily as food.

It is as close as nature comes to that ultimate myth of a one-molecule string. A laboratory recently wished to examine droplets of a certain drug by suspending them from the finest possible thread. The finest man-made thread turned out to be a strand of gold 4 microns thick (a micron=one millionth of a metre). The smallest of all, however, was a thread only 2 microns in diameter produced by a minute spider. It was collected by knocking the creature off a pencil-like bobbin and winding in the thread as the spider fell down it.

PHOTO (TOP) COURTESY OF CAMBRIDGE SCIENTIFIC INSTRUMENTS. PHOTO (BOTTOM) REPRODUCED BY KIND PERMISSION OF THE EASTMAN KODAK COMPANY AND KODAK LIMITED.

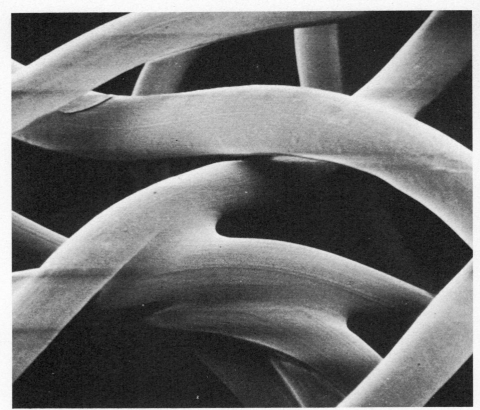

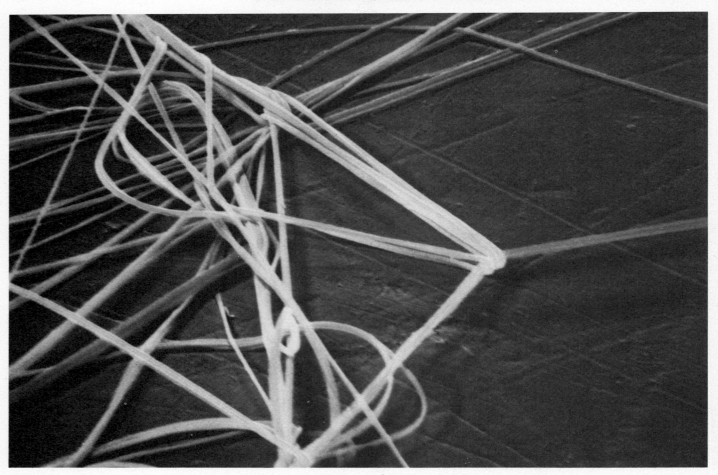

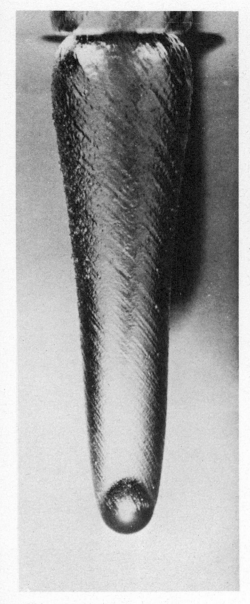 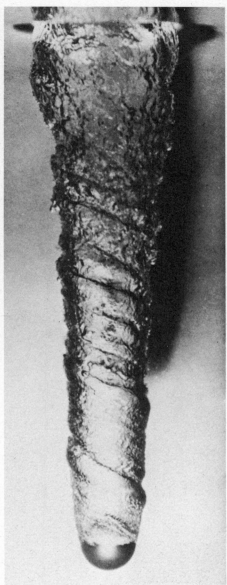 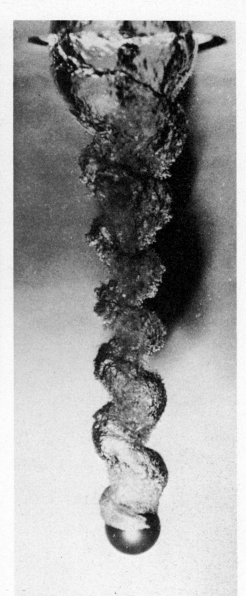

Skin spin. Like the wake of a submarine missile or bathwater spiralling down a drain, a spinning ball dropped into water produces a complex structure of air and liquid behind it, with different kinds of flow and drag superimposed on each other.

When the "skin" of surface tension between air and water is violently stretched, it changes its character. Without any spin the ball produces a cavity with smooth transparent walls. At 24 revolutions per second (left) ridges appear on the walls. At 80 rps (centre) the opaque walls are

"boiling" as the surface breaks down. And at 120 rps (right) there are two cavities, a wide one and a narrow one, wrapped around each other and starting at different points on the ball.

US NAVAL UNDERSEA CENTER, SAN DIEGO.

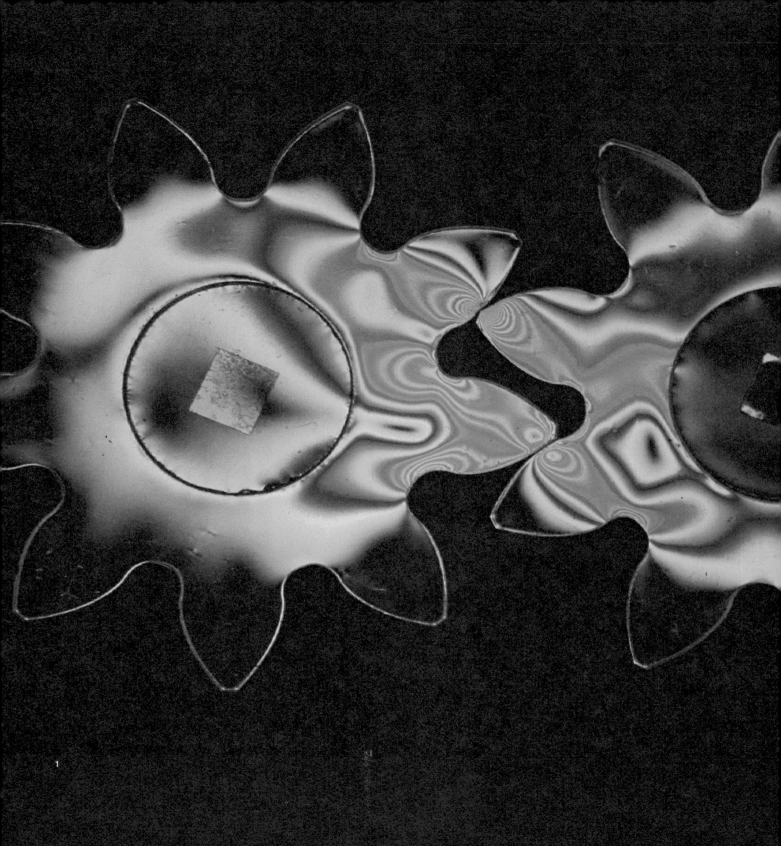

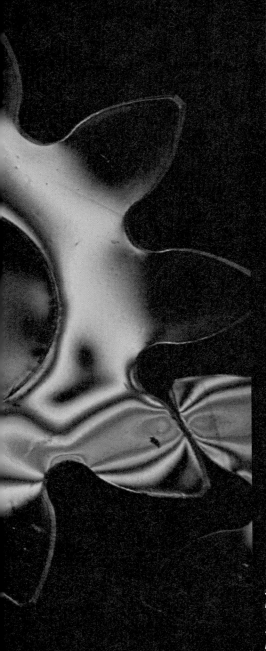

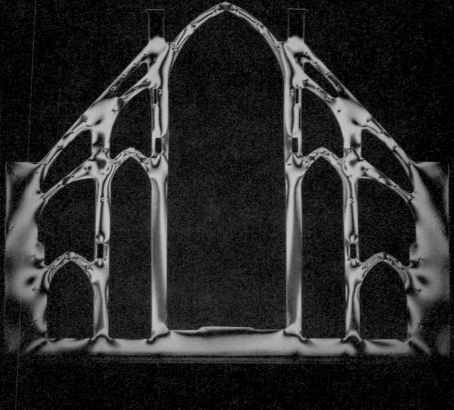

2

The pressures inside solid materials, such as metal or stone, can be revealed by photographing transparent plastic models of the structure. Under polarised light, patterns of stress show up as coloured bands or "fringes."

New industrial or consumer designs are often analysed by this technique. But because it can indicate dangerous weaknesses in a product, the results are usually kept a close secret—especially from rival manufacturers.

1. These anonymous cogwheels show how the stress, flowing from one wheel to the other, is focused at the point of contact.

2. The effect of a 60 mph side wind on Amiens Cathedral, reproduced by a small plastic model of the original Gothic arches. The stress from the wind, and from the heavy cathedral roof, is simulated by loading the model with weights. The coloured fringes show how the load is distributed through the soaring (but practical) columns and buttresses. The pressures are most intense where the pattern is crowded.

Similar experiments on a church in Rouen revealed stresses severe enough to cause cracking, and a check on the building confirmed that the cracks were indeed there.

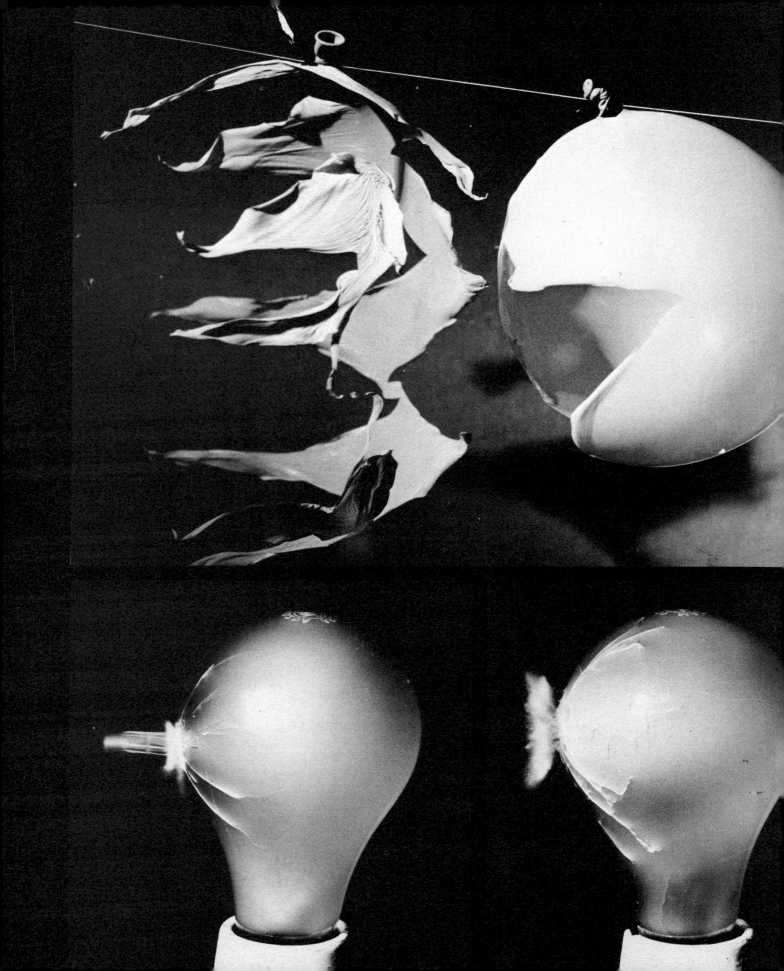

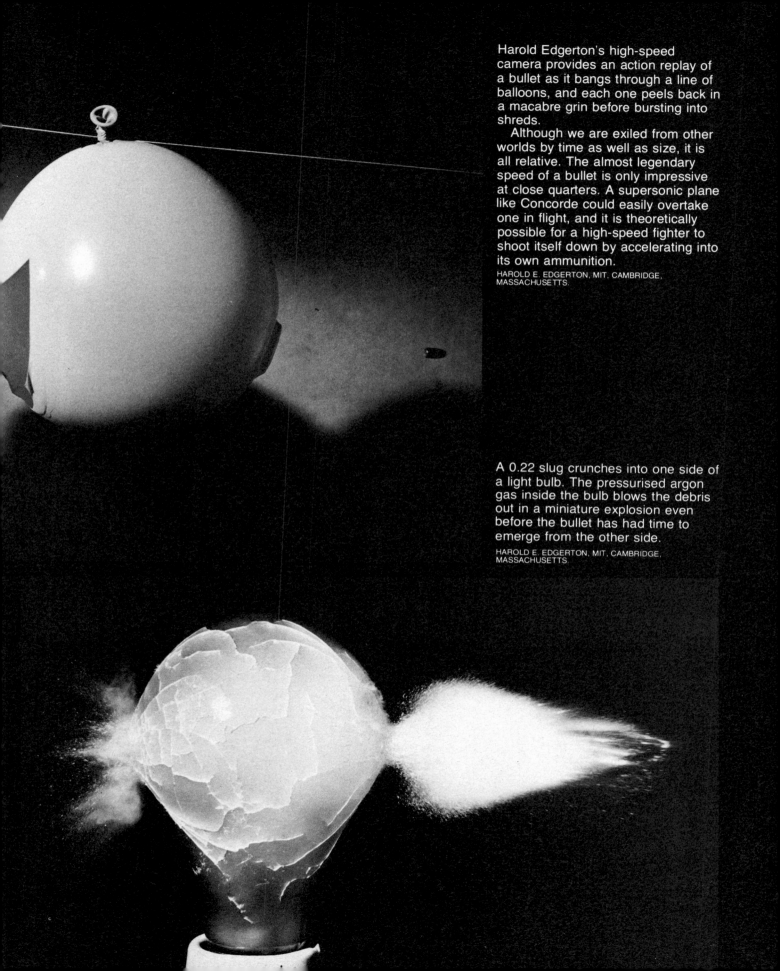

Harold Edgerton's high-speed camera provides an action replay of a bullet as it bangs through a line of balloons, and each one peels back in a macabre grin before bursting into shreds.

Although we are exiled from other worlds by time as well as size, it is all relative. The almost legendary speed of a bullet is only impressive at close quarters. A supersonic plane like Concorde could easily overtake one in flight, and it is theoretically possible for a high-speed fighter to shoot itself down by accelerating into its own ammunition.

HAROLD E. EDGERTON, MIT, CAMBRIDGE, MASSACHUSETTS.

A 0.22 slug crunches into one side of a light bulb. The pressurised argon gas inside the bulb blows the debris out in a miniature explosion even before the bullet has had time to emerge from the other side.

HAROLD E. EDGERTON, MIT, CAMBRIDGE, MASSACHUSETTS.

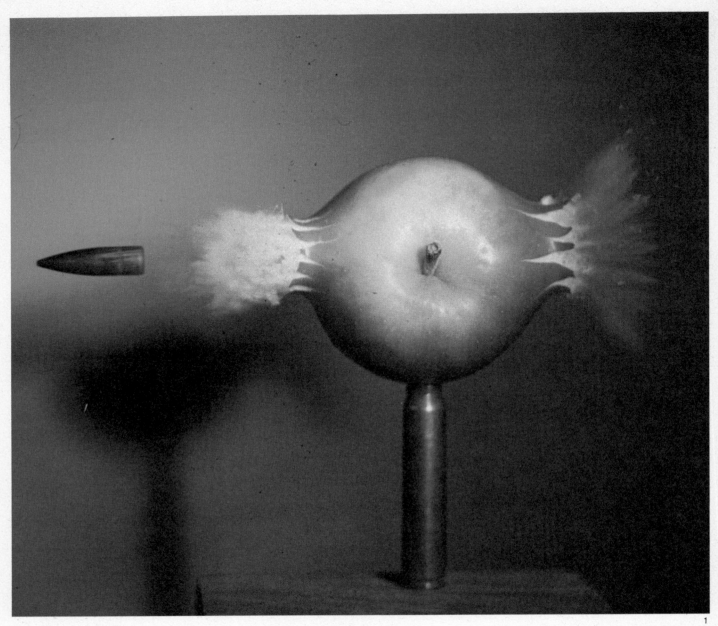

1

1. A .30 bullet acquires a flavour before its target disintegrates.

HAROLD E. EDGERTON, MIT, CAMBRIDGE, MASSACHUSETTS.

2. This picture illustrates the uses of infrared photography in police work. Though the murder victim's body is gone, thermography reconstructs its position from the heat it left on the floor. The policeman sees only a rug; the thermogram sees the heat image of a corpse.

RALPH MORSE, LIFE. © TIME INC., 1977. FROM COLORIFIC PHOTO LIBRARY LTD.

3. Another way to photograph the past is the use of holographs, the astonishing 3-D pictures taken by laser light.

This suspect footprint was made, on a carpet 24 hours previously and once again is quite invisible to the naked eye. But the tufts of carpet take a long time to recover completely and the impression, however slight, is still there. Several holographs were taken of the same spot at twenty minute intervals and the movement of the fibres as they slowly straightened showed up when they were superimposed.

The technique is so accurate that it can register a movement of only 1/100,000th of an inch and could have photographed this footprint on a bare wooden floor.

COURTESY OF EMI ELECTRONICS LTD.

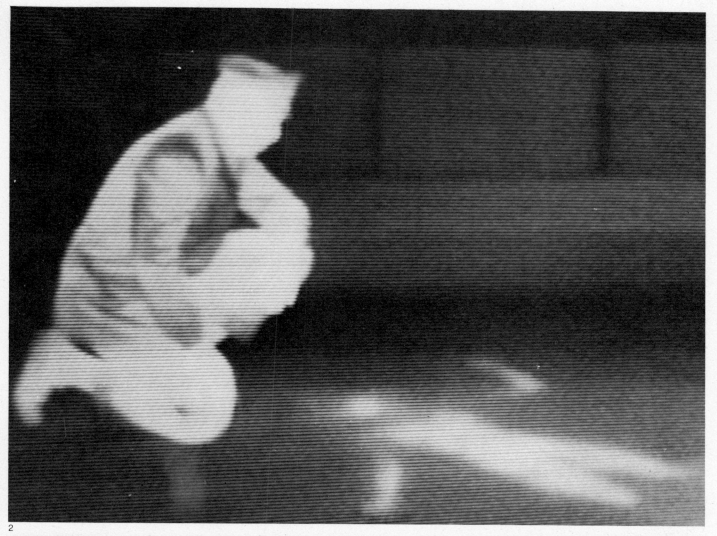

2

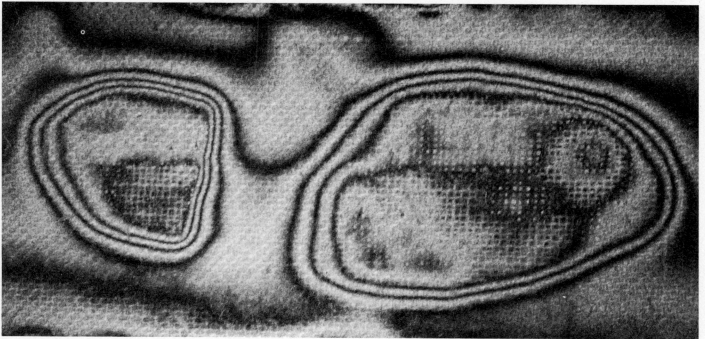

3

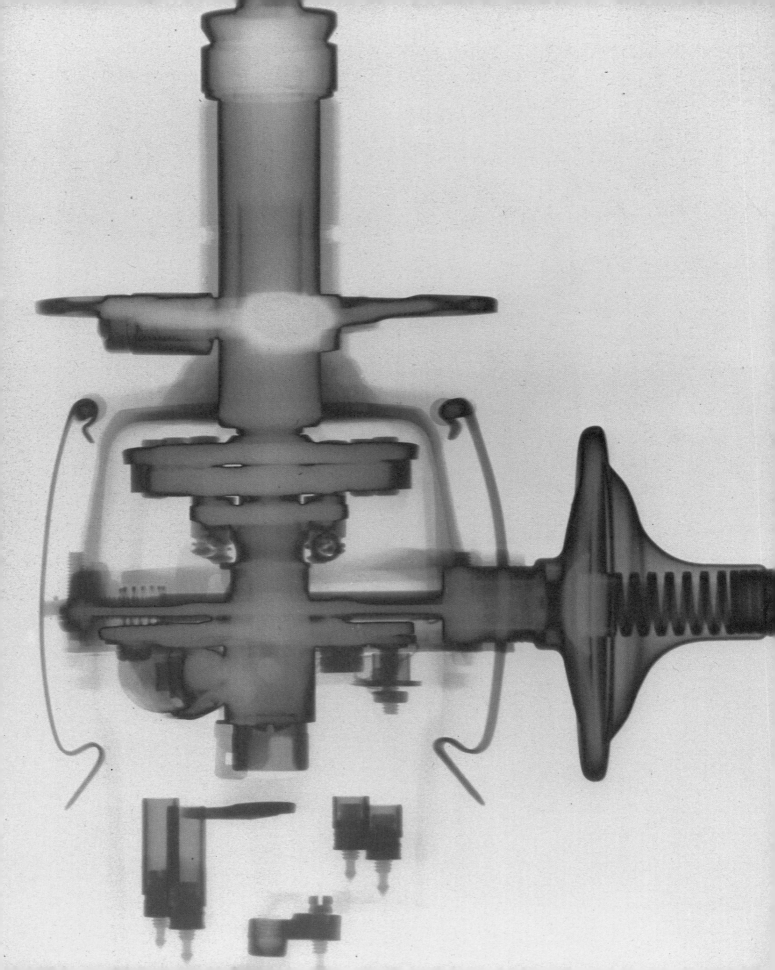

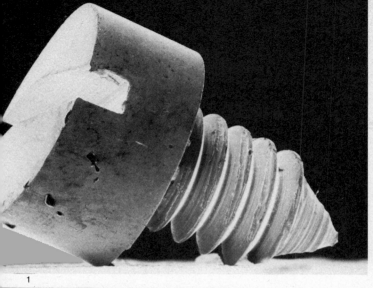

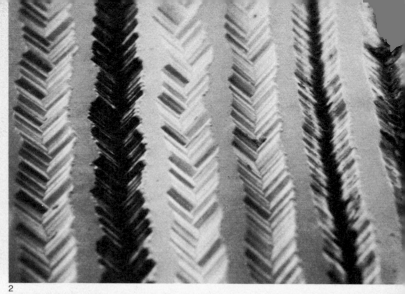

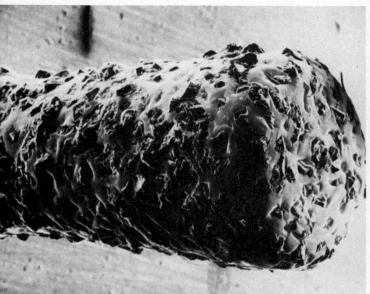

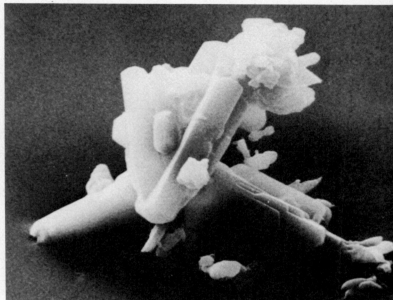

Artificially coloured x-ray photograph of the distributor from an automobile engine.
UNITED KINGDOM ATOMIC ENERGY AUTHORITY.

1. The most delicate precision engineering looks crude in close-up. This, for instance, is the tiny screw from the balance wheel of a watch, enlarged 130 times.

2. Solid sound. The grooves of a phonograph record, enlarged 130 times, are a ridged assault-course along which the stylus is dragged, converting each bump and grind into electrical impulses.

3. Small is not always beautiful. This ugly stump is the diamond-studded tip of a dentist's drill, enlarged 2300 times.

4. The most popular medicine in the world: *acetylsalicylic acid,* better known as aspirin. It is still not understood exactly how it works to block pain and cure rheumatism. It just does. On the other hand it does not, as many people believe, promote sleep or relieve depression.

PHOTOS 1, 2, 3 REPRODUCED BY KIND PERMISSION OF THE EASTMAN KODAK COMPANY AND KODAK LIMITED.
PHOTO 4 BY TONY BRAIN.

When familiar objects go under the microscope, the tricks of scale produce surprising images and textures. 1. The coiled tungsten filament of an electric light bulb. 2. The cutting edge of a dental drill. 3. the translucent matting of kleenex tissue. 4. The stitched network of a nylon stocking.

PHOTOS FROM MICHAEL FREEMAN, DAILY TELEGRAPH COLOUR LIBRARY (1/2), BIOPHOTO ASSOCIATES (3), AND MICROCOLOUR LTD.)4).

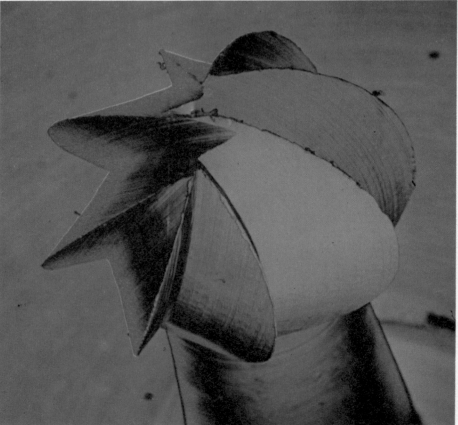

1

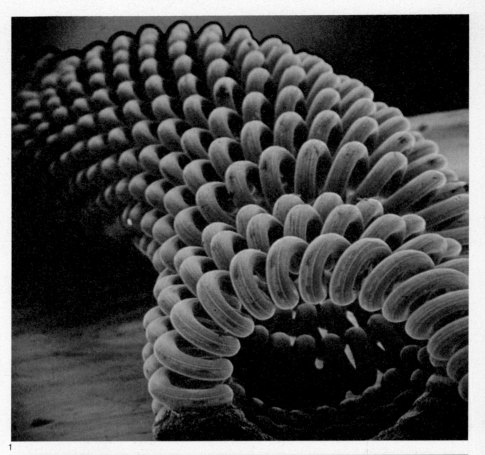

2

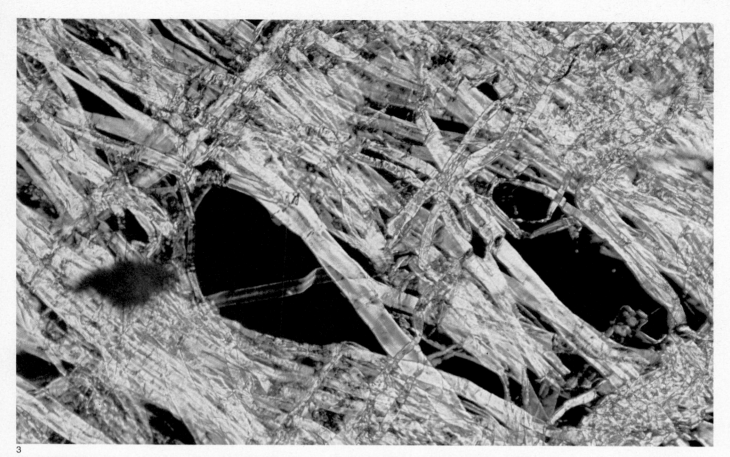

3

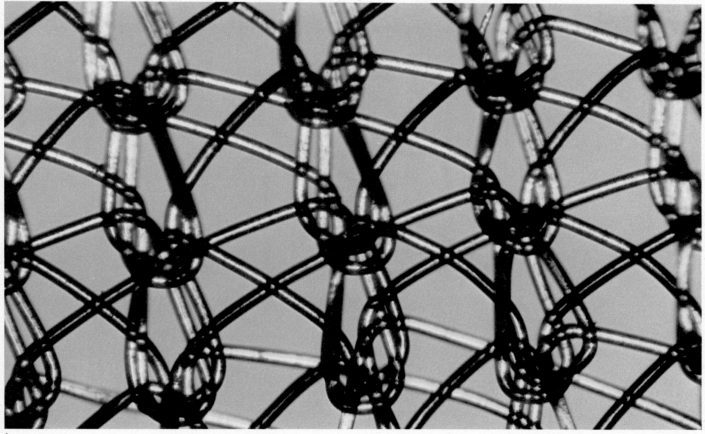

4

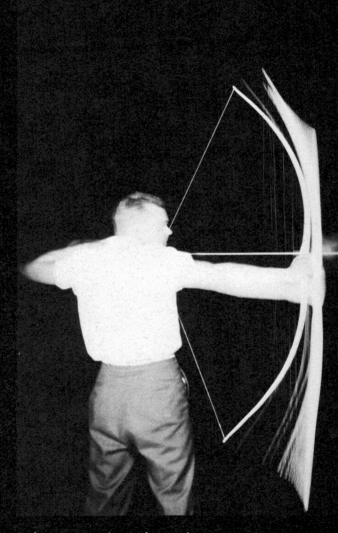

1. As an arrow leaps from a bow,
its flight is captured by a strobe light
flashing 100 times a second. To give
some comparison with the speed of
human reaction, a blink lasts about
1/5th of a second.

HAROLD E. EDGERTON. MIT, CAMBRIDGE.
MASSACHUSETTS.

2. Human precision engineering
compared with nature's: a bee sting
through the eye of a needle.

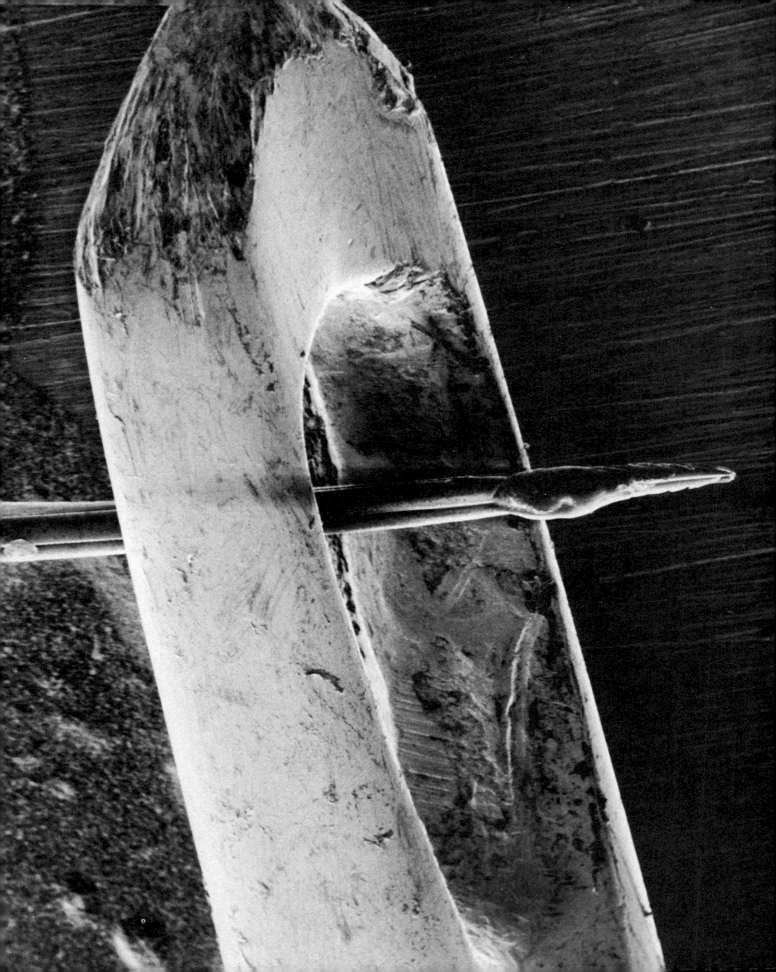

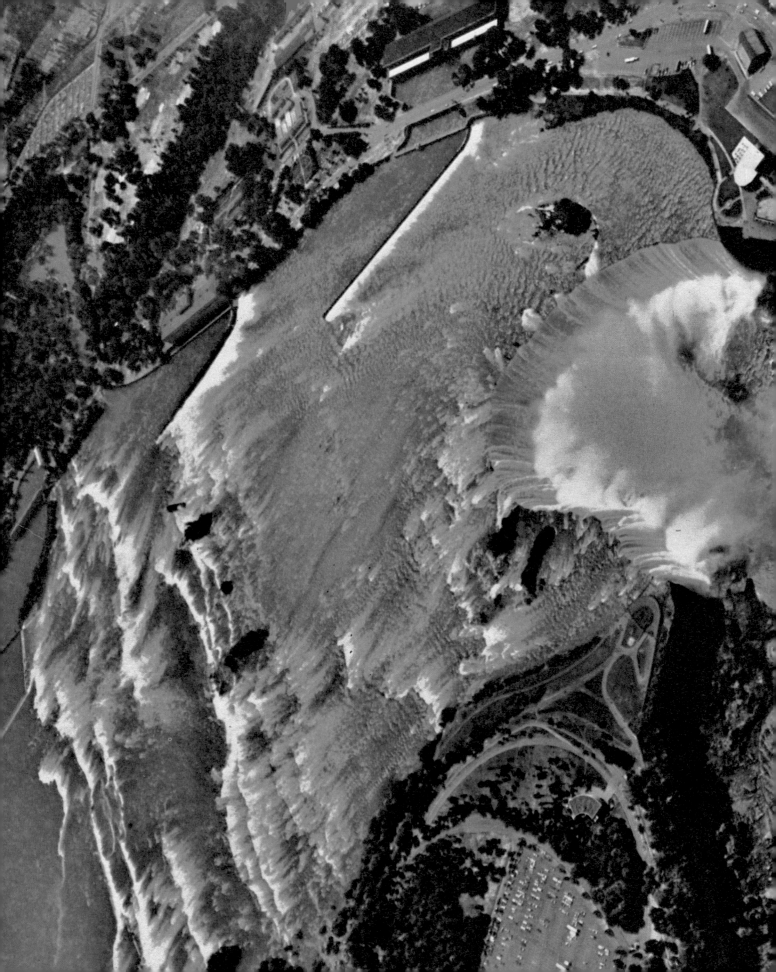

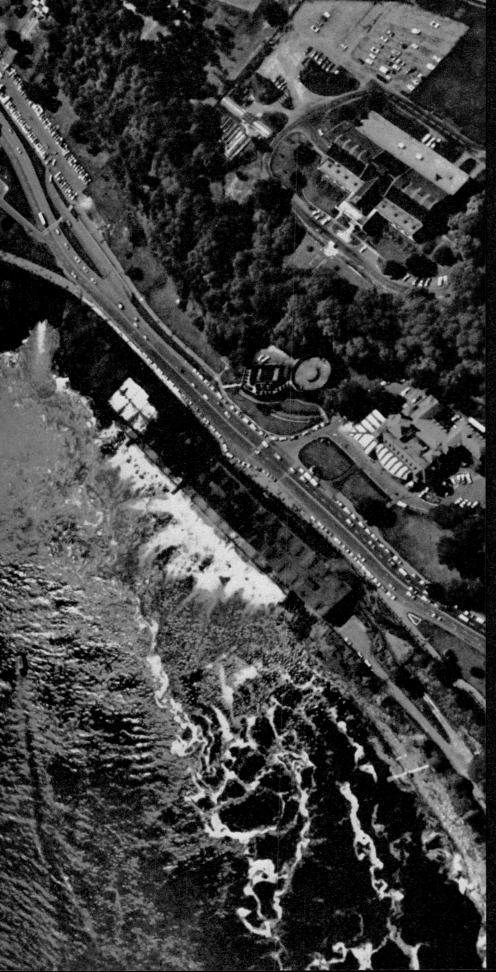

Eyes on the Planet

An infrared portrait of Niagara Falls. Rotate the page, and we're looking upstream towards Canada's spectacular Horseshoe Falls–three thousand feet wide and almost two hundred feet high. Further upstream, rapids churn the Niagara River into a maelstrom of white water. The promontory at centre left is Goat Island, in American territory–the American Falls itself is out of the picture.

Taken by an earth survey aircraft from 2500 feet above the Falls, this photograph was made using colour infrared film, which records reflected light in a normally-invisible part of the spectrum. Vegetation appears in exotic vermilion tones, an indication of how well healthy plant life reflects the infrared component of sunlight.

NASA PHOTO

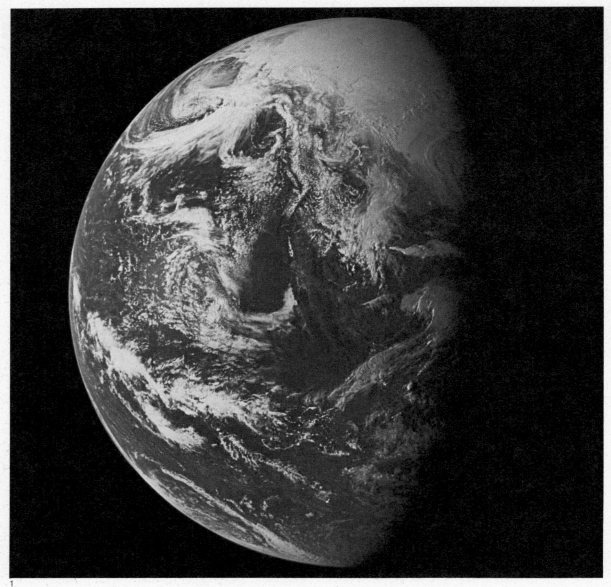

1

"It was a beautiful, harmonious, peaceful-looking planet, blue with white clouds, and one that gave you a deep sense in the gut – a sense of home, of being, of identity. And at the same time, immediately after that, was the sensing that beneath that blue and white atmosphere was a growing chaos that the inhabitants of planet Earth were breeding among themselves – the population and the consciousless technology were growing rapidly way out of control. The crew of spacecraft Earth was in virtual mutiny to the order of the universe."
—Ed Mitchell, Apollo 14 astronaut.

Four steps to Earth:
1. Homeward bound – Earth seen from the returning Apollo 13 moonship. Swirling clouds obscure much of the planet, but the Pacific coastline of North America is visible in the centre.

2. Close-up on California. Robot cameras on board an American satellite map most of the state—an economic entity with a gross national product larger than most countries. Sheltered from the Pacific by an inlet (centre) lies the San Francisco Bay area.

3. The Bay area in detail. Clouds moving in from the Pacific partially obscure San Francisco, but the downtown district is visible (arrowed).

From where this photograph was taken – the orbiting Skylab space platform – even the largest human settlements are dwarfed by their natural surrounds.

4. Suddenly, it's downtown San Francisco. The patterns of nature have been replaced by the quintessential urban landscape – freeways, bridges, city blocks, high-rise offices. Visible in this aerial photograph are waterfront piers, Chinatown, the Bay Bridge from San Francisco to Oakland (bottom right), and the Transamerica Pyramid—identifiable by its triangular apex and shadow.

NASA PHOTOS

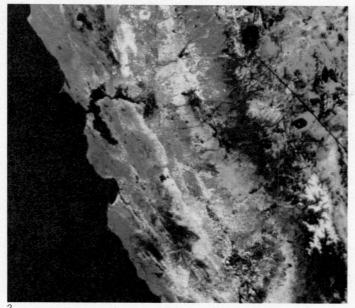

2

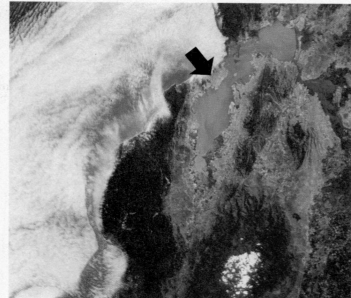

3

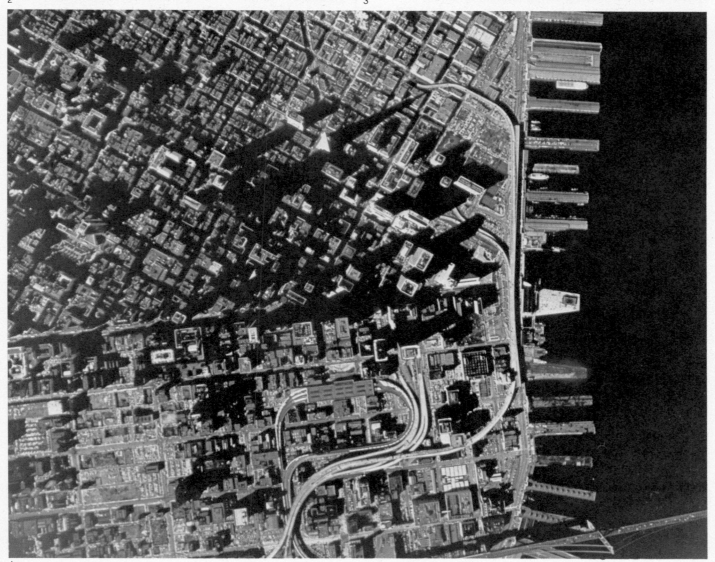

4

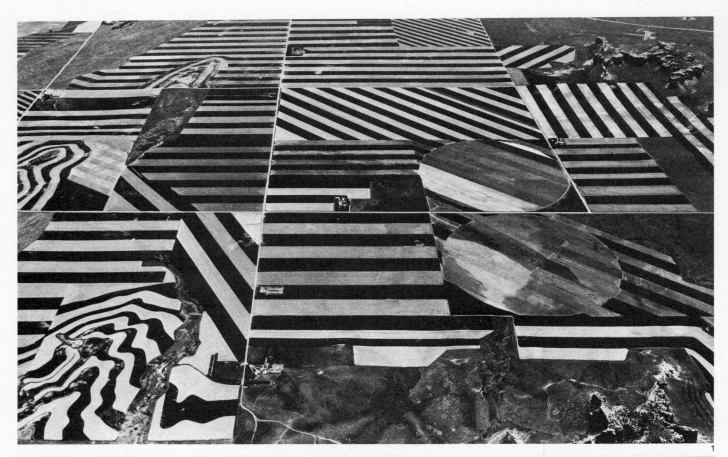

1

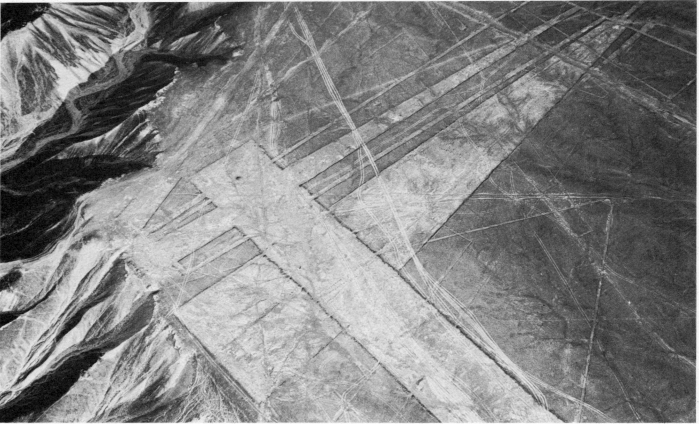

2

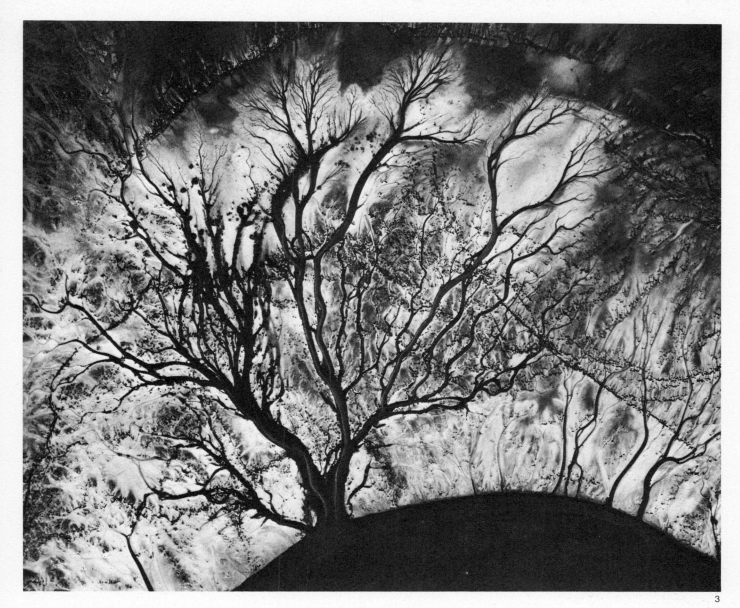

3

1. Summer comes to Nebraska: an agricultural landscape near Scottsbluff. Though the majority of the area is strip-farmed, two new circular corn fields are nearing completion at right. When finished, they will be irrigated by a rotating swivel system: a cheap and efficient way of raising crops.

Strip size and location is influenced by the direction of the prevailing wind, soil condition, and farm machinery. As can be seen, strips are also influenced by the terrain.

© GEORG GERSTER, FROM THE JOHN HILLELSON AGENCY

2. Monument to a forgotten people: prehistoric landscaping on Peru's Nazca plain. Some measure of size

can be judged from the length of the triangle base lines – 390 and 100 feet respectively. Like Britain's Stonehenge, the function of the Nazca shapes remains a mystery, but it seems likely that they were used as "observatories" to predict seasonal cycles for agricultural purposes. However, there is an alternative view, aptly expressed by the photographer, Georg Gerster:

"The unbridled imagination has turned the nonfigurative motifs in the wealth of Nazca earth figures into landing runways and assisted take-offs for extraterrestrial space pilots. It is sad to have to suppose that these super-intelligences from some distant planet had not made a little more progress in their aviatic

technology . . ."

Georg Gerster – *Grand Design: The Earth From Above* (Paddington Press, 1976).

© GEORG GERSTER, FROM THE JOHN HILLELSON AGENCY

3. Aerial photography as art-from-above? "The Burning Tree" is the title given to this picture of the Colorado River delta in the Gulf of California. The river is the black expanse at the bottom of the picture. Its waters branch out through the white sandbars to gain access to the sea at the top.

COURTESY OF AEROSERVICE DIVISION, WESTERN GEOPHYSICAL COMPANY OF AMERICA

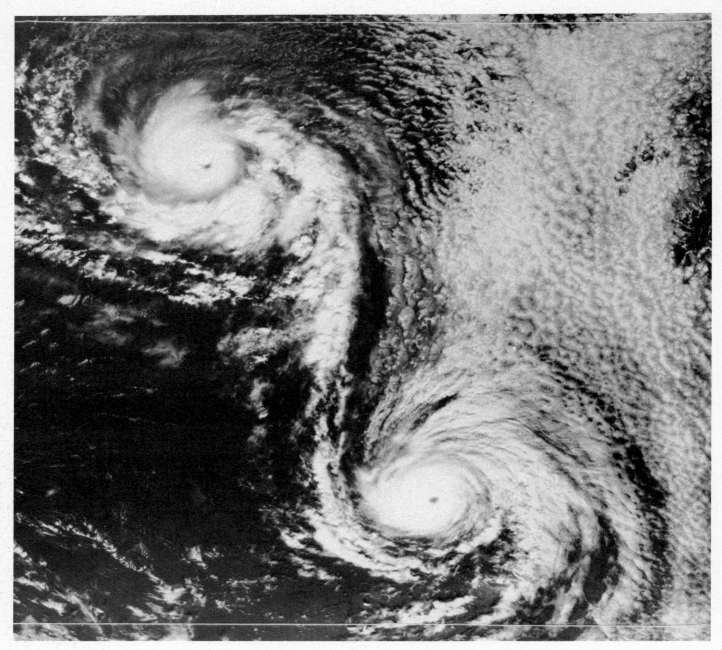

Since the beginning of time, the weather has been of vital importance to man. Agriculture, travel, habitation: all are affected by our solar-powered atmosphere.

Considering the effect it has on our lives, the fact that until recently four-fifths of the planet's weather went unobserved may seem surprising. This state of affairs – due to our inhabiting only 20% of Earth's surface – was changed overnight by the launching of the first weather satellite in 1960. Tiros 1 sent back television pictures which showed vast global cloud patterns. These corresponded so well with the invisible pattern of the weather that meteorologists now view cloud systems as nature's way of drawing a weather map.

Today, advanced generations of weather satellites circle the earth every 100 minutes, sending back detailed observations of global cloud cover every 12 hours.

However, our weather systems are still so little understood that we don't know with 100% certainty what tomorrow's weather will be like.

Twin hurricanes "waltz" directly below an orbiting American weather satellite. Hurricanes – the name comes from "Huracan," the West Indian god of storms – release the energy equivalent of several H-bombs every minute. Though dozens of hurricanes are spawned every year, usually between May and September, twins are a rarity.

US NATIONAL OCEANIC AND ATMOSPHERIC ADMINISTRATION

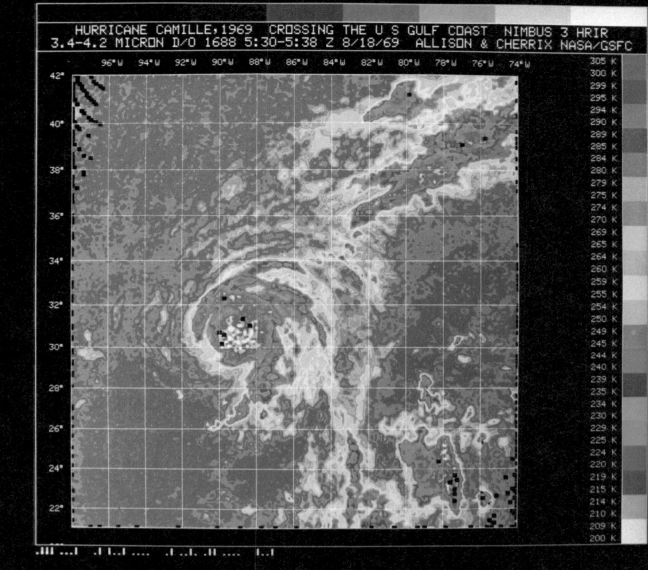

Hurricane Camille—one of the most violent storms ever to hit the United States—pinwheels across the Gulf of Mississippi.

This "picture" of Camille, taken by a Nimbus research satellite, was colour-enhanced to identify the high, cold cloud surfaces of hurricanes and other violent storms. The coldest area is the "eye" of the hurricane (grey-white). Other cold storm clouds (blue) are at top and bottom right, while the warm Gulf waters appear violet and magenta. At top left, the redder portion of the image indicates the relatively "hot" land mass of the Gulf coast.

Nimbus' sensor, called a High Resolution Infrared Radiometer (HRIR), is sensitive to near-infrared radiation. The scanner covers a range from 200-305°K, as indicated on the accompanying scale. At the top of the image, details like time of exposure and operating wavelength are given for easy reference.

NASA/GENERAL ELECTRIC COMPANY

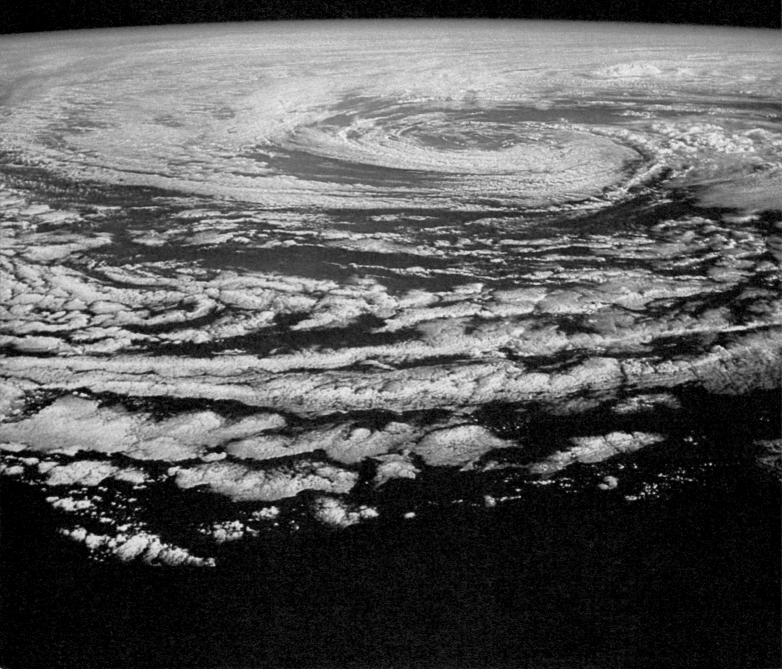

Whirlpool in the sky – a vast cyclonic storm above the Pacific, some 1200 miles north of Hawaii.

1. Born out of the great air masses which girdle the earth, passing in opposite directions to one another, cyclones are the bringers of bad weather, of storms and blizzards.

Cyclonic systems spin around a low pressure area, converging towards the centre. They generally travel from west to east across the sky, rotating counter-clockwise north of the equator, clockwise south of it.
NASA PHOTO

Swords into ploughshares: radar, developed during WWII to give advance warning of bomber raids, now helps the meteorologist to observe and predict the behaviour of tornadoes, hurricanes and blizzards.

High-frequency radar beams are reflected by rain, hail and snow, giving valuable insights into the processes at work deep within the heart of the most violent storm.

A process recently developed at the US National Center for Atmospheric Research now promises to give weather radar a powerful new dimension.

The technique – colour radar – is an innovative blend of existing TV and data processing technology. The radar beam, "bounced" back from a storm's layered structure, is colour-coded via a computer, then flashed onto a TV screen. There is no time delay, and the information can be instantly updated to give a continuous picture of weather conditions over an entire region.

2/3. Colour radar screens map a 100-mile-wide area's weather. The spectrum of colours, 16 in all, are displayed at right. The range runs from rain-heavy thunderclouds (red) to thin, low-moisture mists (green). To measure a storm-cell's velocity and direction, the operator merely flicks a switch and the information is instantly displayed. Using colour radar, meteorologists can give advance warning of tornadoes and hurricanes, thus providing communities in the storm's path with time to seek shelter.

US NATIONAL CENTER FOR ATMOSPHERIC RESEARCH

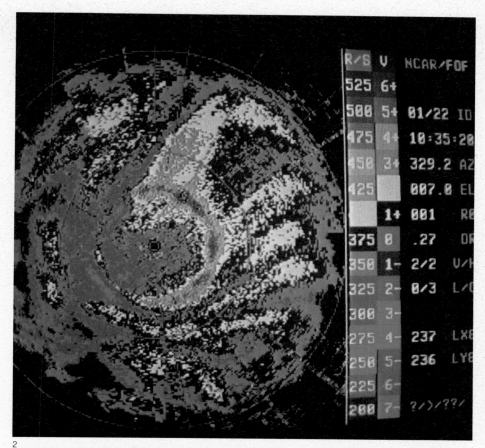

2

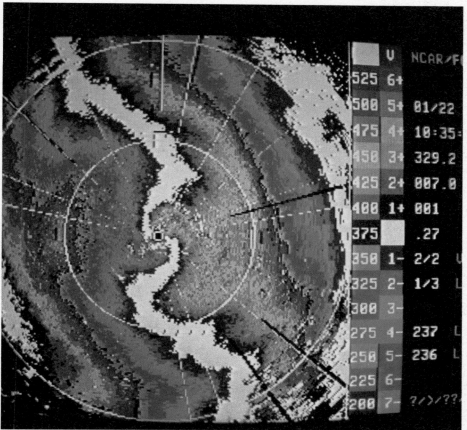

3

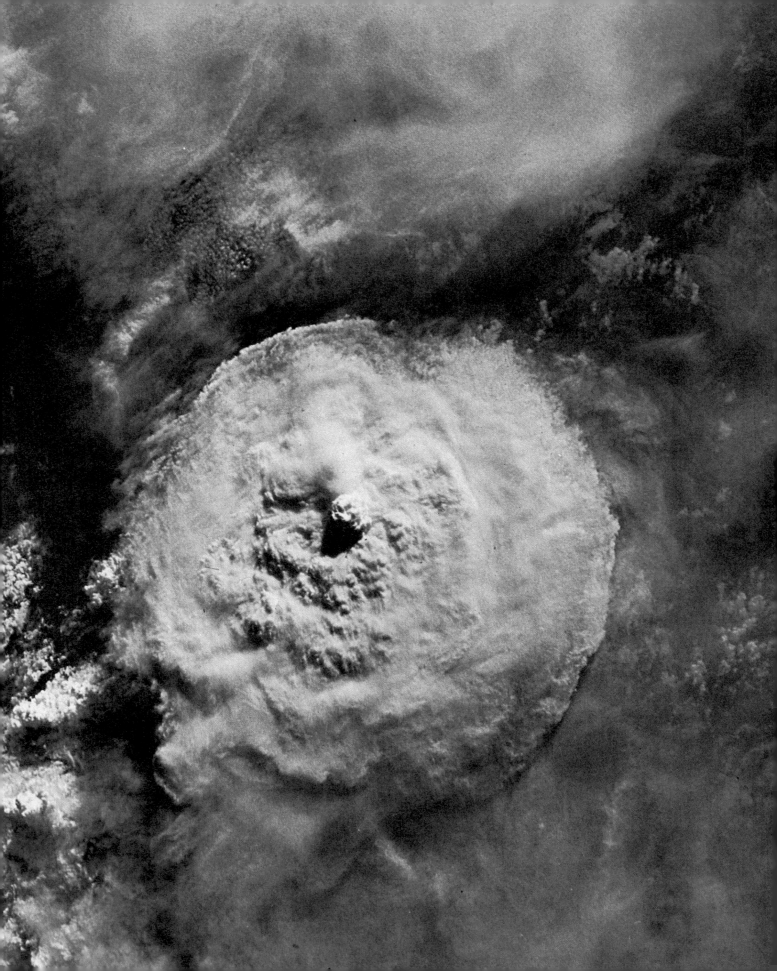

MISSISSIPPI RIVER BELOW MEMPHIS
AS IMAGED BY ERTS-1

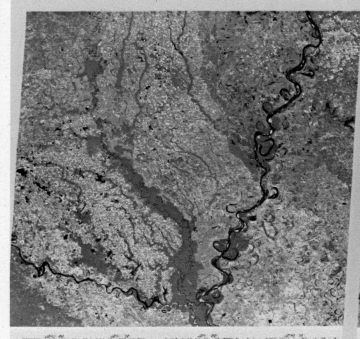

NORMAL LEVEL
Oct. 2, 1972

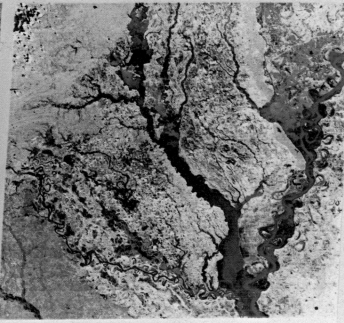

DURING FLOOD
March 31, 1973

Mushroooming thunderclouds over the Amazon basin.

Within the near future, it may be possible to create storms artificially, as a result of experiments carried out in both the US and the Soviet Union. The techniques these countries are developing could herald a new form of warfare in which storms are "manufactured" to ruin crops and paralyse armies, or hurricanes diverted to strike at an enemy's coast. It has been alleged that the US has already used "weather warfare" in Vietnam and to ruin the Cuban sugar harvest.

NASA PHOTO

In July of 1972, the US launched the first of a new breed of "eyes in the sky"–Landsat (formerly ERTS-1), the first earth resources satellite.

Cousin to the Nimbus range of weather stations, Landsat's battery of scanners is aimed at Earth's surface rather than its cloudscapes. Operating over a wide range of the visible and infrared spectrum, the satellite produces photographs of terrain at the rate of some 6 million square kilometres daily, from an altitude of over 900km.

The Landsat experiment has been an unqualified success. For the first time, we can look down on the planet and gather the information we need to understand the vast workings, not only of nature, but of the man-made environment: of urban areas which span hundreds of miles, agricultural regions as big as states, and the effects of pollution and massive civil engineering projects.

Landsat and its successors have given us the perspective necessary to see the dynamics and structures of these giant systems.

These two pictures of the Mississippi River below Memphis, Tennessee, were taken at six-month intervals and dramatically illustrate the effects of one of America's worst floods. The first photograph shows the river's normal state; the second shows the river during the height of the flooding. The pictures were subsequently used by relief agencies and insurance companies to calculate the extent of flood damage. Other damage-assessment uses of Landsat include monitoring the results of earthquakes, strip mining, forest fires and volcanic eruptions. The parallelogram shape of the images is due to a combination of the scanning system and the Earth's rotation.

US GEOLOGICAL SURVEY

To make the most of satellite and aerial photography, a whole new technology has been created to process and enhance remote-sensed information.

When England's Department of the Environment studied Landsat surveys for an urban land-use programme, it was found necessary to improve image resolution.

The satellite's camera system builds up a picture of Earth's surface by measuring the brightness and colour of a 79-metre square unit. Each unit—or *pixel*—is recorded, and transmitted to a ground station. By repeating the process, up to 10 million pixels can be built up into a complete section of territory; but the spacecraft's motion and the number of stages through which each pixel must pass distort the final image.

In a new process, IBM engineers developed a computer system which "cleans" each pixel and locates it in the correct geographical position. The final photographic image can be made direct from the computer, with improved colour contrast and definition. The technique—the results of which are shown here—is so effective that even railroads and buildings can easily be identified.

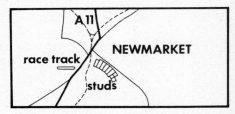

1. The urban area of Newmarket, the centre of English horse-breeding, lies in the middle of radiating grasslands. The town is depicted in black and grey, grassland in red and orange, and arable land in green.

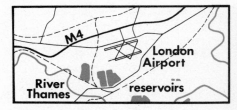

2. Set amidst the suburbs of west London, the runways of Heathrow Airport show up clearly as the yellow "Star of David" in the centre of the picture. The black expanses beneath and to the left of the airport are the King George and Staines reservoirs.

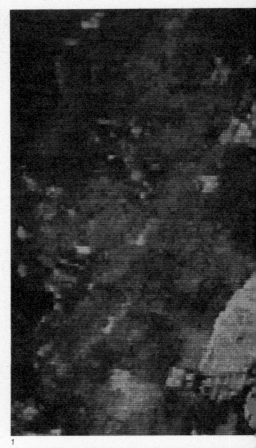

1

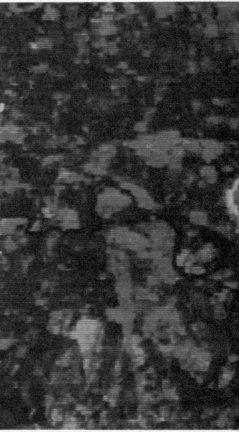

2

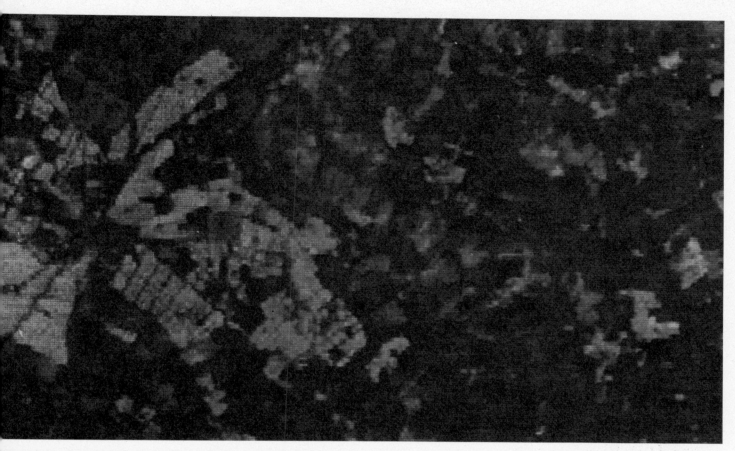

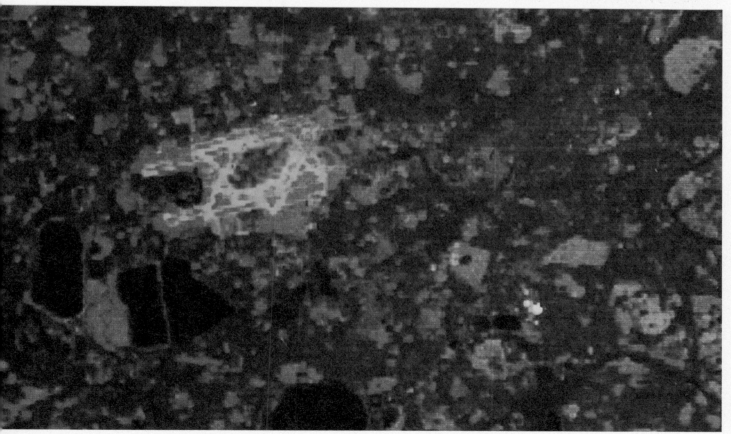

155

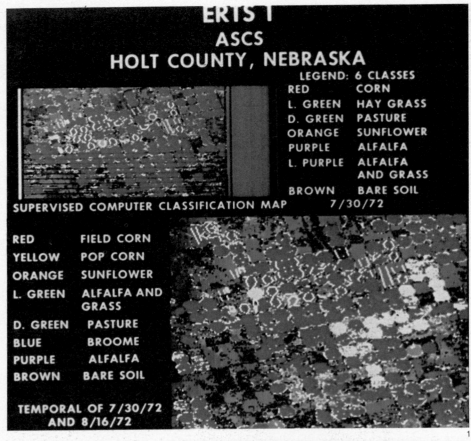

ERTS 1

ASCS

HOLT COUNTY, NEBRASKA

LEGEND: 6 CLASSES

RED	CORN
L. GREEN	HAY GRASS
D. GREEN	PASTURE
ORANGE	SUNFLOWER
PURPLE	ALFALFA
L. PURPLE	ALFALFA AND GRASS
BROWN	BARE SOIL

SUPERVISED COMPUTER CLASSIFICATION MAP   7/30/72

RED	FIELD CORN
YELLOW	POP CORN
ORANGE	SUNFLOWER
L. GREEN	ALFALFA AND GRASS
D. GREEN	PASTURE
BLUE	BROOME
PURPLE	ALFALFA
BROWN	BARE SOIL

TEMPORAL OF 7/30/72 AND 8/16/72

1

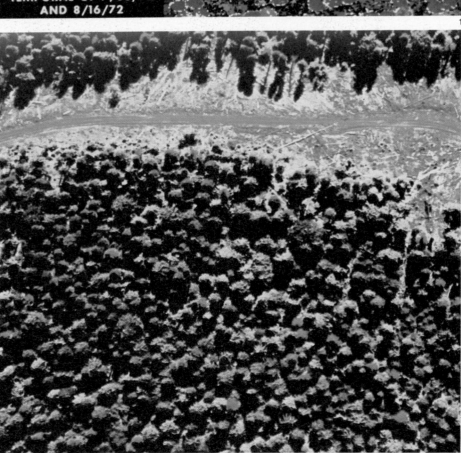

2

Information from resource satellites has contributed to many branches of the natural sciences, including geography – checking and updating existing maps; geology – as an aid in locating faults, mineral deposits, and oil-bearing zones; hydrology—for more efficient management of water resources; and ecology.

Resource surveys can be used to make estimates of major crops, so that farmers can avoid gluts and shortages. Agricultural land can be classified into crop types accurately and quickly: using Landsat data, foresters were able to classify 5500 acres of woodland into tree types, pasture and water in less than 30 minutes. Vegetation maps for areas like central Africa and Alaska, where conventional techniques would require years of work and cost millions, can be made with the minimum of time and expense. Such surveys can also be used to detect fraud: an Indian Landsat survey showed that landlords had been swindling the government for years by planting fewer trees than they had been paid for.

1. Data from Landsat's sensors was computer-enhanced to produce these maps of fields in Holt County, Nebraska. Each particular crop has its own "signature," and the computer hunts for similar signatures then classifies them by colour. The method is analogous to giving a dog a bone and then sending it off to find more of the same. The top map is derived from a single Landsat pass; the lower map, of the same area, was combined with the next Landsat pass 18 days later. The result was a crop map which identified field corn as opposed to pop corn. Several other crops can also be identified.

NASA PHOTO

2. Remote sensing of vegetation can be used as an "early warning" system against insect attacks and crop damage. Satellites and aircraft with infra-red scanners detect diseased vegetation before the blight becomes apparent on the ground. In this aerial survey of Oregon timber stands, healthy trees appear red or pink, while insect-infested timber stands out in blue or green.

US GEOLOGICAL SURVEY

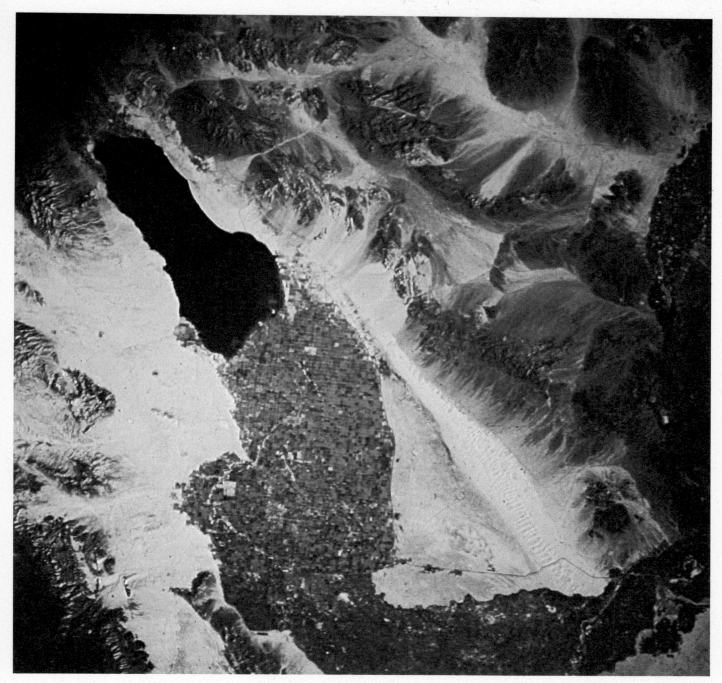

California's Imperial Valley: 500,000 acres of fertile cropland and the largest single irrigated area in the western hemisphere. Here, the US shares a border with its poor southern neighbour, Mexico. The border line runs across the lower quarter of this Apollo 9 infrared photograph, and neatly divides healthy US crops (red squares) from the sparsely cultivated Mexican fields (blue-green), which are lying fallow after the harvesting of the cotton crop.

Imperial Valley has been intensively studied by resource satellites. One scheme matched computer-stored imagery from each Landsat pass (Landsat covers an area once every 18 days) with a previously known "crop calendar," a table listing which crops grow at what time of year in a given area. The crop calendar showed what *should* be growing; Landsat showed what actually *was* growing. Discrepancies between the two could be used to rapidly identify bad

irrigation or insect attack.

There is, of course, a negative side to satellite crop-watching. Countries with access to resource surveys can predict whether unfriendly states will have good or bad harvests. That information can prove invaluable for political and economic bargaining.

NASA PHOTO

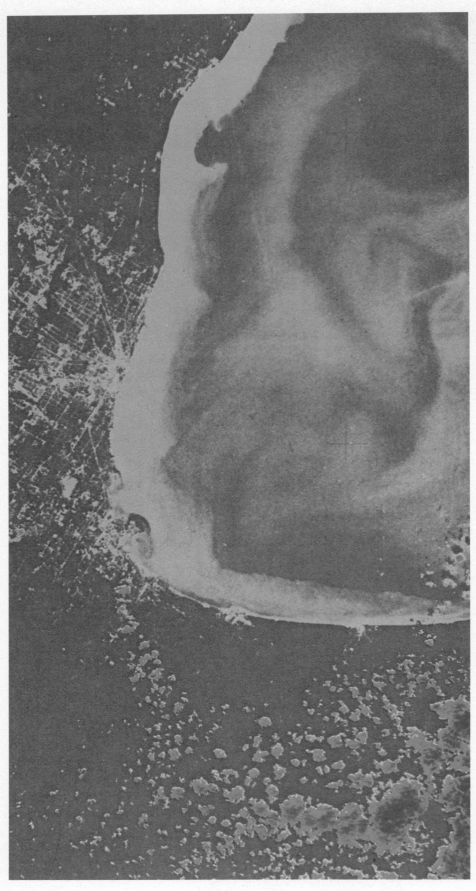

During an experiment to space-test earth resources technology, Skylab plumbs the depths of Lake Michigan.

From a height of 270 miles, the spacecraft's camera battery exposed miles of film, covering ten percent of Earth's surface.

This picture demonstrates how image treatment can "bring out" selected items of interest: in this case the swirling deep-water circulation patterns off Chicago's polluted waterfront. The animal, vegetable and mineral debris dumped into Lake Michigan reflects near-infrared, water absorbs it; and processing of Skylab's film in the laboratory enhances this distinction.

For earth resources researchers, this photograph shows that maps which include both land and water can be easily updated using near-infrared photography. For the rest of us, it's a reminder of the extent to which a city's garbage can damage the natural environment.

NASA/ITEK CORPORATION

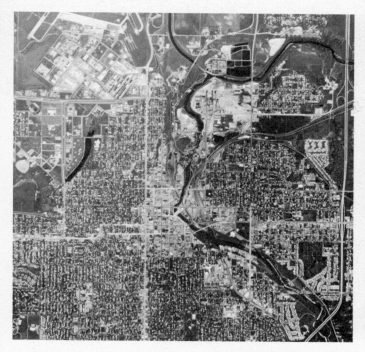

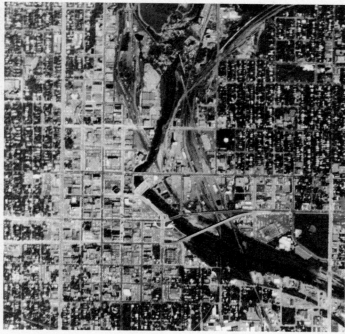

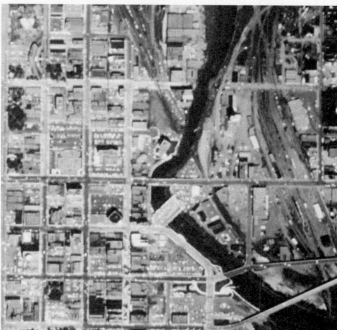

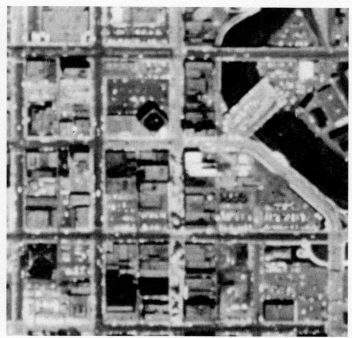

Sioux Falls, South Dakota, from a high-flying US reconnaissance aircraft.

This demonstration reveals, through successive enlargements from a single print, the resolving power of a modern aerial photographic system. On the final blow-up, street details can be clearly seen, including parked cars. The plane's altitude? Over fifty thousand feet, or almost twice the height of Mt. Everest.

Even more powerful cameras exist, but they remain closely-guarded military secrets. Spy planes and satellites carry equipment capable of resolving ground details a few feet across from heights so great they are immune to retaliation. It is even rumoured that the current generation of American spy satellites can actually "read" the insignia and number plates on Soviet military vehicles.

US GOVERNMENT PHOTOS.

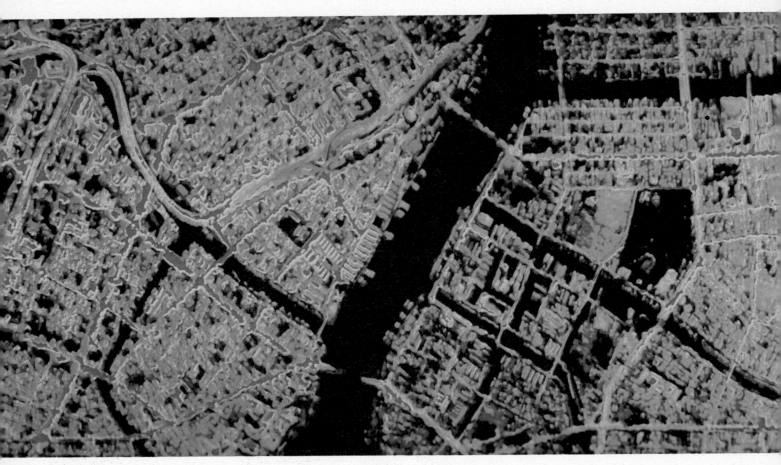

A city's invisible heat pattern, detected by the "eyes" of an airborne thermal sensor.

This is eastern central Tokyo at three on a late summer's afternoon. The Sumida River runs from top to bottom through the centre of the picture, crossed by two bridges. Wharfs and moored boats line the banks. The other dark areas are canals and inlets, coolly contrasting with the hottest areas picked out in red: roads and parking lots. At top left, an expressway interchange is highlighted in yellow, while the dark patch at right of centre is Kiyosumi Garden.

The aircraft sensor, operating in the *thermal* infrared (rather than the *near* infrared, which records light reflectance), detects small variations in heat emission from the ground. In order to make them more apparent, the variations are enhanced by a film printing system, Digicolor, whose "thermometer" runs from black (coldest) through magenta, blue, green and yellow to red (hottest).

The ease with which a city can be heat-classified using thermal infrared sensors is an invaluable aid to urban planners. The high yellow content left of the river and on the far right, for example, points to high density areas, which give off more heat than the less crowded neighbourhood on the right bank of the river (blue and magenta).

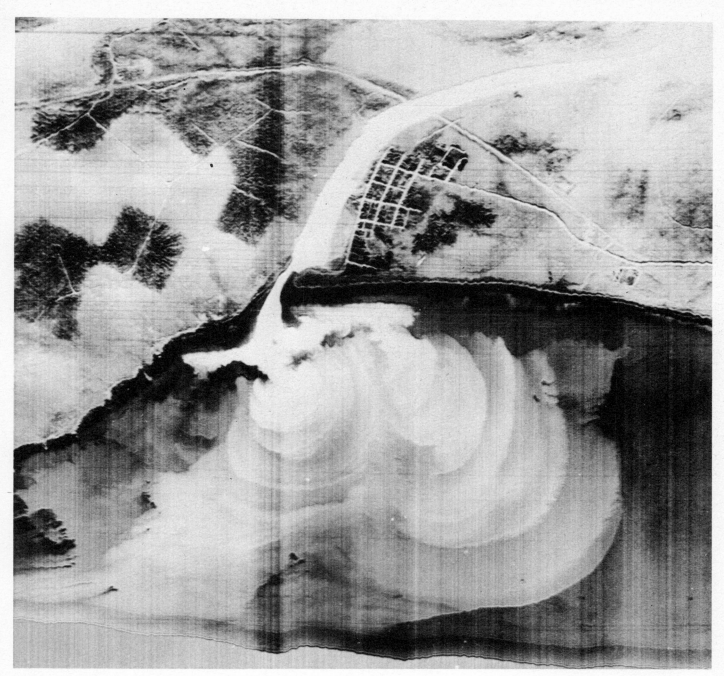

Some thermal infrared images need colour-coding to show up minor differences in temperature. Where thermal contrasts are readily apparent, however, simple black-and-white enhancement is sufficient: as in this heat-scan of the Quinault River entering the Pacific at Taholah, Washington State.

The river, heated by upstream sewage outfalls or power station cooling water, flows out into the relatively cooler waters of the ocean. Thermal infrared analysis is now an established procedure for locating heat pollution in rivers, lakes and estuaries.

Other remote sensors can locate chemical pollution in land, water or atmosphere. In what was probably the world's first satellite law-suit, a Landsat image showed that a paper mill in New York State was polluting waters belonging to neighbouring Vermont. Using the Landsat data, Vermont successfully proved its case and obtained a court injunction against the mill. Other satellite and aerial surveys have detected atmospheric pollution resulting in weather changes, sea pollution caused by sewage and waste dumping, and vegetation damage caused by chemicals used in strip-mining. Illegal waste dumping has also been detected by Landsat, leading to an interesting phenomenon—polluters are learning to dodge satellite detection by timing their activity according to Landsat's 18-day cycle, so that waste disposal occurs while the satellite is over the horizon.

NASA PHOTO

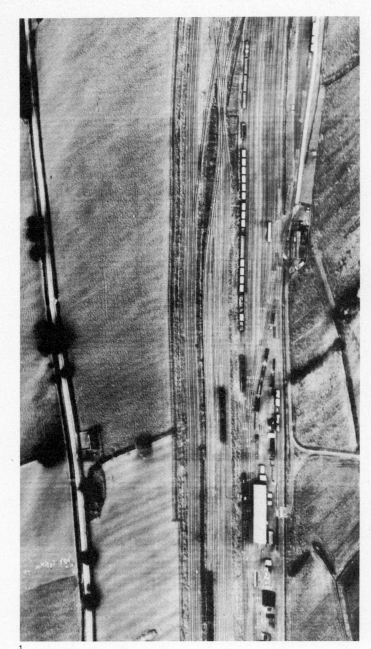

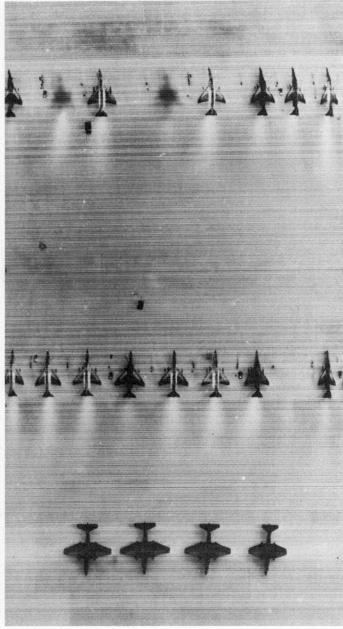

1   2

In the automated warfare of the 1970's, armies rely on robot spies – ranging from satellites to tiny hovering drones – to supply information on enemy formations and movements. Because most military activity produces heat energy in the form of infrared radiation, these robots are equipped with heat-detecting electronic "eyes" so sensitive that even body heat from hidden soldiers can be registered.

1.   In a demonstration run, infrared detectors on board a reconnaissance aircraft pick out nighttime details of a railway marshalling yard. The infrared device, Linescan, needs no form of illumination, and is thus impossible to detect.

2.   Linescan catches aircraft in readiness for take-off. Full fuel tanks show up as light patches on the wings, warmed-up engines can be detected by bright streaks along the fuselage. Two aircraft from the top row have already left, but their "thermal shadow" – an invisible heat imprint on the tarmac – betrays them. Thus, an astute intelligence officer can work out the real number of aircraft on an enemy's airfield, even though some may have left hours ago.

COURTESY OF HAWKER SIDDELEY DYNAMICS LTD.

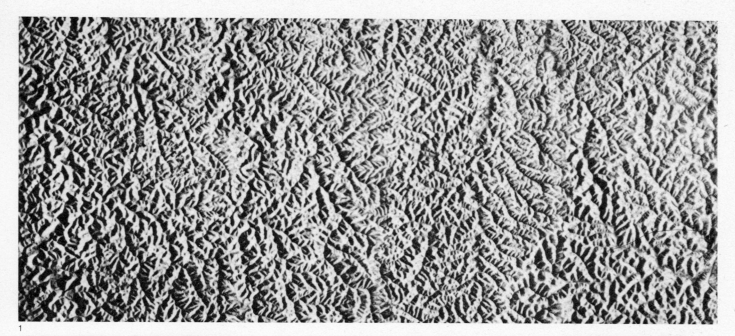

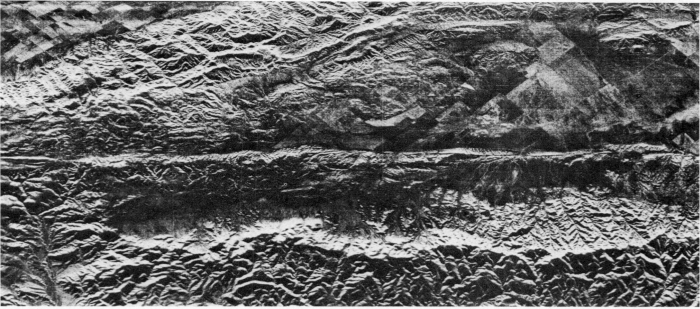

Much of Earth's surface is so consistently covered by clouds that aerial photography is impossible. Yet these areas – mainly around the equator – desperately need the resource and mapping information that airborne surveys can provide.

That information can now be gathered by a specialised sensing system known as SLAR – Side-Looking Airborne Radar. SLAR sends out a narrow beam of pulsed microwave energy to one side of the carrier aircraft. The beam, having grazed the terrain surface, returns to the aircraft and is translated electronically onto film. Unlike conventional aerial photography, SLAR operates by day or night, through dense cloud cover and rainfall, and can even penetrate vegetation. In addition to mapping, SLAR's potential uses include monitoring sea traffic, tracking oil slicks, and observing sea and ice conditions.

1. Nature at work: a SLAR mosaic of Sandy Hook, Kentucky, shows how rainfall and drainage over millennia have landscaped Earth's surface.

US ARMY ENGINEER TOPOGRAPHIC LABORATORIES

2. A small part of the notorious San Andreas Fault, which many Californians (and some scientists) think will one day topple their state into the Pacific Ocean. The build-up of pressure in the fault has caused many devastating earthquakes, including the one in 1906 which destroyed San Francisco. SLAR's 3-D effect is particularly useful in detecting and mapping geological fractures and faults.

COURTESY OF THE WESTINGHOUSE ELECTRIC CORPORATION

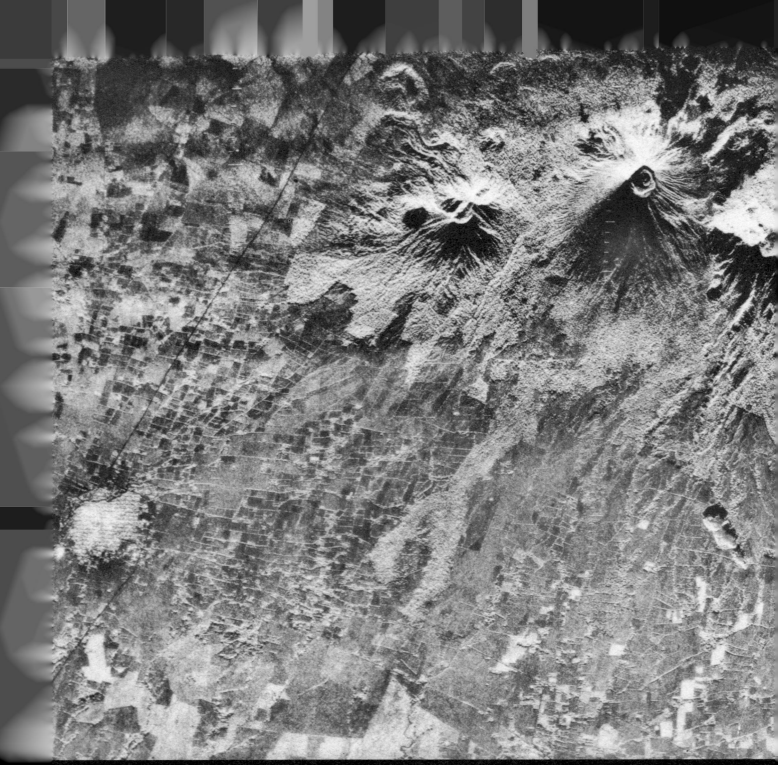

From 20,000 feet, SLAR maps a swathe of western Nicaragua through as many as three separate cloud layers. San Cristobal volcano and its associated landscapes are at top centre, the town of Chinandega is at lower left, tarmac highways show up as dark lines and cultivation patterns can be clearly seen.

San Cristobal's northern slopes are brightly lit, not by the sun, but by SLAR's own radar beam, transmitted from an aircraft flying from right to left far beyond the top of the photograph. SLAR "sees" a different version of reality, because the properties of radar are different from those of light. One interesting SLAR

effect is that at near distances facing hill slopes become foreshortened, while far slopes appear elongated. In effect, the hill appears to lean *towards* the observer, rather than away from him. For a demonstration of SLAR's distortion of perspective, turn the page upside-down.

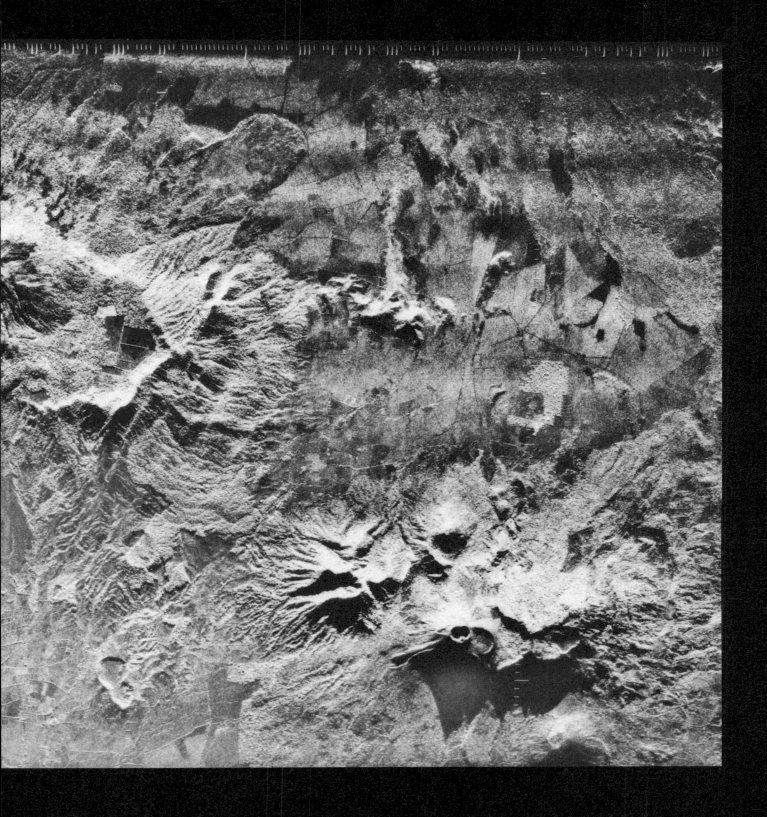

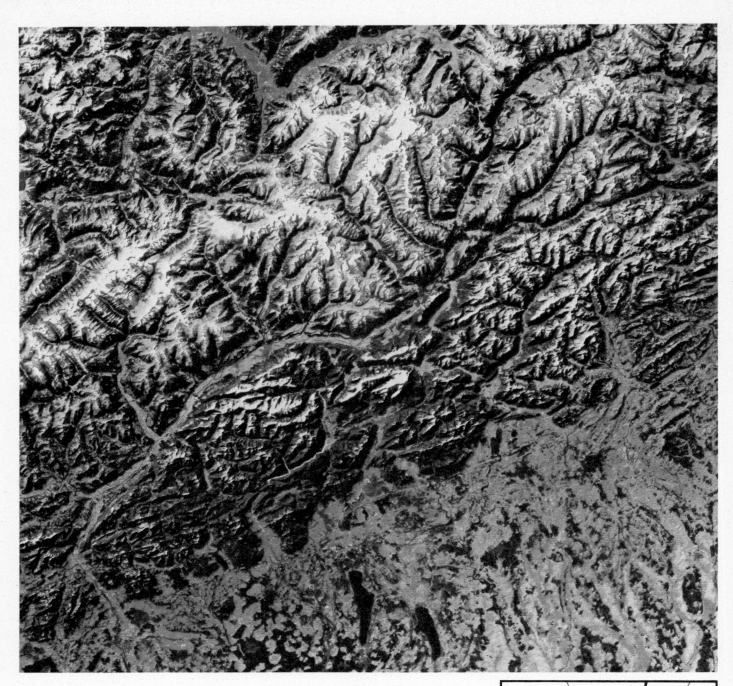

It's a clear, sunny winter's morning in the Austrian Tyrol. The low sun casts long shadows off the Alpine mountain tops, their upper slopes covered by snow.

Looking down from 500 miles over four European countries: Germany, Austria, Italy and Switzerland. (For clarity, the usual geographic conventions are reversed—south is at the top.) The famous Austrian ski resort of Innsbruck is clearly visible: so are rivers, lakes, even roads. The equally famous Brenner Pass, however, is obscured by cloud.

This infrared false-colour image demonstrates the unique potential of Landsat. Photographs like this serve as instant "maps," and can be made into mosaics of regions and entire countries. Conventional maps are often out of date by the time of printing: Landsat continuously updates its images and, compared with conventional maps, satellite photographs are cheaper, have more information content and can be produced by the thousand.

NASA PHOTO

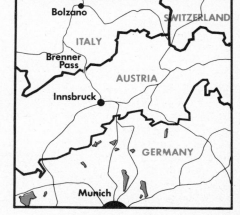

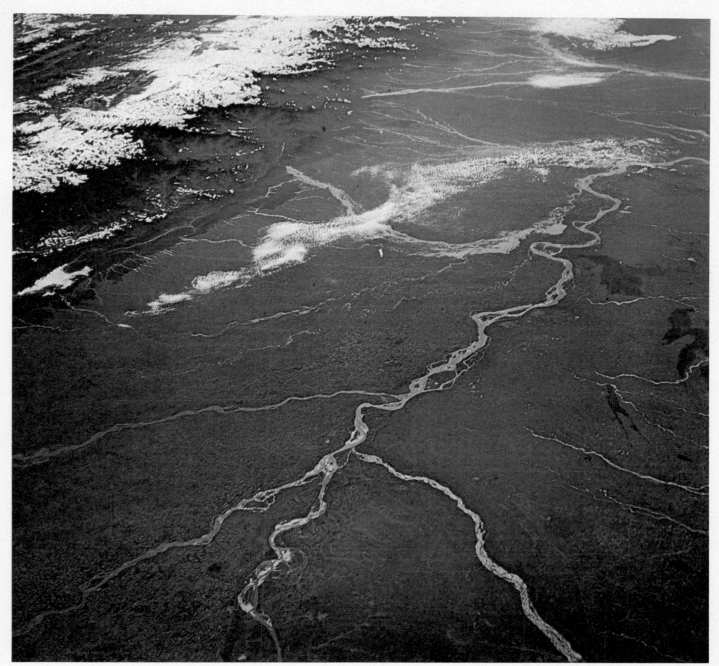

Looking across the roof of the world: the snow-covered Himalayas rise up out of the north Indian plain.

The Ganges and its tributaries – the four holy rivers of India (the Ganges, Gandak, Gogra and Son) – flow south-east (towards top right) to the immense Ganges delta and the Bay of Bengal.

The picture, taken from Apollo 7 in Earth orbit, shows the eastern half of the Ganges plain shortly after the summer monsoons. The river, which at its widest is some 20km across, snakes its way through the oldest settled area on Earth. It's also the most populous, with nearly 500 people to every square kilometre.

Rising from top left, striding in parallel, are the Himalayan ranges, with their entire peak region deep in an unbroken cover of snow. Behind them is Tibet. In front, dropping down towards the Ganges plain, are the foothills of Nepal.

NASA PHOTO/PICTUREPOINT LTD.

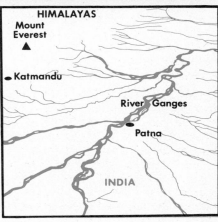

HIMALAYAS
Mount Everest ▲
• Katmandu
River Ganges
• Patna
INDIA

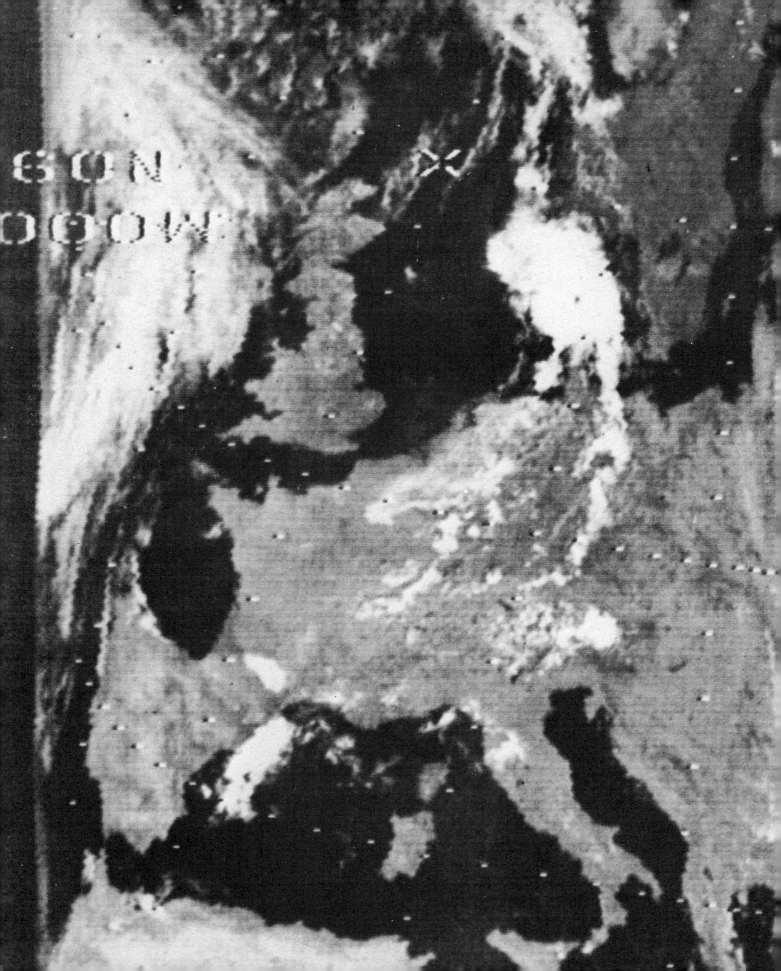

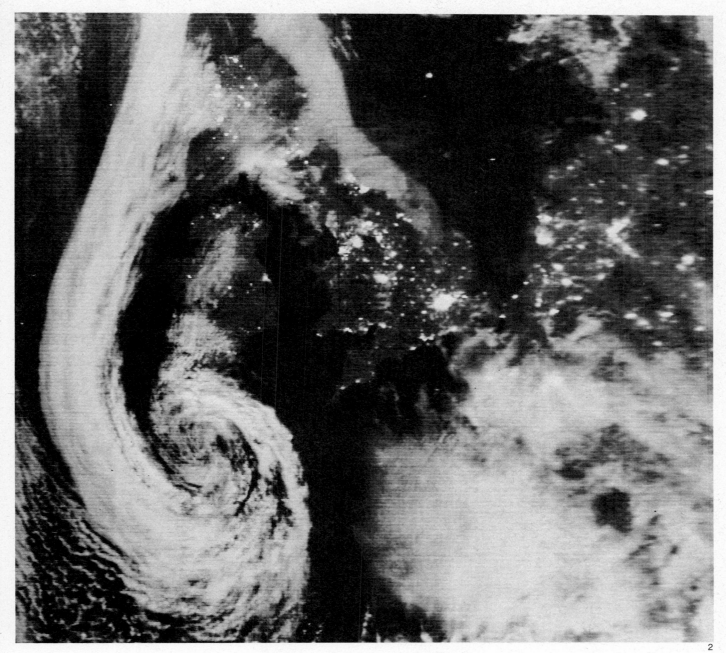

2

1. It's a fine day over much of Europe. Seven hundred miles up, Nimbus III looks down on the continent that once ruled the world.

NASA/GENERAL ELECTRIC COMPANY

2. City lights: the United Kingdom and north-west Europe from an orbiting US Air Force satellite.

It's ten in the evening, and the craft's sensors, operating in both visible light and the near infrared, pick out the night life of a continent's teeming cities.

The lights are on in London, Birmingham, Liverpool and Manchester; the pubs are filling up in Belfast and Dublin. A short hop over the North Sea takes us into Amsterdam, Rotterdam and the Hague. Stout burghers in both Germanies are at work and play: Berlin shines through a thin cloud covering (top right) and the industrial megalopolis of the Ruhr – where machines run through the night – sweeps round in a boomerang of light. The French are almost entirely cloaked in cloud, while fog shrouds the north-east coast of England and Scotland.

US AIR FORCE WEATHER SERVICE

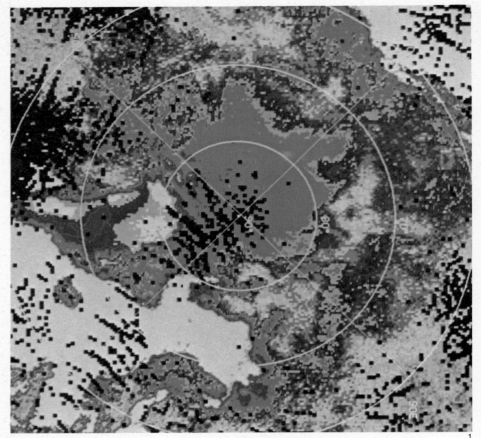

Ice world: the North and South Poles from an orbiting weather satellite.

The images bear little resemblance to conventional photographs, for the technique records a quantity known as "brightness temperature," not light. Brightness temperature is the relationship between an area's surface heat and the rate at which that heat is emitted. The satellite sensor detects the ground's output in the form of microwave emission, from which brightness temperature is calculated.

The resulting pictures are used to contrast open sea, seasonal ice and permanent ice coverage. Such information is of prime importance to shipping and weather forecasters. Though both polar regions are usually obscured by clouds, microwaves penetrate the cloud cover and allow ice changes to be monitored free from atmospheric interference. The results are impressive, colour-enhanced portraits of the planet's two great ice zones.

1. The most striking feature of this picture of the Arctic is the great contrast between land and water. Open sea is shown white; land masses of North America (top left corner), Russia (bottom right corner) and Great Britain and Scandinavia (bottom left corner) appear yellow-orange. The Arctic ice is blue.

2. Antarctica, the last great uninhabited continent. The Weddell Sea is at the bottom, the Ross Ice Shelf upper right. Surrounding the continent is seasonal ice; further inland vast ice sheets permanently cover the Antarctic's surface. The brightness temperature variations from dark blue to magenta are not yet fully understood.

NASA PHOTOS

3. Artificially-enhanced colour photograph of the *geocorona*, a thin shell of hydrogen gas which surrounds Earth. Sunlight shines from the left, so the geocorona is brighter on that side. Astronaut John Young took this photo, in ultraviolet light, from the Apollo 16 moonship.

NASA PHOTO

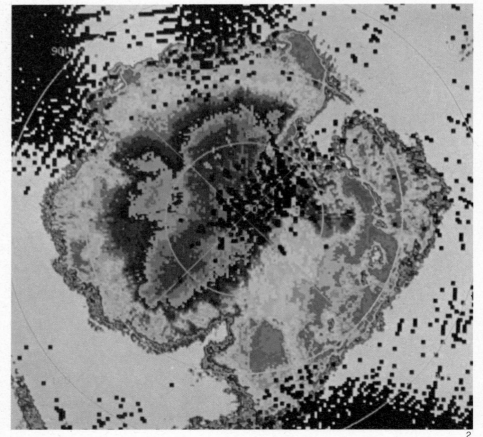

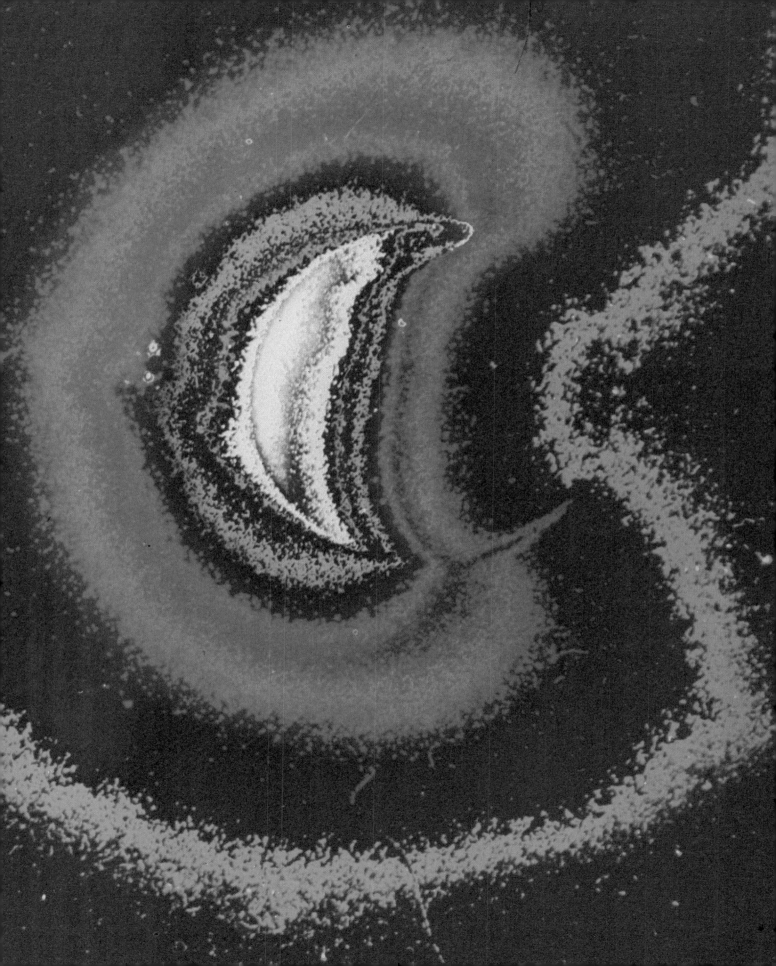

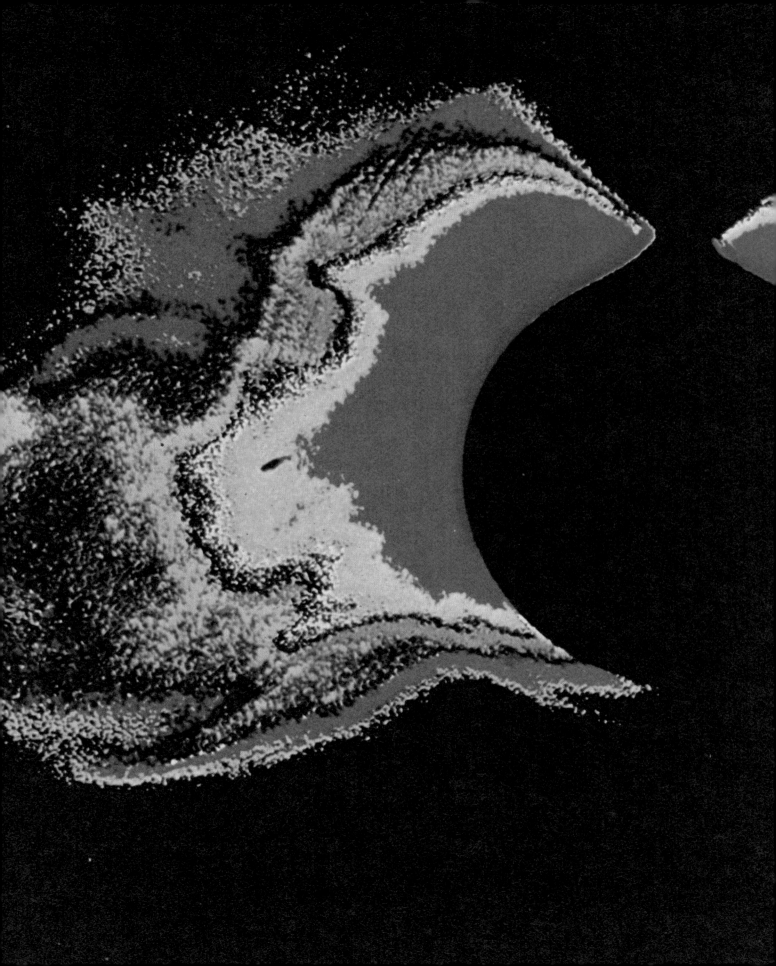

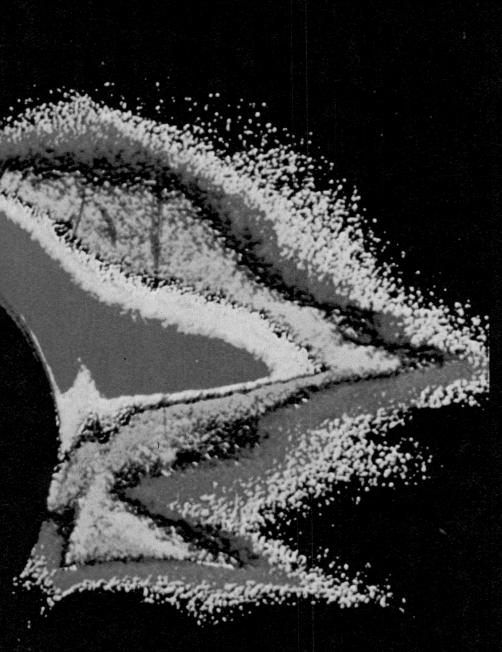

Out Into Space

America's Skylab spacecraft, launched in May 1973, lofted tons of scientific instruments into Earth orbit. From this space platform, far above the atmosphere, cameras captured the life-processes of the sun. The result: a stunning visual portrait of our nearest star.

Crowned by petal-like streamers, the pale cloud of the sun's outer atmosphere reaches a million miles into space. The corona, a thin mist of gas, is normally invisible from Earth because of the intense light from the sun's surface. To take this rare photograph, colour coded by brightness, instruments aboard Skylab created an artificial eclipse to mask the sun's disk. Skylab provided solar scientists with 8½ months of continual observation of the corona – compared with less than 80 hours from all natural eclipses since the use of photography began in 1839.

NASA PHOTO

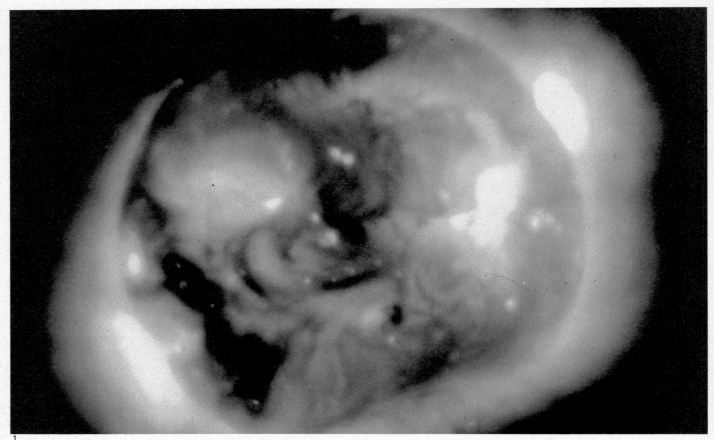

1

Though spacecraft have given us spectacular new views of the sun, what goes on inside has become more mysterious. The confident belief that the sun shines by thermonuclear fusion has been challenged by recent findings, resulting in a crop of bizarre solar theories. Is the energy source a "black hole" in the sun's centre? Was the sun formed at two different times? Are the processes at work within the sun unknown to science? Some theorists suggest that the sun does not burn evenly and the reactions within the solar core are temporarily "running down." When this effect reaches the sun's surface it could, perhaps, cause a new ice age on Earth.

1. The sun's atmosphere, seen in this Skylab x-ray photograph, is a turbulent swirl of incandescent gas. Waste heat and light are carried by convection from the sun's interior, emerging as the bright patches at top right and lower left. From here, this excess energy will be radiated into space as sunlight and heat.

NASA PHOTO

2. Ground-based telescopes capture the total eclipse of 1966, framing the solar corona against a backdrop of space.

NATIONAL CENTER FOR ATMOSPHERIC RESEARCH (NCAR), BOULDER, COLORADO.

3. The living sun. This photograph, taken in the light of hydrogen, reveals the sun's inner atmosphere or *chromosphere*. The peculiar surface texture is caused by gas geysers up to 500 miles across, which roar through the chromosphere by the thousand, their tops appearing as "grains." The bright areas are solar flares, while the black patches hover above sunspots. Though there is some uncertainty about sunspots, they are known to follow a regular 11.1 year appearance cycle – a cycle that is apparently linked with such diverse terrestrial phenomena as the price of corn on the New York stock exchange and the incidence of car accidents.

THE HIGH ALTITUDE OBSERVATORY OF THE NATIONAL CENTER FOR ATMOSPHERIC RESEARCH.

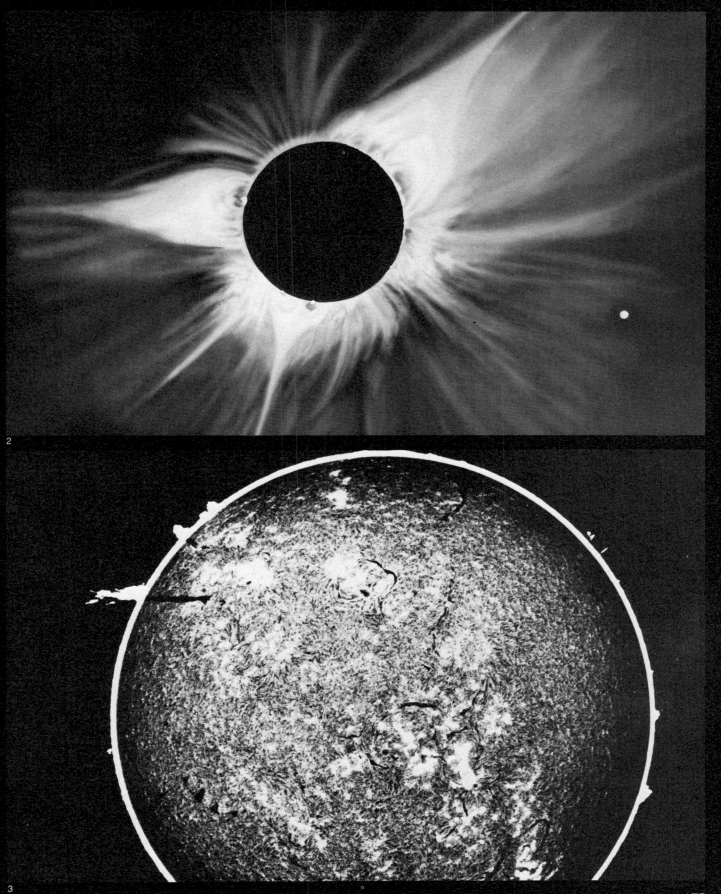

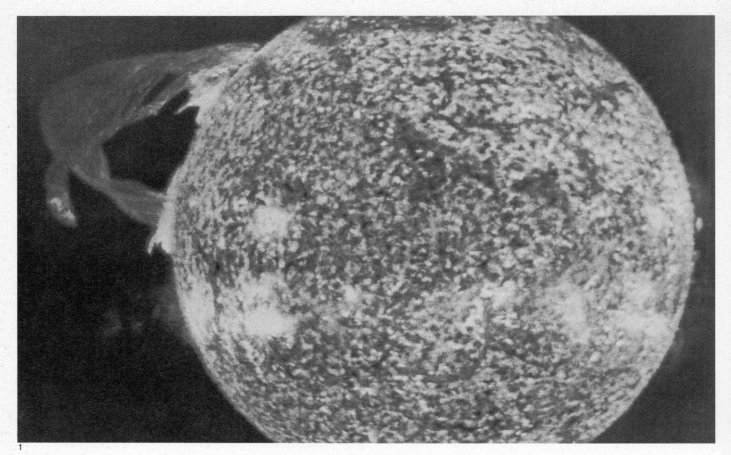

1

Solar flares begin their brief lives near a group of sunspots. Suddenly, the magnetic field associated with the group will be transformed into kinetic energy, and an explosion of vapour rockets up through the chromosphere at a third of the speed of light. Following this comes a slower, secondary burst, and sometimes a "third stage" of high-energy electrons. Meanwhile, the primary explosion has created an expanding shock front which travels out through space and will reach Earth some 24 hours after the event. A shock wave launched by the great solar flare of 1972 was tracked from sun to Earth by an orbiting US satellite. Travelling at a speed of 780 miles a second, the shock's arrival coincided with the beginning of a storm in Earth's ionosphere – the first direct proof that terrestrial magnetic storms, which disrupt radio communications, can be triggered by events on the sun.

1.   Caught in the act by Skylab 4, a giant solar flare arches 360,000 miles across the sun's surface.

2.   A cascade of helium vapour rises high above the sun. Ghost images of the solar disk linger on in this Skylab ultraviolet photograph.

3.   Detail of the helium eruption. Each colour represents a particular density range: the darker the colour, the thicker the eruption. On the scale of this picture, Earth would be a dot no larger than a full-stop.

NASA PHOTOS

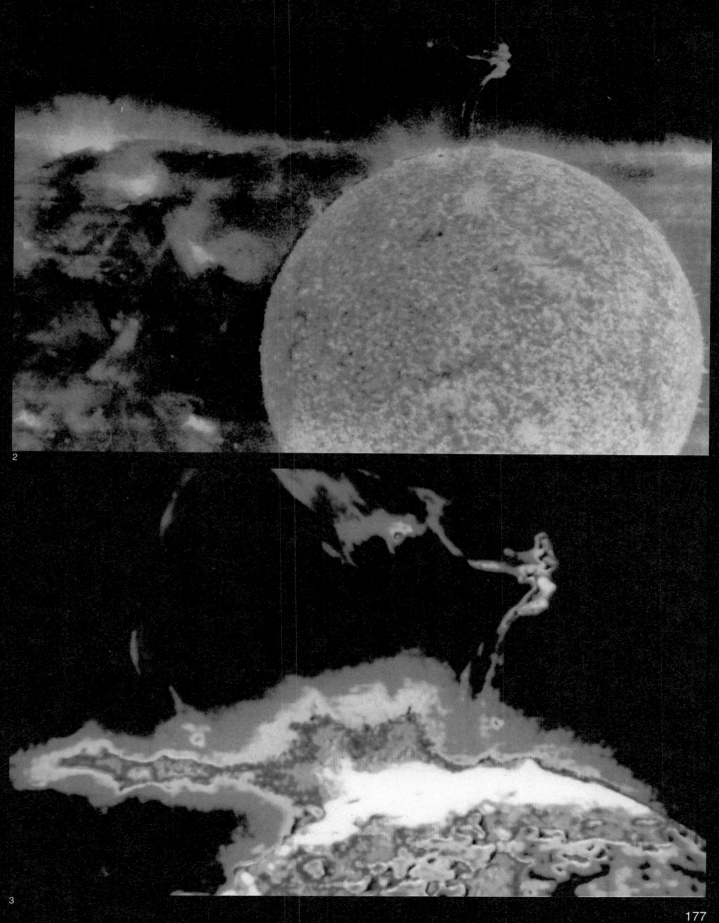

2

3

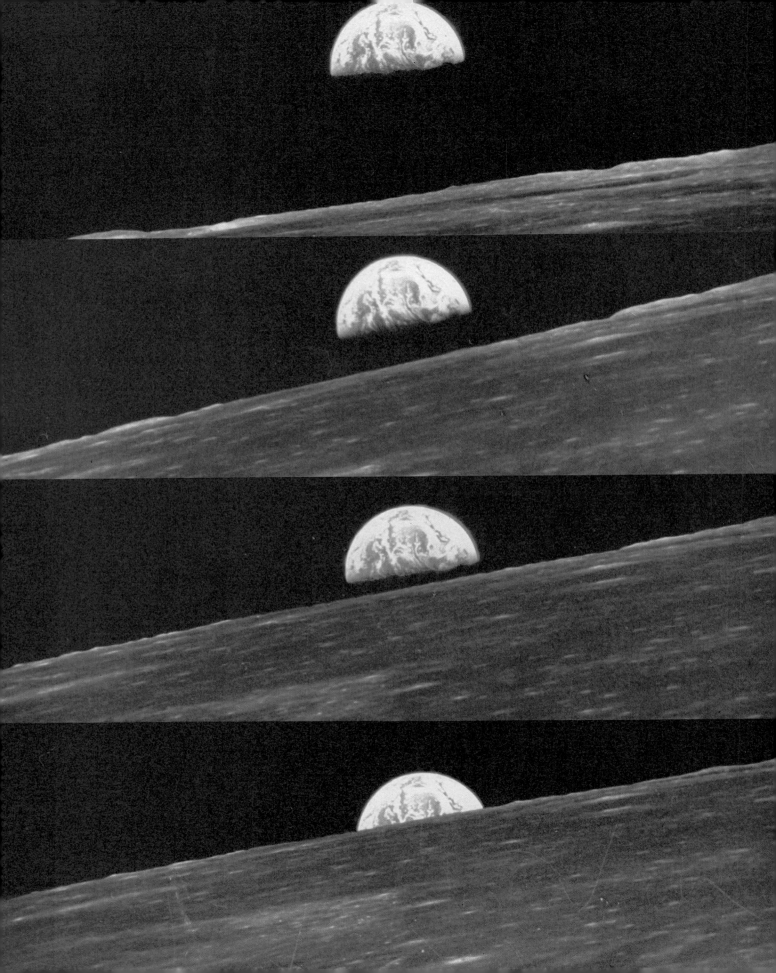

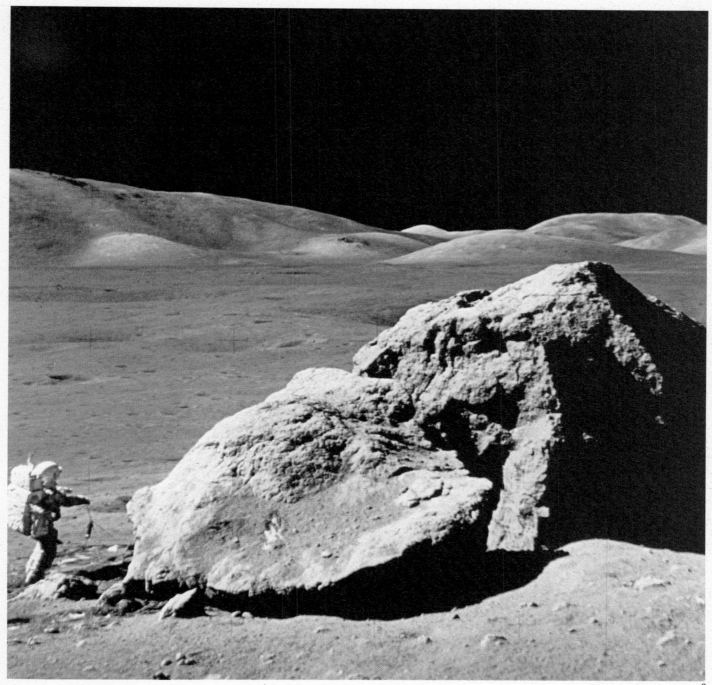

1. Earthrise. One of the most rewarding results of the Apollo space expeditions was to see Earth as a planet. The growing awareness that we are aboard a "giant spacecraft" in orbit around the sun, needing to maintain our life-support systems from the resources of a finite planet, was best expressed by the new views of our world brought back from the moon. The fragility and beauty of the planet—its cloudscapes hiding the ugliness of war, exploitation and corruption—brought home to us the fact that we are all custodians of an abundant but finely-balanced ecosystem.
NASA PHOTO

2. Home movies from the moon. Astronaut Eugene Cernan snaps buddy Harrison H. Schmitt during the Apollo 17 walkabout in December 1972. The large boulder provided one of the many samples of lunar rock brought back to Earth by robot spacecraft and astronauts. Cosmic history is written in these few hundred pounds of moonrock, for the erosion-free lunar environment has preserved evidence of events long since wiped from the face of Earth.
NASA PHOTO

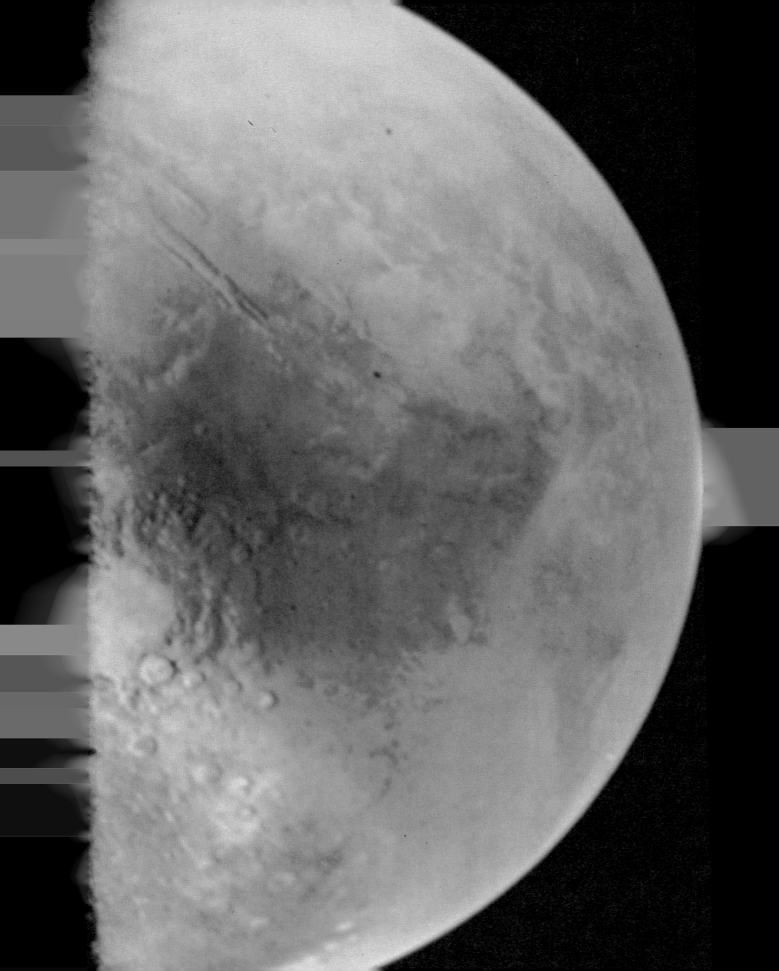

2

1. As Viking 1 nears its rendezvous with Mars, cameras map the approaching planet from a distance of 200,000 miles. This photo, a composite of three separately filtered images taken seconds apart, shows that Mars is indeed the Red Planet. As in terrestrial deserts and red bricks, the mineral limonite supplies the colouring.

The central dark area is the Mare Erythraeum, long visible by telescope. Between Erythraeum's south-western "coastline" and the Martian night is Argyre, made bright by ground frost or haze. The great gash running into Erythraeum's north-western region is the Valley of the Mariners, the nearest Mars comes to the "canals" beloved of fantasy writers. This Martian version of the Grand Canyon measures up to 100 miles from edge to edge, is 20,000 feet deep and extends 2,500 miles across the planet's surface.

2. Sunset over an alien planet. This is Mars at dusk, recorded by the Viking 1 lander on August 20, 1976.

Each Viking carried two scanners, which used a combination of mirrors and light-sensitive devices rather than the vidicon plate of a conventional TV system.

Some four minutes after the sun had dipped below the horizon, Viking began scanning from left to right for ten minutes. By the time the image was completed, the sun had fallen far from sight and the horizon appears as a black silhouette. The sky colour grades from blue to pink across the image. unlike the "moody" halo around a terrestrial sunset, this is a camera effect. The Martian sky is, in fact, pink.

NASA PHOTOS

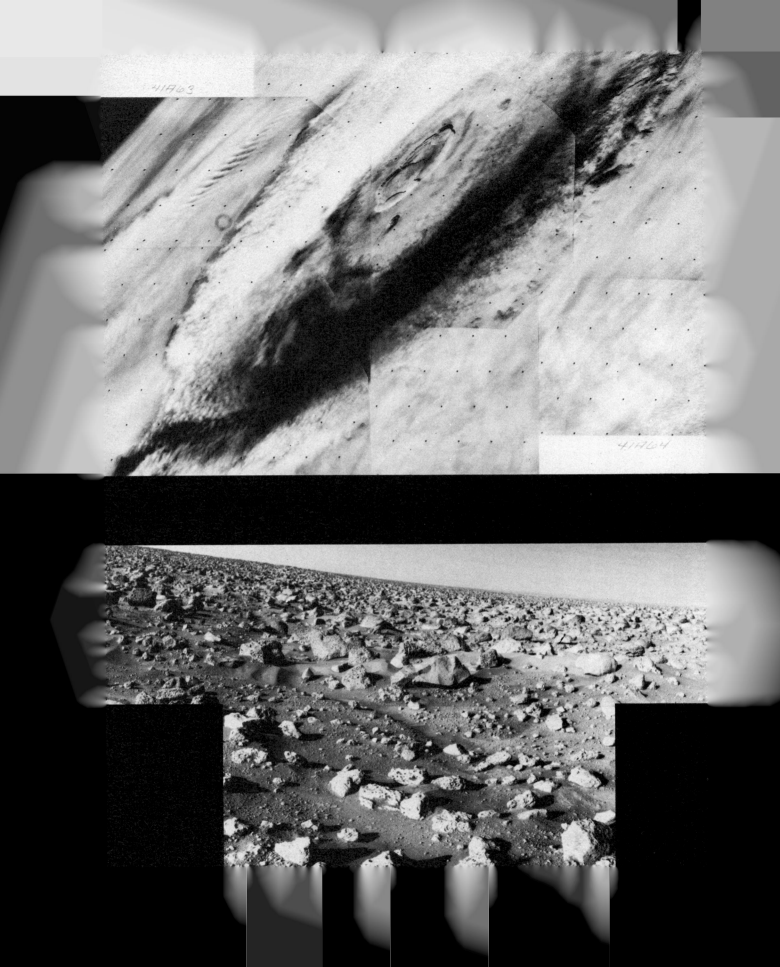

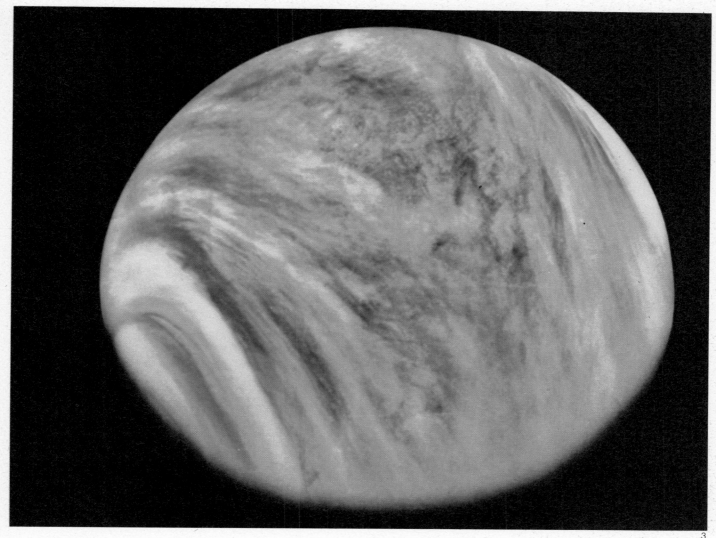

3

1. Olympus Mons – the largest volcano on Mars and, for that matter, anywhere in the solar system. Measuring nearly 400 miles across and rising to a height three times that of Mt Everest, Olympus' slopes are ringed with clouds in this mid-morning photo by Viking 1. The volcanic crater, itself 50 miles in diameter, pushes cloud-free into the Martian stratosphere. To the left, a train of clouds extends several hundred miles beyond the mountain. The clouds are thought to contain mostly water ice, condensed from the atmosphere as it cools while moving up the slopes of the volcano. By the Martian afternoon, the cloud cover will be visible from Earth. The volcano itself is extinct.

NASA PHOTO

2. "On a clear day on Mars, you can see tens of thousands of rocks."

Two high-resolution scans by Viking 2 were combined to create this Marsscape, looking north-east to the horizon some two miles away. What seems to be the dried-up channel of a small stream winds from upper left to lower right, confirming the astronomers' belief that Mars was once a watery planet. Today, however, it's a bleak and lifeless vista. The Martian atmosphere is almost pure carbon dioxide. Winds range up to 300 mph (though this picture was taken in calm weather) and the average temperature is far below freezing. To the disappointment of scientists on the Viking project, neither of the two craft landed on Mars in 1976 found any conclusive evidence of life on the planet.

NASA PHOTO

3. Deep in interplanetary space, Mariner 10's TV cameras map Venusian weather patterns in ultraviolet light.

A blanket of clouds hides the surface of Venus. Unlike Earth, however, these clouds contain no water vapour. The Venusian atmosphere is mainly carbon dioxide, mixed with a dash of sulphuric acid, and the resulting clouds are best described as thick, oily smog. Forty miles high, this cloud layer traps sunlight, producing a "greenhouse effect" which turns the surface of Venus into an inferno. Spiralling 200 mph winds carry heat from the Venusian equator towards the long cirrus-like streaks near the poles.

NASA PHOTO

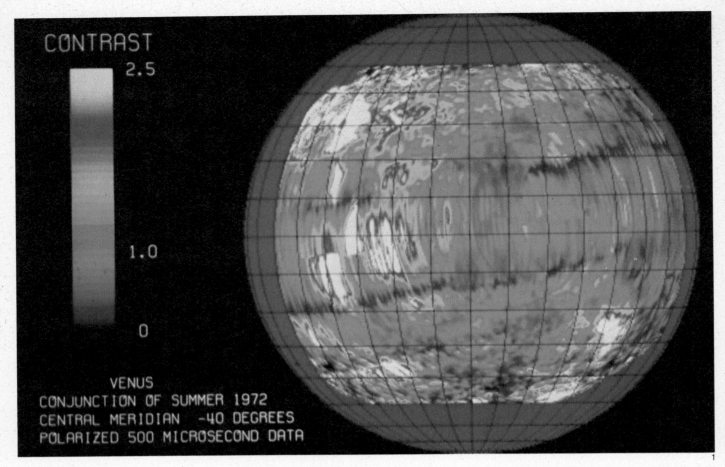

CONTRAST

2.5

1.0

0

VENUS
CONJUNCTION OF SUMMER 1972
CENTRAL MERIDIAN -40 DEGREES
POLARIZED 500 MICROSECOND DATA

1

1. Using a radio telescope carved from the natural amphitheatre of a defunct volcanic crater, astronomers bounce radar signals off the planets.

This radar map of Venus was made using a specially developed transmitter, the S-band, with a power output of nearly half a million watts. Beamed from the 1000ft diameter dish of the Arecibo radio telescope in Puerto Rico, the radar pulses scan the surface of Venus, perpetually hidden by clouds. The S-band has already revealed a lava flow the size of Oklahoma, and an impact crater as large as Hudson Bay.

Developed by NASA scientists, the S-band was launched in style, sending a coded message across the galaxy to possible extra-terrestrial civilisations. Travelling at lightspeed, the message will take some 20,000 years to reach its destination: the globular star cluster known as M13. While the message was being transmitted, scientists estimated that, along the beam's path, Earth blazed brighter than the sun in the S-band frequency.

COURTESY OF DR D. B. CAMPBELL, ARECIBO OBSERVATORY.

2. Enigmatic Jupiter, largest of the planets. Though we have studied it for over 300 years, we are still far from understanding the giant's peculiar nature. Why does Jupiter give out twice as much heat as it receives from the sun? Why is the planet surrounded by "space reefs" of lethal radiation?

Jupiter, according to some scientists, may well be a thirty thousand mile deep ocean of liquid hydrogen. We can never see the surface of this ocean, for the entire planet is covered by a thick atmosphere of ice and ammonia crystals, capped by hydrogen gas; a raging blizzard of 400mph gales, Earth-size tornadoes and great electric storms.

Pioneer II soared out of Earth's orbital plane to snap this hitherto unseen view of Jupiter's northern hemisphere. The north pole itself is in darkness, and the areas surrounding it are broken and mottled into what scientists believe may be the Jovian version of "blue sky." Here, far from the great convection currents (pale yellow zones and reddish-brown belts) which girdle the equatorial regions, life may be possible. The forms it might take, however, would be completely alien to us.

NASA PHOTO

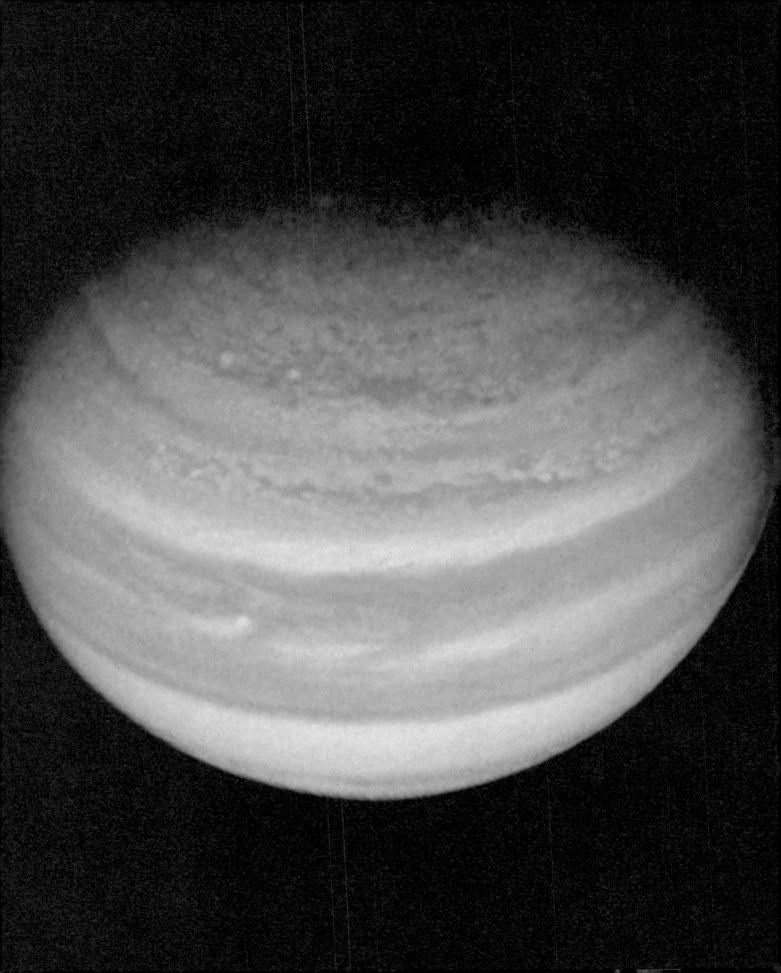

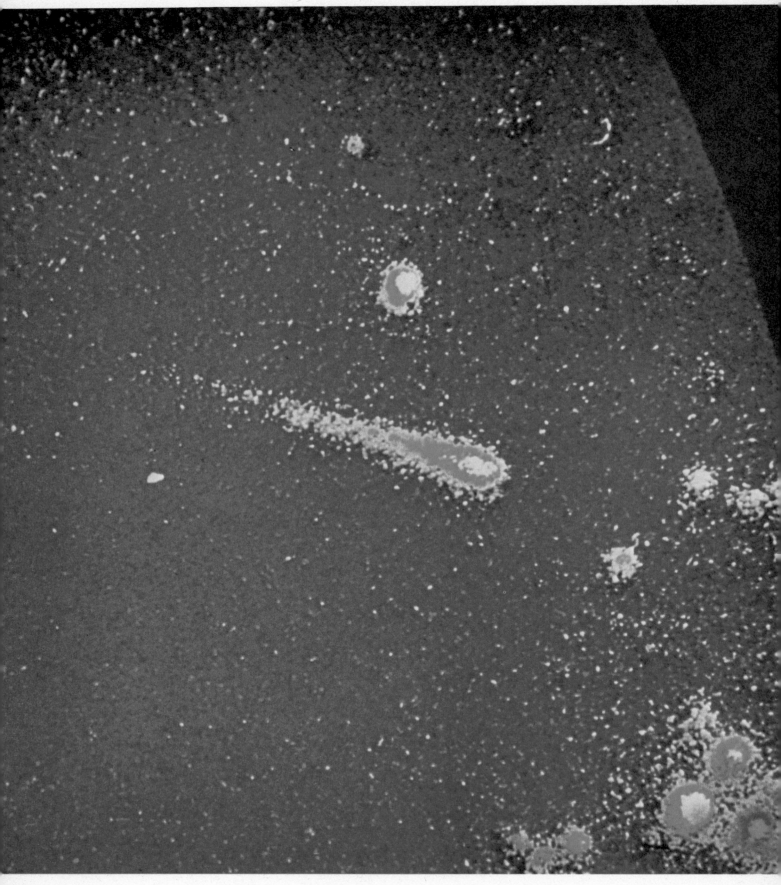

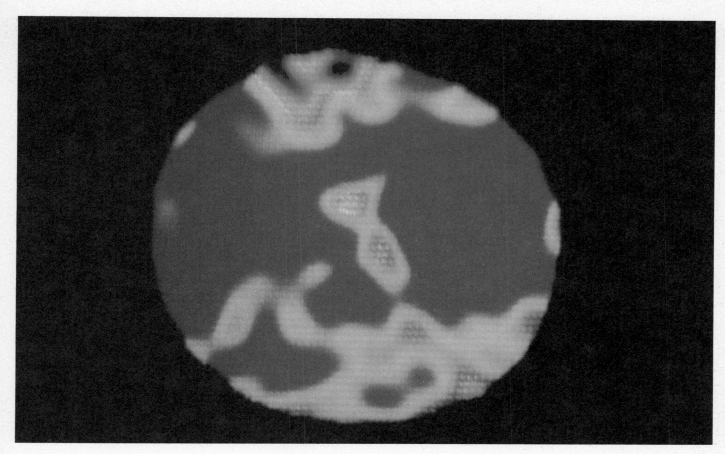

Left. Christmas Day, 1973—and space-walking astronauts on the Skylab 4 mission snap comet Kohoutek as it approaches the sun. Taken in ultra-violet light, the colour enhancement highlights Kohoutek's three million mile tail against a background of stars in the constellation of Sagittarius.

Though many space objects radiate heavily in the ultraviolet band of the spectrum, Earth's atmosphere blocks out most of the radiation. For this reason, much of the work done in ultraviolet astronomy is carried out above the atmosphere, by balloon, rocket and satellite.

NAVAL RESEARCH LABORATORY/NASA

Speeding at 186,000 miles a second, light takes 8½ minutes to cross from the sun to Earth. The nearest star lies approximately 4.3 light years away. Yet to travel the full length of our galaxy—the Milky Way—a ray of light would need 100,000 years to complete the course.

The galaxy is full of such cosmic superlatives. It holds a hundred billion stars, arranged in two great spiral arms surrounding a central core, itself ten thousand light years across and five thousand thick. The solar system lies in a spiral arm that runs in the general direction of the constellation of Orion. We are in a galactic suburb: neither out at the edge of the mammoth disk nor near the expanding cloud at its centre. We revolve once around the galaxy every two hundred million years. At this leisurely pace, we have made 20 such revolutions in the estimated 4.6 billion years of the solar system's existence.

Above. This computer-enhanced image, from America's Kitt Peak Observatory, is our first glimpse of the surface of a star other than the sun. The star is Betelgeuse, in the constellation of Orion – a red-hued supergiant one thousand times larger than our sun. The quality of the image – which shows huge convection regions in Betelgeuse's atmosphere – may leave much to be desired. But, as scientists point out, seeing the surface of a star 500 light years away is about as easy as picking out details on a grain of sand in the next county.

© BY THE ASSOCIATION OF UNIVERSITIES FOR RESEARCH IN ASTRONOMY INC., THE KITT PEAK NATIONAL OBSERVATORY.

Overleaf. Looking towards the galactic centre. This starfield in the constellation of Sagittarius—crossed by the track of a passing satellite—lies between us and the galaxy's hub. We can never see into the heart of the galaxy, because of great clouds of dust and gas which are present throughout the Milky Way.

US NAVAL OBSERVATORY PHOTOGRAPH.

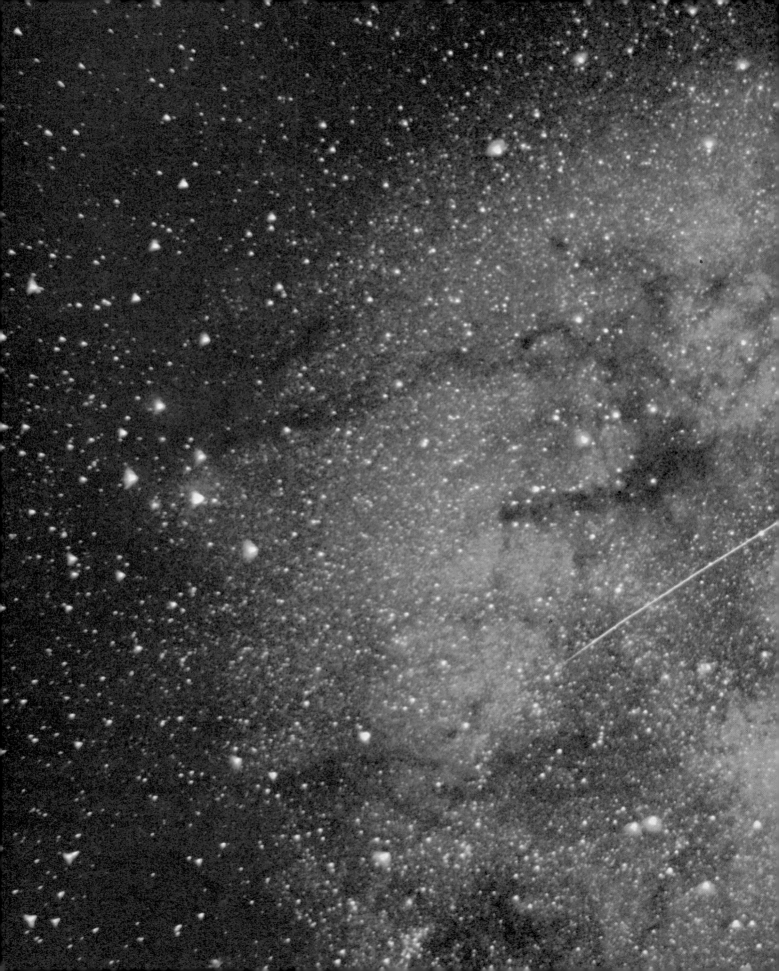

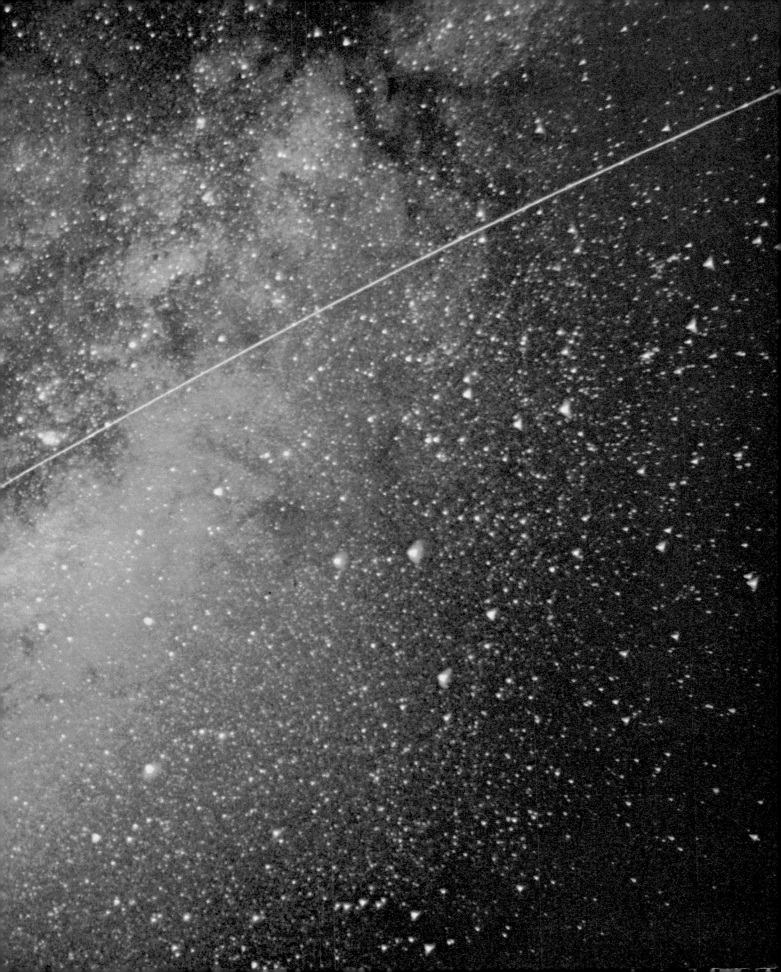

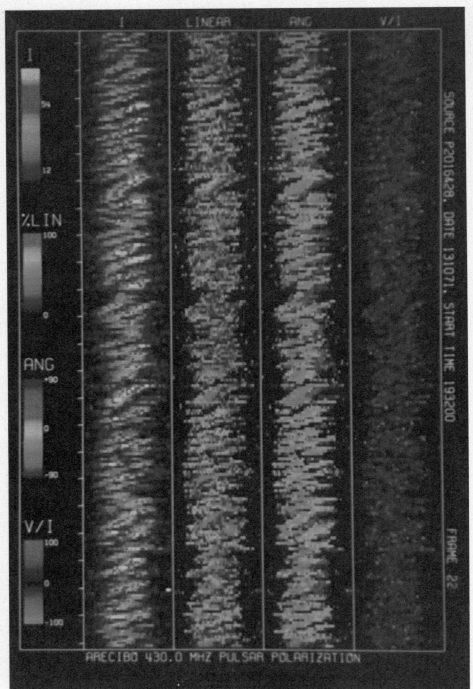

The incoming signal from pulsar P2016. The star's "flashes" are represented by the sideways peaks and troughs on these four colour-coded variations of the signature. During the few seconds of this recording, P2016 has pulsed several dozen times.

Pulsars, or "pulsating radio sources," broadcast great bursts of radio energy with the precision timing of an atomic clock. There is much speculation about their origin and nature, but they are generally believed to be the remnants of collapsed stars, crushed by the force of their own gravity into rapidly-spinning balls of matter under such enormous pressure that a million tons of pulsar would fill the volume of a pea. The rapid spin and intense magnetic field combine to beam out energy pulses from these stellar lighthouses. Pulsars are travelling at such speed that they have thrown off the gravitational bonds of their galaxy. One intriguing explanation suggests that pulsars are propelled by the energy of their own pulses, rocketing across the galaxy like giant catherine wheels.

COURTESY OF DR JOHN RANKIN, ARECIBO OBSERVATORY.

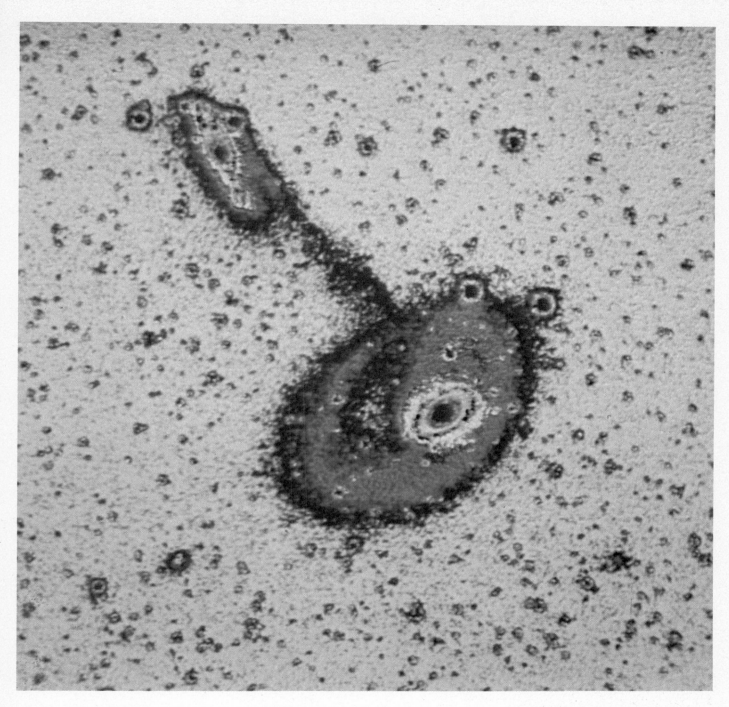

Galaxies that pass in the night. Though no one has ever recorded a pair of colliding stars, "crashes" between galaxies are relatively commonplace. The distances between individual stars are so vast that two galaxies may even pass gracefully through each other without any of their stars ever meeting. Collisions do occur, however, between gas clouds within the galaxies, creating patches of high density material in which, it is believed, new stars will rapidly be formed.

Two galaxies pass at a distance. Taken at Cerro Tellolo Observatory in Chile and enhanced at Kitt Peak, the photograph shows a bridge between the star-hosts, the result of gravitational attraction. The bridge, some 5 million light years across, may already contain a new stellar population.

Overleaf. Streamers of star matter distort the shapes of these two galaxies, nicknamed "The Mice." The photograph was taken by the Kitt Peak Observatory's 4-metre telescope, then colour treated to show brightness levels.

PHOTOGRAPHS (ABOVE AND OVERLEAF) © BY THE ASSOCIATION OF UNIVERSITIES FOR RESEARCH IN ASTRONOMY INC., THE KITT PEAK NATIONAL OBSERVATORY.

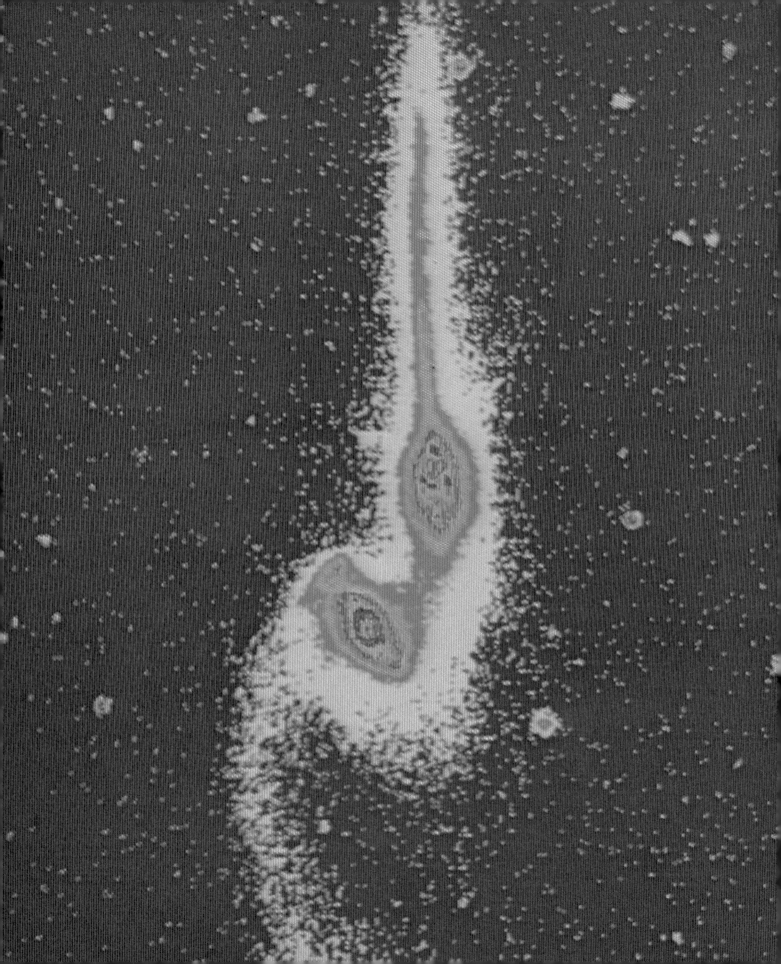

Technical
Appendix

Spectrum

FREQUENCIES
cycles per second

WAVELENGTH

ATMOSPHERIC TRANSMISSION

DETECTING SYSTEMS

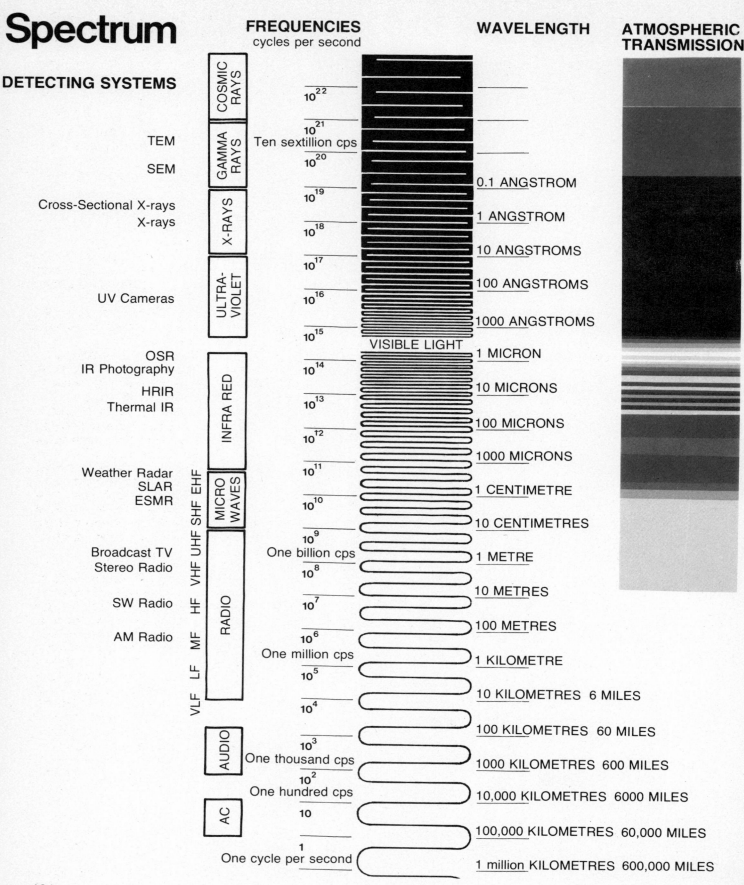

DETECTING SYSTEMS	Band	Frequencies	Wavelength
	COSMIC RAYS	10^{22}	
TEM	GAMMA RAYS	10^{21} Ten sextillion cps	
SEM		10^{20}	0.1 ANGSTROM
Cross-Sectional X-rays	X-RAYS	10^{19}	1 ANGSTROM
X-rays		10^{18}	10 ANGSTROMS
	ULTRA-VIOLET	10^{17}	100 ANGSTROMS
UV Cameras		10^{16}	1000 ANGSTROMS
		10^{15}	VISIBLE LIGHT
OSR	INFRA RED		1 MICRON
IR Photography		10^{14}	10 MICRONS
HRIR		10^{13}	100 MICRONS
Thermal IR		10^{12}	1000 MICRONS
Weather Radar	MICRO WAVES	10^{11}	1 CENTIMETRE
SLAR		10^{10}	10 CENTIMETRES
ESMR			
Broadcast TV	RADIO	10^{9} One billion cps	1 METRE
Stereo Radio		10^{8}	10 METRES
SW Radio		10^{7}	100 METRES
AM Radio		10^{6} One million cps	1 KILOMETRE
		10^{5}	10 KILOMETRES 6 MILES
		10^{4}	100 KILOMETRES 60 MILES
	AUDIO	10^{3} One thousand cps	1000 KILOMETRES 600 MILES
		10^{2} One hundred cps	10,000 KILOMETRES 6000 MILES
	AC	10	100,000 KILOMETRES 60,000 MILES
		1 One cycle per second	1 million KILOMETRES 600,000 MILES

VLF LF MF HF VHF UHF SHF EHF

THE RADIATION UNIVERSE

The photographs in this book are the results of our first crude attempts to explore areas of the spectrum outside our narrow, light-oriented world. They are the scans and shadows and echoes from beyond our senses—crude, certainly, but as exciting as the first spices from the Indies or rock samples from the moon. And for once they are not material treasure, but information, images, a wider view of things. Understanding.

The divisions of the spectrum are no more than a convenience. Radiation frequencies all run into each other and many of them have particular characteristics which overlap. They form a continuum, with no discernible upper or lower limit.

Although our eyesight cuts off at the 0.4 and 0.7 micron wavelengths, light exists beyond this and is perfectly visible to other animals. These adjacent areas of ultra-violet and infrared have been well researched. The really alien territory begins where the cameras cease to function and the light microscopes cannot reach, in the frequencies which only electronics can record. And most of the equipment involved is designed to translate the information back into light.

Radiation of every wavelength is all around us. It pours down on us from the sun and is emitted by everything on Earth. It is refracted and reflected back into space, scattered by atmospheric particles and absorbed by water vapour and gases.

For scientists such as doctors, who work at close quarters with radiation, the whole spectrum is available and "active" sensing — for instance projecting radiation through a subject (x-rays, injected radioactive isotopes) or bouncing it off the subject (electron microscopes) — is possible. But with the exception of radar, long range uses are essentially "passive" because of the distances involved and interference from turbulent exchange of energy in the atmosphere.

This absorbent blanket around the Earth has shielded us from the more dangerous frequencies in space, such as ultra-violet, but it has also severely blocked our view, and it was not until the satellite cameras rose above it that

astronomers could take the first UV-photographs of the sun.

The Windows

Certain bands of radiation, including light, find it relatively easy to penetrate the atmosphere, and these wavelengths, which form an irregular pattern on the spectrum, are known as "windows."

Satellites can use windows in, say, the thermal-IR band, to get a clear view of Earth's surface, or they can deliberately use one of the absorbent bands, to study different layers of the atmosphere itself.

Black Bodies

The spectrum disappears into infinity at either end, beyond the range of our instruments. We have no idea what hyper regions exist above cosmic rays or what indefinitely long wavelengths (such as the hypothetical "gravity waves") might be like. This presents a problem because, with no limits, it is difficult to tell where you are. So scientists have established certain norms or standards against which they can measure radiation.

There is, for instance, the "black body," which is used to quantify the reflection or emission of radiation. A black body is an ideal object which absorbs all the energy it receives and reflects nothing at all. In terms of infrared, therefore, it is also very hot. A "white body" is the opposite, reflecting everything; and since it absorbs no radiation, its surface temperature remains unchanged. Real objects are "grey bodies" which both absorb and reflect radiation at a variety of different wavelengths.

Ground Truth

One advantage of the new radiation sensors is that many of them can operate at great distances. But this in turn presents another problem. A doctor using radiation equipment can easily check on its accuracy and learn to interpret the results, by carrying out other tests on the patient. But when the sensors are five hundred miles above an inaccessible part of Earth, it can be difficult to know exactly what is being recorded. So the concept of "ground truth" is vitally important to aerial and

satellite photography. It simply means that sample sites are carefully monitored at ground level and then checked against the photographs or radiation scans. Once the chemical composition of a rock is matched to its reflective qualities as recorded from space, or a type of plant to its colour on infrared film, the information is stored for use in future interpretations.

Signatures

All bodies with temperatures above absolute zero give off energy. The array of wavelengths and intensities of real-world radiators can be very complex, and they are as distinct as fingerprints. Banks of these spectral signatures are now being built up from measurements in space, cross-referenced against ground truth and factors such as weather conditions and the angle of the sun.

One of the first steps in taking a radiation fingerprint is to measure the *albedo,* or the proportion of radiation an object reflects or absorbs. For instance, fine sand reflects 37% of short wave radiation, whereas moist black soil only reflects 8%. Washington DC in September reflects 12%, whereas Yuma, Arizona, reflects 20%. Dense, clean dry snow reflects 86-95%, sea-ice 36%, oak trees 18% and heather 10%. And this is only in the short-wave band. The albedo for light, microwaves and ultra-violet are all different.

Radar can produce radiation patterns indicating the windspeeds in the heart of a hurricane. Infrared can tell if buildings are inhabited and how recently roads and airfields were used. The spectral signatures recorded by satellites show whether a piece of territory is granite or basalt, whether it is growing wheat or corn, how much of the forests are softwood or hardwood, and how good or bad the harvest will be. They detect the warmth, water content and height of clouds, can tell the difference between snow and ice, the depth of coastal waters, the temperature and shape of its currents, and even the degree of salinity of water used for irrigation. They alter maps, record urban development, survey natural disasters for insurance companies and relief agencies, and track nuclear missiles.

We are learning to "see" in radiation.

The Limits of Light

SPACE CAMERAS

The equipment which took many of the pictures in this book would not be recognised as cameras – or the processes as photography – and most of it has only recently been developed as a direct result of space technology.

In view of the results, it is surprising that the potential of space photography was not fully appreciated until as late as 1963, when the first Gemini astronauts took hand-held Hasselblad cameras with them into orbit. But by the end of that project thousands of pictures had been taken and (in NASA jargon) "earth photog" was no longer "requested" but "required."

Cameras are now standard equipment on space flights, in a variety of specialist forms. The most useful development is probably the multi-spectral camera, a bank of half-a-dozen cameras in a single mount, photographing the same area on different types of film. Each filter or film responds to a different wavelength and picks out specific features. For instance, rock markings may be clearer in green, while vegetation and water stand out better on infrared film. The results are often combined as composite images, such as that of Imperial Valley (page 157) taken by the multi-spectral camera on Apollo 9.

Another ingenious development was the ultra-violet camera, which was first flown on Apollo 16, and later on Skylab, where it took the comet picture (page 186). UV is another "invisible" form of light that can be recorded on film but, unlike IR, it has to be focused electronically.

The image is first focused through a normal lens system onto a scanning detector which is especially sensitive to the UV content, and separates it from the light wavelengths. The electrical signals from it direct an electron-beam of varying intensity back and forth across a strip of film to produce the black-and-white image of the original scene, in ultra-violet light.

LIGHT FANTASTIC

Light itself is being stretched into some strange shapes by technology. The use of polarised light (in which the light waves are roughly parallel) and "coherent" laser light (in which the exact frequencies are in step), not to mention high-speed strobes and fibre optics, demonstrate the sort of control we have over no other form of radiation. But it is holograms, above all, which capture the imagination. As someone said of Einstein's Theory of Relativity, "It's easy enough to understand. The difficulty is believing it."

If you look at an object, the space in between is filled with lightwaves at different frequencies, all going in different directions. These are what the eye, or camera, take in and focus into a picture. A hologram, however, is a cross-section through that space, recording the random pattern of light waves. When "pure" light is shone through it, from behind, it recreates those original waves and they "resume" their journey towards your eyes. You "see" exactly what you would have seen then, in three dimensions. Look around it, as you could have done then, and you "see" another side.

Making the first holograms was a delicate process, because the slightest movement destroyed the effect. Everything had to be bolted down, and only inanimate (and therefore immobile) objects could be recorded.

The introduction of pulsed lasers now makes slight movements acceptable, and the first holographic portraits were made recently in California – of Salvador Dali among others. It is even possible to produce cylindrical holograms with overlapping plates, so that when a laser is shone down into it, there appears to be a complete "person" inside. In one of these experiments the subject, a girl, happened to smile as the last plates were being exposed. When the hologram was reassembled, so was her movement. Walking around the cylinder at a steady pace, you actually saw her "smile" at you.

Holograms have other curious properties. If you break a holographic plate in half, you have two identical holograms. If you look through even a very small fragment, the whole scene will still be visible. The image may be less three-dimensional, but the basic information about the original is still coded into every part of the hologram's surface.

HOLOGRAMS

The principle of three-dimensional holograms was set out by Dennis Gabor, of the British-Thompson Laboratories in Rugby, in 1948, and he was awarded the Nobel Prize for his discovery in 1971.

Although his theories were correct, Gabor's early holograms were not very effective because he was limited to the weak and diffuse light of mercury-vapour lamps. Not until lasers became available in 1960, was it possible for the first real holograms to be produced by Emmett Leith and Junis Upatineks at the University of Michigan.

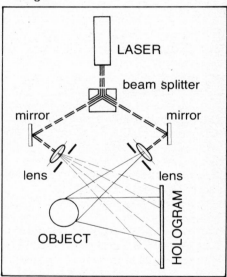

It requires two beams from the same laser to make a hologram. One of them illuminates the object and the light from it is scattered in all directions, some of it hitting the holographic plate. At the same time the other beam shines directly onto the plate, setting up interference with lightwaves from the object. It is this pattern which the plate records.

When it is developed, the opaque chemicals in the emulsion, such as silver, are bleached out, leaving behind the transparent swirls of bromide crystals on the surface.

If a laser is then shone through it, the varying thickness of bromide acts as an elaborate lens, scattering the light in the original directions so that an observer "sees" the original object.

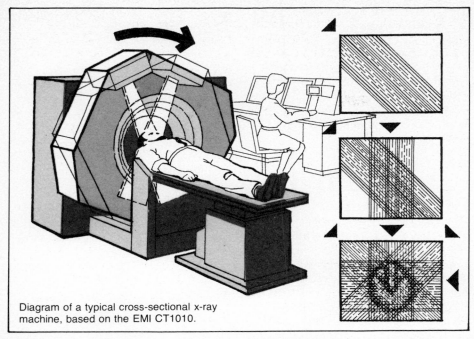

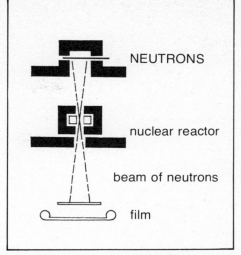

Diagram of a typical cross-sectional x-ray machine, based on the EMI CT1010.

See-through photography

CROSS SECTIONAL X-RAYS

Cross-sectional x-rays, known as "tomographs," are probably the greatest advance in diagnostic medicine since the invention of x-rays themselves.

A modern tomograph machine consists of a scanning frame with an x-ray tube mounted exactly opposite an array of 30 or more highly sensitive crystal detectors. The patient lies inside the frame while a fan-shaped beam of x-rays, between 10 and 15 mm thick, is projected through his body from a number of angles about 10° apart. The entire scan takes roughly 20 seconds, although more detail is revealed in, for instance, brain tissue with a 4 or 5 minute scan. The information is then fed to a computer where each strip of x-rays is "projected" as a pattern of lines, intersecting those of the next strip, to build up the complete tomograph. As each strip contains up to 250,000 absorption measurements, a computer is essential to "clean up" the resulting picture. This can then be displayed on a TV screen, colour-coded and analysed. As with most electronic

devices of this sort, the operator can "zoom" in on any detail, enlarging it about four times, to full picture size.

In spite of early fears about possible tissue damage, tomography was first used for brain scans in 1972 and proved so valuable that it is now in regular use at hospitals around the world.

"TOMOGRAPHY. A technique for using x-rays for photographing one specific plane in the body for diagnostic purposes."
— The Penguin Medical Encyclopedia.

NEUTROGRAPHY

The technique of neutron "photography" was conceived in 1932, shortly after the discovery of the neutron itself. But it was not until the early 1960s that technology caught up with the possibilities and scientists at General Electric and the Argonne National Laboratory developed the first neutron radiograph facilities.

A neutrograph is made by passing a beam of neutrons from a nuclear reactor through a test object. Neutrons are those particles in the atomic nucleus which have no charge and, because they are not affected by electromagnetism, they ignore the electrons which orbit around each atom. Only the nucleus itself affects their passage. This means that they can go right through heavy elements

like lead, which blocks normal x-rays, and yet can be stopped by light-weight hydrogen or carbon atoms.

Neutrons will not react well with the emulsion of films and in some cases, such as when the test object itself is radioactive, direct contact is impossible. So the film is usually covered with a plate or foil. When the neutrons emerge from the test object, the beam strikes the plate and is converted into ionising radiation (electromagnetic waves) and this secondary radiation is photographed on normal x-ray film.

Neutrography is expensive because it requires costly nuclear reactors, so its applications are limited to certain critical areas. It has been used for checking explosives and inspecting elements of aero-space technology, especially ceramics.

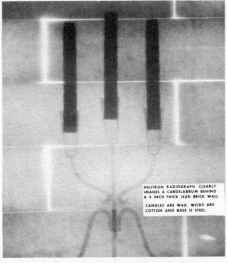

The extraordinary qualities of neutrography are demonstrated by this picture of wax candles taken *through four feet of solid lead.*

Microscopes

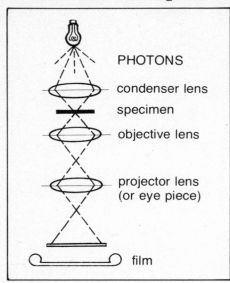

PHOTONS
condenser lens
specimen
objective lens
projector lens
(or eye piece)
film

LIGHT MICROSCOPE

Although its origins go back to the early 17th century, the microscope was first put to scientific use by a Dutchman called Leeuwenhoek in 1683. His instrument only had a magnifying power of X275, but it was enough to reveal the tiny organisms in a drop of water and open up whole new worlds of discovery.

Since then, though the principles have remained the same, microscopes have been developed to the resolving limits of light itself. This allows a magnification of roughly X2500, revealing details about 1/125,000 of an inch across. Beyond this horizon, the wavelength of light is so large in comparison with the subject that the image breaks up.

In a compound microscope the final magnification is the product of its lenses. If one is X10 and the other is X8, it will result in a magnification of X80. The short focus produces such a shallow depth-of-field that the picture is virtually two-dimensional. On the other hand, the SEM, with roughly 300 times the depth-of-field, produces comparatively 3-D pictures of subjects.

The technique of "dark field" illumination has extended the range of microscopes by making transparent (or unstained) objects visible. By putting an opaque stop in the path of the light just in front of the condenser lens, the light can be prevented from going through the instrument, and passes obliquely through the edges of the lens. The only rays which can be seen are those which bounce off features of the specimen and are deflected from the path. The fine details then show up as bright outlines against a black background.

TEM

The Transmission Electron Microscope.

The first transmission electron microscope was built in Berlin, in 1932, by Max Knoll and Dr Ernst Ruska. It attempted to overcome the limits of normal microscopes by using a beam of charged electrons, focused through magnetic "lenses," instead of light.

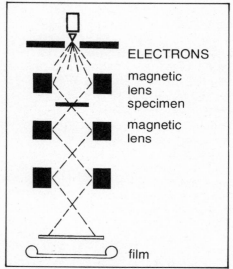

ELECTRONS
magnetic lens
specimen
magnetic lens
film

Light microscopes cannot resolve anything smaller than the wavelength of their radiation, about half a micron. But this was 5000 times larger than the diameter of an atom, and at least 20 times bigger than viruses and many structures in living cells. The shorter wavelengths of, say, x-rays, would enormously increase the resolving power, but no one had yet discovered the necessary lenses and optics to control x-rays.

Then, in 1927, atomic physicists confirmed the astonishing wave/particle theory: that particles such as electrons could act *either* as a wave *or* a particle at any given time. Electrons with an energy of only a few thousand volts act as if they had a wavelength roughly the same size as an atom, and, unlike x-rays, electrons can be controlled. It set Knoll thinking about a microscope with an inconceivably greater resolving power than even x-rays.

The pictures produced by the first TEMs were enlarged to a revolutionary order of magnitude. But the magnetic lenses proved to be less efficient than hoped for, and this prevented TEMs from resolving objects smaller than about 50 times the size of atoms.

So Max Knoll set about devising a more efficient method of using the electrons.

SEM

The Scanning Electron Microscope.

The principle of the scanning electron microscope was outlined by Max Knoll in 1938, and again a year later by Manfred von Ardenne. But no prototype was built. Perhaps because of the success of the TEM, or the war which intervened, nothing was done until 1948, when C. W. Oatley of Cambridge revived the idea. The first models reached the market in the late 1950s.

The "more effective" method made use of new electronic developments. A fine beam of electrons was scanned across the specimen in a raster pattern similar to a television image. Electrons leaving the object (not necessarily the same ones which hit it) were scanned in the same pattern by a sensitive detector that turned them into electrical impulses. They were used to modulate the flying spot of a cathode ray tube to produce a very much larger image.

But there was one drawback. While the whole of the TEM image is "illuminated" by electrons all the time, the beam of an SEM, racing back and forth, only "illuminates" each part for a fraction of the total exposure time. This limited the resolution of the SEM to about 100 angstroms, even with a long exposure of nearly two minutes. The problem was solved in the early 1970s, with the development of brighter and more sharply focused electron guns based on the same principles of field emission which led to the FEM.

The resolution of SEMs are now comparable to the transmission systems, and the inherent advantages of scanners are beginning to tell. When electrons are transmitted through an object, some of them are bound to emerge with less energy than others. If they then have to pass through a magnetic lens their paths will bend slightly more than the energetic ones and they will come to a focus at slightly different points, blurring the image. But in SEMs all the focusing is done before the beam hits the object. All that remains beyond is a scanner, which can be as close as one likes to the specimen and is (theoretically) capable of recording every single electron. It would be impossible to ask more of any observing instrument.

The SEM could not match the quantum leap of the TEM – from the resolving power of a light microscope at 2000 angstroms, to one of only 2 or 3 angstroms. One can only break the light barrier once. But the SEM achieved something at least as valuable. By enormously increasing the depth of field, it gave the microworld a new dimension and reality.

It also saved time. Previously, when an investigator wanted a complete view of a specimen, he had to preserve it, cut it into hundreds of slices on a device called a microtome, mount each one on a slide, photograph them one by one, and then painstakingly attempt to reconstruct the original object from the cross-sections. It was like printing an entire pack of playing cards in order to find the shape of their box. No single person could hope to study a large number of specimens like this.

But the SEM made it possible in one step. Nowadays large-scale surveys are not only possible, but easy.

The specimens for SEMs are treated in an entirely different way. First they must be protected from the fierce beam of electrons, which can damage them and are liable to set up static in some materials, blurring the image. So the specimen is "fixed" to retain its size and shape, and then the whole object is metal-plated – coated with a layer of gold (or some other good conductor) only a few atoms thick. This used to be done by heating a sheet of gold foil in a vacuum until the atoms on the surface boiled off, and evaporated as a fine mist over the object. But a device has recently been developed which "blows" it on directly.

Within an hour, the specimen, now looking like a marvellously detailed jewel, is ready to go under the SEM. Because the machine is electronic, the controls are very flexible. The investigator can look at the whole specimen, change his angle of view, move from part to part and zoom in on any interesting details. When he finds a picture he wants, he just presses a button and it is automatically photographed.

FEM

The Field Emission Microscope

The radiation that "illuminates" an FEM, like that of medical gamma-ray cameras, comes from within the object itself.

The fact that in an electrical field a test object can be made to project electrons from its surface was discovered in Berlin in 1876, when E. Goldstein saw the blurred likeness of a 10-penny coin used as a cathode on the fluorescent glass wall of his discharge tube. In 1936, Erwin W. Mueller realised that electrons flying off the surface in this way carried the pattern of the original atoms from which they came and "magnified" the atomic structure of the surface.

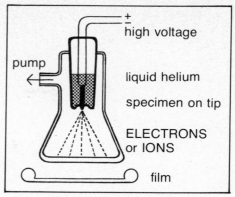

His early FEMs produced blurred and very faint images. Development work was interrupted by World War II, but in 1941 Mueller made an important discovery—that if the electrical field he had used to generate the electrons was *reversed,* whole atoms (charged ions) could be torn off the surface. Because these were more powerful, the image would be much brighter, and since they had a shorter "wavelength" than the electrons they would give much finer resolution.

After the war many technical improvements such as image-intensifiers and freezing techniques to stabilise the surfaces became available. In 1950, Mueller's field electron microscope proved its worth by photographing individual molecules and a year later his new field ion microscope produced the first faint pictures of a metal surface in true *atomic* detail. In 1958, at an international conference, Mueller was able to show his fellow scientists the first motion pictures of atoms migrating across a metal surface and evaporating.

In 1967, Mueller developed what he called the "atom probe," which he described as "the ultimate micro-analytical tool, 10 orders of magnitude more sensitive than any other." He linked his field ion microscope to a mass spectrometer which can measure the atomic weight of individual atoms in flight (the lighter they are, the faster they fly). The atom, as Mueller points out, is no longer "merely a concept, more or less convincing by its billionth of a contribution to a dim diffraction spot. Besides seeing atoms within their environment, we can now experiment with single atoms, follow their path, pick one up at will and identify its chemical nature by its atomic weight."

ELECTRONS
magnetic lens
scanner
amplifier
detector
specimen

199

THE FINAL CLOSE-UP

The ultimate goal for microscope technology is still to photograph a single, tantalising atom. Scanning electron and field emission microscopes have got as close to it as any technique, but x-ray crystallography is just behind, and there are holographs ahead.

X-Ray Crystallography

This was the technique which helped to unravel the double helix of DNA. It was originally designed to study the regular structure of atoms in crystals by shining x-rays through them and analysing the resulting diffraction patterns. The patterns produced by irregular organic molecules, like DNA, were thought to be too complicated to be understood. But nowadays one can analyse almost any molecular structure—with computers to read the images, deduce the angles and carry out the nightmare calculations necessary to work out the shape which caused the diffraction in the first place.

"Increasing vision is increasingly expensive."
—R. A. Janek.

Atoms in 3-D

"In the past all we have been able to do is produce a score. Now we can produce real music."
—George Stroke, University of New York.

One of the most exciting developments in atomic imagery is the recent use of holograms to produce truly three-dimensional pictures of atomic structure.

The complicated geography of molecules must be carefully explored if we are to understand their functions, and this has been made easier by the technique, invented by George Stroke and his colleagues at New York's Electro-Optical Laboratories, for turning x-ray diffraction pictures into holograms. The clue is that diffraction images already carry a form of interference pattern very similar to holograms.

"We realised," said Strokes, "that a crystal, in which the atoms are arranged in a repeating array, can be made to produce a three-dimensional display of data. What we've figured out is a way of viewing it."

Computers analyse the diffraction pattern (like the picture on page 15) and design a hologram based on its relative densities. Lasers are shone through it in the usual way, but the light is then focused by a lens, acting as an optical computer, and projected onto a screen.

SONOGRAPHY

The use of ultra-high frequency sound to probe the most sensitive tissues of the body was pioneered by British scientists in 1959, for use in obstetrics. Proposals to use it in brain studies gave rise to objections in the medical press and interest waned. But it was revived again in the early 1970s, when more sophisticated visual displays and colour-coding became possible, and is now in use in many areas of medicine.

Sonography has two advantages over other means of examination. It can be focused on minute and delicate parts of tissue like the eyeball, and it is continuous, so it can monitor internal movements such as the heartbeat of an unborn baby. X-rays are kept to very short exposures for safety reasons and thermographs only register surface effects, but sonography can provide an action replay of any internal activity. A probe called a transducer, on the end of a long flexible arm, is simply pressed against the patient's body. The sound frequencies it emits at over 1,000 cycles a second are safe and "silent," and the echoes it picks up are accurate enough to enable doctors to distinguish muscles from soft tissues and organs. Sonographs can detect tumours as small as a quarter of an inch in size long before they would show up on other equipment. The technique is rapidly superseding x-rays in the study of obstetrics, and has revolutionised eye surgery to the extent that lasers are now being used to produce experimental 3-D *sound* holograms.

KIRLIAN PHOTOGRAPHY

Kirlian photography started out as do-it-yourself science, though it has since acquired academic

credentials. Amongst other research projects, it is being studied by Drs Thelma Moss and Kendall Johnson at the UCLA Neuro-Psychiatric Institute and by William Tiller, a materials scientist at Stanford University, who is attempting to quantify the electronic effects. NASA is investigating its use in detecting microscopic fissures in metal.

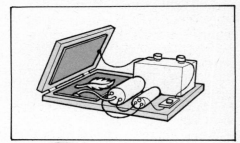

However, it is still possible for anyone with minimal scientific knowledge to construct a cheap and effective Kirlian camera of their own. All that is required is a controlled source of high-voltage electricity (which is harmless because of the low current levels involved), electrodes or condenser plates, and film.

It is, in effect, a form of field emission (see FEM) which records the interference patterns and diffraction produced by the electro-chemical structure of the specimen.

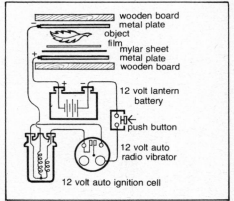

The apparatus should be set up in a dark room (with a safe-light), and a piece of film, or better still a good photographic paper, placed emulsion side up on the myla insulator covering the bottom electrode plate. To photograph, say, the fingertips, one places the thumb on the top (grounded) plate and the fingertips on the film, and presses the "start" button for a one or two second exposure. The result will be a negative image that will require printing in the usual way to produce a positive image.

Beyond Light

FALSE COLOUR

Infra-red film records a mirror-image world where red is green, and black (if hot enough) is white. The use of "false colour" and "density slicing" techniques are changing the meaning of "colour" itself. Red can mean growth as well as fire, and black can indicate either the presence or absence of radiation.

"The human eye can perceive between ten and twelve intensity levels in a normal black and white photograph, but only after careful scrutiny of the photograph. In terms of perceiving the *distribution* about the photograph of a specific intensity level, this becomes even more difficult."

—J. A. Swift and A. C. Brown, Unilever Research Laboratory. Journal of Microscopy Vol. 105.

A black-and-white world would not only be boring, but also intolerably vague. Without colours and with only 16 shades of grey to rely on, we would lose much of the meaning in our surroundings. Colours are the mental code we use to distinguish between different frequencies of radiation, and if we were deprived of them we could only register the intensity of light without knowing its wavelength.

This is a problem with pictures taken in bands of the spectrum other than light. Although it is possible to measure the wavelength, we have no mental colours to recognise it by. So all the pictures come out the same—variations of intensity in shades of grey.

Colour Conscious

Colour did not evolve in the first place because it made the world more beautiful, but because it made it easier to interpret. Boundaries are sharper, distance and movement clearer, and areas easier to estimate. It literally helps us to get more out of a picture, by assisting the curious ability of our brains to recognise patterns, i.e. to absorb complex information without going through it step by step.

All these advantages apply to monochrome radiation pictures if colours are substituted for the shades of grey. If, in other words, the pictures are "coded," quite arbitrarily, with "false colours."

Electronic Colour

Since most radiation records start life as magnetic tape, the easiest way to colour them is electronically. There are different kinds of hardware available to do this, but the principles are usually the same.

The information is scanned line by line electronically to the shade of grey, or intensity of each portion. The first run through, or *slice,* records the brightest areas, the second the less bright, and so on. Each "density slice" is then allocated a colour and a composite picture is projected on a colour television screen.

Nowadays this process is neatly packaged in a piece of equipment called an analyser which has a keyboard console containing several colour channels, each with red and green colour control. At the touch of a button the operator has the choice of hundreds of colours.

Between four and eight slices are normally used, but if the picture is reduced to only two or three colours, they can be turned into beautiful abstract shapes.

NASA scientists first experimented with colour coding in order to get more information from photographs of the surface of the moon. But the twin techniques of density slicing and colour coding were so successful that they were rapidly adopted by other professions—and entrepreneurs.

Sliced Art

"The analyser keyboard is the artist's palette and the cathode ray tube is his easel. The challenge is to combine both creative and technical skills."

—Howard Sochurek

Howard Sochurek, the American photographer who is responsible for many pictures in this book (pages 92, 108, 119, 126-7), was one of the first to recognise the art potential of density slicing. He bought himself a $35,000 analyser and established a prosperous business turning ordinary black-and-white photographs into instant graphics for the covers of *Time* and *Newsweek,* and the lobbies of oil company offices.

Digicolor

If the end product is to be on film, there are systems like Digicolor.
This is designed to process the magnetic tape record from airborne scanners. A tape of, say, thermal-IR reading, is converted into monochrome film, after correcting the distortions due to aircraft drift, and then into six temperature-related film strips. These are then electronically combined and photographed on to 70mm colour film.

Infrared Film

In the case of infrared, it is also possible to photograph the radiation directly, with an ordinary camera, but using special infrared film. This has layers of emulsion that respond to different strengths of radiation.

Using the convention of a positive (white) signature for strong radiation and a dark one for weak, some strange effects are produced. Water, which absorbs almost all the infrared, comes out dark blue or black, whereas green vegetation, which is burning up energy, develops right through to the base layer and comes out bright red or white.

The Eye Opener

"False" colour coding has now become essential wherever an exact density has to be mapped, from measuring the distortion of fuel rods in a nuclear power station to seeking the exact site of a pituitary tumour for a surgeon's cryogenic needle.

But perhaps the last word should go to a scientist whose work has been revolutionised by it—a radar meteorologist.

"Colour display," says Robert Serafin of the US National Center for Atmospheric Research, "is an innovative use of existing technology. It combines integrated circuit technology and commercial television know-how. A single picture represents a tremendous condensation of information—a quarter of a million bits or more—available in a form that can be analysed easily by the observer. Many of us who have been working with radar for many years share the same feeling that a blindfold has just been removed from the eyes of the weather radar observer."

Scanners

INFRA-RED

If non-smokers puff through half a cigarette, the temperature of their fingertips drops dramatically by 2½°C. The change is caused by the constricting effect of nicotine on the tiny blood-vessels in the hand and is often used to demonstrate the remarkable sensitivity of "heat cameras," those versatile tools which are becoming standard equipment in jungle-warfare, skin-graft units, industrial espionage and satellite surveillance.

Anything that "works" has a distinctive heat signature. A thermal infrared picture can outline the tumours in body tissue as clearly as it can identify the presence of a tank or aero-engine from a spy-plane miles above.

There are two forms of infrared. They are not so much "colours" as quite different types of radiation. One form, like the examples above, is radiant heat, the other is reflected light.

Near infrared, which is usually recorded from 3-4.5 microns wavelength, is an element of reflected sunlight, just below the visible red band in the spectrum. *Thermal infrared,* further down the spectrum and usually recorded from 8.5-14 microns wavelength, is heat. It may be absorbed from that same sunlight and slowly given off, or generated in the first place by the metabolism of plants and animals, and by man-made engines.

Since near infrared is a form of light, it can be photographed by ordinary cameras and it is widely used for surveillance because of its ability to penetrate through haze or clouds. Thermal infrared, on the other hand, is much more temperamental. It is badly affected by such factors as atmospheric conditions and whether the subject is wet or dry. It can only be recorded by electronic devices, and thermal-IR surveys are normally flown at night to avoid interference from sunlight which can warm up one side of a subject and cast cool "shadows" on the other.

One of the first applications of these wavelengths was their use by the military, during World War II, to spot camouflaged equipment. Healthy plants reflect near-IR from a layer below the chlorophyll in their leaves. A damaged plant rapidly loses this ability, and camouflage netting doesn't reflect it at all. This phenomenon has since been put to other uses, including sophisticated crop analysis.

Many of the military developments of IR technology are now well known, from "black" searchlights (near-IR) to sniperscope sights and heat-seeking missiles (thermal-IR). One example of its use in battle conditions was during the Arab-Israeli Six Day War in 1973, when satellite surveillance kept the Russians and Americans better informed than either of the combatants. The Israeli High Command even ordered its tank crews to turn off their engines whenever it was known that Russian satellites were over the horizon, so that their presence would not be detected.

At the moment there is special interest in thermal reconnaissance because it may provide a basis for the identification of "cruise missiles." Tactical cruise missiles, which carry a conventional warhead and travel only short distances, have engines which emit more heat than strategic cruise missiles, which travel thousands of miles and carry nuclear warheads. Because of this difference IR-equipment on satellites may be able to distinguish the two.

The medical uses of IR are almost entirely limited to the thermal range. The ability of thermal-IR to detect minute changes of temperature is particularly useful in monitoring growth patterns of tumours or grafts, or in studying circulatory disorders such as varicose veins and the effects of drugs on the blood supply. For instance when a regular smoker has a cigarette the temperature of his fingers only drops ¼° to ½°C, which suggests that the sort of permanent change has taken place that may be associated with coronary disease.

The infrared waves are now so well explored by scientists that the results are filtering back into everyday life. IR is, for instance, ideally suited to tracking down thermal pollution, and infrared pictures have been accepted as legal evidence in environmental court cases. The practical advantages of themographs are also demonstrated by the fact that NASA now does a brisk trade selling copies of IR aerial surveys to householders for do-it-yourself energy conservation.

But perhaps the most important role (as we shall see) is the part played by infrared in surveying Earth from space.

ELECTRONIC VISION

With radiation other than light, cameras must give way to electronics. This is partly because we have no adequate "optics" to focus it in the same way as light. But there are also considerable advantages to having your record in the form of electrical impulses.

In scanners, lens systems are replaced by oscillating mirrors and other devices which expose an electronic sensor to brief bursts of radiation. As the scanner collects energy along a track at right angles to the aircraft or satellite (or medical probe), its forward motion brings another strip into view and the scanner moves back to "start."

The sensor, which replaces the film emulsion, is tuned to pick up precise frequencies or wavelengths. It turns the radiation into electrical signals which can be stored on magnetic tape, analysed by computer and, unlike film, transmitted instantly over long distances. Retrieving film from an unmanned satellite involves shooting a package through the atmosphere, whereas electronic data can simply be radioed down to the nearest receiving station. Airborne scanners and ground-based ones (where no retrieval problem is involved) usually have built-in facilities for turning the signals into pictures on film or a video screen.

The scanners operate in three different ways: *broad waveband sensing* —in which non-specific sensors integrate energy from many wavelengths, e.g. across the visible light band; *narrow waveband sensing*—where most radiation is recorded at just a single wavelength; and *multi-spectral sensing*—in which objects are studied at several non-adjacent wavelengths and the results compared.

Most objects give off energy across a wide range of wavelengths, but they tend to have a peak wavelength at which the maximum radiation is reflected or emitted.

THE LINESCAN

It is impossible to describe all the scanners used in the book, but the Hawker Siddeley Linescan, which took the pictures on page 162, is typical.

The heart of a heat-camera is the sensor—a thermo-sensitive transducer—which converts heat into electricity. In the same way that film emulsion must be kept in the dark, a heat sensor has to be kept cold, and the cadmium mercury telluride detector in the Linescan is chilled to $77°K$ by liquid nitrogen.

Beneath the sensor is a four-sided revolving mirror. Each time it turns the sensor catches a glimpse of an area below, and records its average temperature as a "bit" of electronic information. The Linescan mirror revolves 125 times (producing 500 scans) per second, to an angle $60°$ either side of vertical. The signal is amplified and used to activate a white light source, which is focussed on to 70mm film as a spot travelling back and forth, synchronised to the scanning mirror.

The faster the mirror spins, the smaller is the area covered and the better the resolution of the final picture. There is no focusing as such, and therefore no lens. An electronic detector is simply exposed to a series of flashes and turns them into electrical impulses.

THE MULTI-SCANS

In order to "see" in other types of radiation, we must do what the eye does with light—learn to discriminate between, and simultaneously compare, as many wavelengths as possible. For this reason most surveillance equipment in space is now in the form of multiple units and many of the photographs in the book are composites of different images.

Like the cameras in satellites, scanners are now often mounted in arrays of two or more, called Multi-Spectral Scanners or MSS units. The reason is the same as that for multi-spectral cameras; to compare the different information from different wavelengths, and to obtain additional information by superimposing several synchronous views of the same subject.

For instance, the data from one MSS band may provide information on ground moisture and this, in turn, will affect the interpretation of data from another band measuring the thermal emission of rocks, because dry rocks emit more infrared than wet ones. And this data may then be combined with other information such as atmospheric conditions, the satellite's height, local time, and so on, to provide a single complete analysis.

Such comparisons indicate the depth of readings; and because they enable light pictures to be compared with microwave, thermal and near-IR, and ultra-violet frequencies, extraordinarily accurate energy "signatures" can be built up.

It has even been possible to superimpose data from quite different sources, as in the recent operation involving Landsat and a Nimbus weather satellite. They both monitored a 100 hectare region around the western fringes of the Ahaggar massif in Southern Algeria. Landsat recorded the patterns of vegetation while Nimbus monitored the precise rainfall, and when the results were compared with ground tests they were found to be remarkably accurate.

MSS units have so far been limited to the central bands of the spectrum from ultra-violet to infrared. But as techniques improve, their use is expanding.

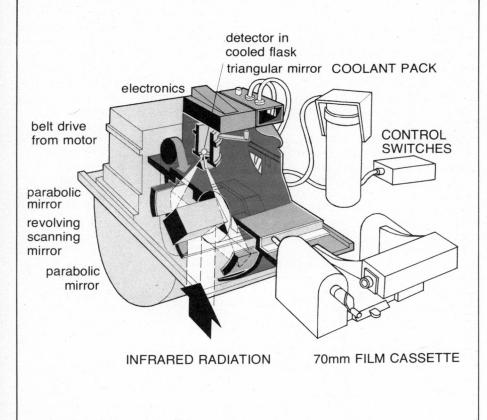

detector in cooled flask

triangular mirror   COOLANT PACK

electronics

belt drive from motor

CONTROL SWITCHES

parabolic mirror

revolving scanning mirror

parabolic mirror

INFRARED RADIATION   70mm FILM CASSETTE

A simplified diagram of the Linescan 212 by Hawker Siddeley Dynamics Ltd.

The Earth from Space

Many of the pictures in this book were taken from the LANDSAT and SKYLAB space platforms and a list of some of their equipment illustrates the range of scanners and cameras now aloft.

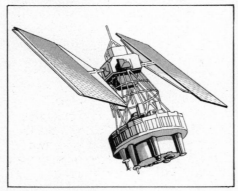

Landsat carries an MSS unit with separate scanners for red light, green light and two bands of near-IR, a vidicon system (no longer working), and a relay unit picking up signals from automatic ground stations in remote areas.

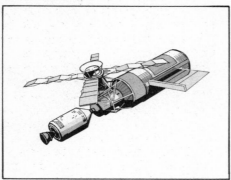

Skylab, among its unclassified equipment, carries a very high resolution camera (using 5" film, and with the incredible focal length of 18"), a multi-spectral unit with a bank of six cameras shooting on 70mm film in b/w, colour and near-IR, an L-band radiometer, a microwave radiometer, an infrared spectrometer, and a huge MSS with no less than 13 detectors including one for thermal-IR—not to mention the astronomical equipment with its telescopes, cameras, x-ray gear and spectrometers. And that was just its original unclassified equipment.

LANDSAT

The first LANDSAT satellite (then called ERTS 1) was launched by NASA in July 1972, and after a highly successful programme was followed by LANDSAT 2 in January 1975.

It has a circular orbit of 570 miles above the Earth, and crosses the Equator at roughly 9.30 am every morning on each north-to-south daytime pass. The sensory equipment transmits its information to receiving stations in Alaska, California and Maryland, among others; it is then unscrambled at the Goddard Space Flight Center; and, should you be interested, is on sale as photographs or "computer compatible" tapes at the EROS Data Center, Maryland, about 30 days later.

This delay indicates a fundamental problem with modern science. The limits are now human rather than technical, since our ability to gather data far outstrips our ability to process and study the vast flood of information pouring in.

The Landsat images overlap each other by about 10% and it requires 470 of them to cover the land mass of the United States, resolving objects down to 300 feet across. For black-and-white pictures the red light band gives the best general-purpose view of Earth's surface. But it is Landsat's MSS "false colour" composites which have proved so useful to resource planners all over the world.

SKYLAB

SKYLAB was primarily designed as an astronomical observatory. Although its Earth Terrain Camera, which can resolve objects down to 20 or 30 feet, has been put to good use, most of its important scientific instruments point out into space, free of atmospheric pollution for the first time.

Skylab was originally placed in orbit as an unmanned spacecraft in February 1973, and was occupied by a number of manned missions during the following year, which included the longest mission in space.

It travels in an orbit 270 miles out, covering most of the inhabited areas of Earth between latitudes 50°N and 50°S.

THE LANDSAT RECORD

Landsat has contributed to projects around the world. These examples, from the United States alone, give some idea of the range of its operations.

A single Landsat image revealed unsuspected grasslands in the Kenai Peninsula of Alaska, which can form the basis of a red-meat industry.

A study of Landsat photographs of Lake Michigan showed smoke from the steel mills of Gary, Indiana, aligned with cloud patterns along the eastern shore. This led to the hypothesis that rising and dispersing smoke formed the nuclei on which water condensed—producing a man-made weather-system that even deposited snow on the coast and inland.

43 forest fires were monitored by Landsat in Saskatchewan, in 1973, and this became the basis of a regular fire-monitoring programme.

Earthquake measurements in Alaska were compared with Landsat imagery and 4 out of 5 epicentres were found to be on previously unknown fault lines in remote areas.

Although Landsat has had its successes, it is by no means the only earth resources satellite. India, for instance, has its own, the Aryabhata, launched for them by the Russians. And another is planned for 1978, to conduct soil and land-use surveys, and to monitor the Himalayan snow cover to help predict the non-monsoonal flow in India's northern rivers.

EYES IN THE SKY

Scanning and other detector units come in a wide variety of packages with a bewildering litany of acronyms.

In an attempt to clarify matters, here is a simple run down of some of the systems used in the book, together with a few definitions.

Definitions

SPECTROSCOPE. An instrument which analyses a wide band of

radiation (such as light) and breaks it down into its various wavelengths.

SPECTROMETER. A type of spectroscope for measuring *reflective indices* or the energy distribution of a particular type of radiation.

RADIOMETER or radiomicrometer. A sensitive instrument for measuring heat radiation statistically, rather than as a direct image (although it can be turned into one). They usually consist of a thermocouple connected to a single copper loop forming the coil of a very accurate galvanometer. Both spectrometers and radiometers are used as detectors in scanning equipment.

VIDEO. The signal which transmits both the picture and the synchronising information in a television system.

RADIO. The scientific definition of radio is slightly different from its common usage. In technical terms, radio covers not only the broadcast frequencies (long, medium and short waves), stereo (VHF) and television (UHF), but also the microwave bands (SHF and EHF), which include radar.

ESMR

Ice-scan by Electronically Scanning Microwave Radiometer. Page 170.

The ESMR device on board the Nimbus 5 satellite measures microwave radiation from Earth's surface, using a metre-square scanner and a sensitive 1.55 cm wavelength receiver.

As the scanner sweeps from side to side, an on-board computer halts it for a fraction of a second, makes a measurement, and resumes the sweep. Each line of the image is made up of 78 such stops, completed every four seconds. At the wavelength used by ESMR, radiation penetrates the cloud cover and allows the surface brightness to be measured. The result is a map-like image recording neither heat nor light, but a quality known as "surface brightness temperature"—the relationship between the physical temperature of the target and the rate at which it gives off energy in the 1.55 cm band of the spectrum.

WEATHER RADAR

One of the more recent developments of radar is its use in monitoring weather conditions which need an instant "real-time" image, such as hurricanes and tornadoes.

A colour-coded radar picture of a typical thunderstorm shows a full range of reflections from dense clouds (red) to thin ones (green), as well as measuring rainfall, hail or turbulence. At the flick of a switch, it also gives the Doppler velocities.

This last, extraordinary facility records the wind speeds at the heart of a storm, from zero to 60 mph, as they move towards or away from the radar antennae. It does so by measuring the minute Doppler shift in the return signal.

SLAR

Rock-scan by Sideways Looking Airborne Radar. Pages 162, 163.

If you wanted to illuminate the ground beneath a high flying aircraft, it would not be much use shining light or heat down on it. Radar, on the other hand, can floodlight hundreds of miles from a single small source, because there just happens to be an atomospheric "window" in that part of the spectrum which lets the relatively long microwaves through. This makes radar the only active Earth scanning system now in use. The other scanners passively record radiation, SLAR generates its own.

SLAR is operated from high-flying aircraft which project a beam down to Earth that is highly directional horizontally, but fans out to 50° of vertical. As the aircraft moves forward, the SLAR covers a swathe from 20-40 kms wide.

Fixed antennae are used instead of the usual rotating radar aerials, because they are larger and more sensitive. The receiving equipment, either on board the same plane or one flying alongisde, times the lag between the transmission and the return of the signal.

The images are then built up on a continuous strip of film moving at a rate proportional to the plane's speed, with an on-board computer compensating for changes of altitude and for drift.

HRIR

Sea-scan by High Resolution Infrared Radiometer. Pages 149, 168.

HRIR does for heat what ESMR does for microwaves, measuring the relative brightness of radiation. It records how much of the available heat is reflected from clouds and how much from the surface at sea level—the sort of information which is invaluable in, for instance, the study of ocean currents.

HRIR equipment, such as that on the Nimbus 3 satellite, once again replaces the TV cameras carried by early weather satellites with electronic sensors that convert the infrared energy directly into modulations of the output signal. The information from the scanners is stored as a video signal for two orbits and transmitted back to Earth in a single ten-minute burst.

OSR

Cloudscan by Oscillating Scan Radiometer. Page 169.

The study of clouds alone can now provide detailed world weathercasts, and part of the hardware responsible for this revolution is the OSR equipment on board a US Air Force satellite whose existence was first revealed in 1973, though its information is now widely available.

The "oscillation" is between two sets of scanners, one adjusted for daytime and the other for twilight and night conditions. This is because the spacecraft has a curious orbit, wobbling 6° back and forth across the terminator line, partly in day and partly in night, with a permanent fix on the sun, and Earth turning at 15° an hour beneath it.

Each set has two scanners, a light sensor to record the lower, denser clouds, and an infrared sensor which is needed to record the icy temperature of the almost invisible clouds in the upper atmosphere.

It has a typical scanner layout, with the high-resolution IR sensors cooled to −15°C, and with mirrors revolving at 1.78 revs per second. The electronic response is translated into video signals, radioed to earth and printed out on 9½" wide film for distribution to weather stations.

Astronomy

KITT PEAK

The 14 astronomical telescopes at the Kitt Peak National Observatory form the largest and most effective concentration of instruments in the world. The observatory, with its own self-supporting community, is sited on land leased from the Papago Indians, 6875 feet above the Sonora Desert, near Tucson, Arizona.

The main instrument is the 4-metre (158-inch) Mayall Telescope, which is housed in its own 19-storey tower (visible in the centre of photograph on pages 10-11). It went into operation in March 1973, and concentrates on the study of remote objects such as quasars, whose light started out before Earth was even formed.

Kitt Peak also houses the world's largest solar telescope, with tracking mirrors on top of a 110-foot tower which reflect light down a 500-foot shaft, most of it cut through solid rock.

CERRO TOLOLO

Many of the most interesting objects in space are only visible from the southern hemisphere, including the nearest galaxies to our own, the Magellanic Clouds. So the complex of telescopes at the Cerro Tololo Observatory, 300 miles north of Santiago, in Chile, is particularly valuable.

Its viewing conditions are superb, 7000 feet up in the Andes on the edge of the Atacama Desert, chilled by the Humboldt Current sweeping up from Antarctica, and with such dark transparent skies that objects as small as 0.5 seconds of an arc are easily visible. There are seven main telescopes, ranging from a 61cm instrument originally used for planetary observations at Flagstaff, Arizona, to the 4-metre giant built to the same design as the one at Kitt Peak and considered by many astronomers to be the finest in the world. It weighs 375 tons, with a 15-ton 24"-thick Cer-Vit mirror, and began operating in October 1974.

ARECIBO

The Arecibo radio telescope is one of the wonders of the world—a 1000-foot bowl carved out of the remote mountains of Puerto Rico, with a dish larger than the collecting areas of all telescopes ever built. It has increased the sensitivity of radar astronomy by a factor of two thousand.

The dish is covered with 20 acres of aluminium reflector panels, each one adjusted to the correct angle by a laser beam from the receiving and transmitting platform suspended 500 feet above. The telescope can receive a wide range of radio signals from space and has four different types of radar transmitter—yet the whole installation can, if necessary, be operated by a single person.

Arecibo had barely been completed, in 1963, before starting the extraordinarily successful research programme which continues today.

In April 1975, for instance, it mapped the surface of Venus, through the planet's cloud cover, using 12.6 cm radar, and discovered in the process that it was the only planet which spins in a clockwise direction (page 184).

But the main work at Arecibo has been the study of pulsars (page 190). When these strange signals were first received in 1967 they were thought to indicate the presence of intelligent life, but Arecibo established the source as a neutron star in the Crab Nebula, part of the remnants of a stellar explosion in 1054 AD. Since then the telescope has located and analysed many other similar phenomena.

THE "OTHER" ASTRONOMIES

In addition to light waves, there are now two other bands of radiation used by astonomers, which not only enable them to see further into space, but to "see" different things.

The Radio Sky

"If our eyes were sensitive to radio wavelengths, we could see through walls and furniture, but would be unable to look through the holes in a metal chain-link fence."
—Robert Sheaffer, *Astronomy* magazine.

Just over forty years ago, a radio engineer called Karl G. Jansky discovered radio waves reaching Earth from space. Until that time

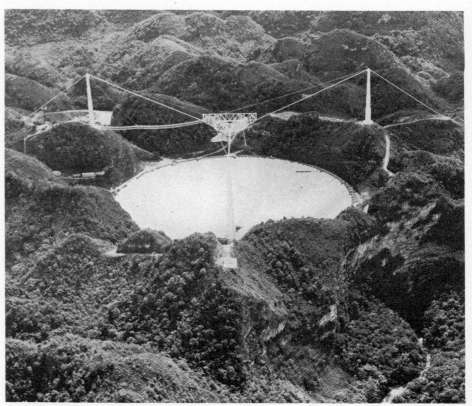

The Arecibo dish, set in the Puerto Rican mountains.

scientists only had one "window" through which to view the universe. Jansky opened a second, much larger window, since radio occupies a much wider band of the spectrum than light.

The radio sky is very different from the one we know. The familiar stars and constellations disappear. The moon and planets are almost invisible. But the Milky Way is far brighter than it appears in ordinary light, and it shares the sky with a host of new cosmic radio sources.

Observation of them is difficult, however, because they shed so little power onto Earth—only a few watts—which limits us to enormous, expensive (and definitely Earth-bound) arrays of aerials.

But once we penetrate Earth's atmospheric blanket, and move into space, it is possible to tune into the one really powerful form of radiation which illuminates the universe —x-rays.

The X-ray Sky

If you dropped this book on the surface of a neutron star, it would release the energy of an atomic explosion and a brilliant flash of x-rays.

In the same way that infrared indicates organic growth on Earth, x-rays are a sign of the huge gravity-powered processes in space. Quasars, black holes and the super-dense neutron stars which suck material in from millions of miles away, are so violent that they shock-heat gases to a temperature at which they emit x-rays.

The first x-ray satellite, UHURU (1970), discovered many of these new phenomena, and those that followed (Copernicus, ANS, UK-5 and SAS-3) discovered even more, including mysterious x-ray sources which flicker on and off. The largest x-ray satellites yet are due to be launched over the next few years as part of the HEAO programme. These 10-foot long unmanned observatories will be sneaked into orbit just below the Van Allen belts (which will protect them from unwanted cosmic radiation), carrying multi-sensors designed to map x-ray sources in the "soft gamma ray" bands and study the diffuse x-ray background in space.

SUNLAB

"To the romantics among us—and I am one—the Skylab success may not seem a pleasant victory. The ATM succeeded in large measure by impersonalising astronomy—replacing single efforts and more limited crusades with the staggering power of regimented attack. Skylab seized the remaining momentum and paraphernalia of the Apollo lunar programme and applied it to loft a battery of the world's most advanced solar telescopes to the ideal observing site; then, from an extensive group control centre manned by professional astronomers and supported by observatories around the world, the ATM team collectively directed their instruments with careful strategy and unerring aim."

—Dr. John Eddy, High Altitude Observatory, Boulder, Colorado.

The Apollo Telescope Mount (ATM) was the innocuous title for Skylab's main astronomical experiment—the first comprehensive study of the sun. It cost 10% of Skylab's $2.6 million budget, recorded the transit of Mercury, the passage of Comet Kohoutek (page 186), two eclipses, and vast amounts of other solar information including some spectacular photographs (pages 173, 174, 176-7).

Only 5 of the 30 cameras took photographs in ordinary white light, These were to study the sun's outer corona, which has weak atomic emissions and is best observed by reflected light at about the 6000 angstrom wavelength. The rest of the equipment was devoted to x-ray and ultra-violet frequencies.

The two x-ray telescopes were used to study the corona, in depth, at 0.15 and 2.5 angstrom wavelengths. The pictures they produced altered many previous assumptions, showing the whole corona to be composed of closed-loop systems of gas, patterns of "storms" across the entire solar disc, and "coronal holes" which emitted such violent belches of solar wind that they caused strong fluctuations in Earth's magnetic field. These had previously been attributed entirely to the solar "flares."

Below the corona is the chromosphere, where highly ionised helium gases emit brilliant ultra-violet. The ATM package had two spectrographs (with nine 35mm cameras) and an electronic spectroheliometer focused on this region, recording the spicules and flares from the giant cellular network beneath, and taking spectral analyses at each level. One of the extraordinary events they recorded was a huge bubble of gas the size of the sun itself, which slipped out of the chromosphere and into space at a million miles an hour.

SPACE PROBES

Spacecraft are essential for close-up astronomy. Only by actually going there could we sample the atmosphere of Venus or tell whether the polar cap on Mars was frozen CO_2 or (as it turned out) water ice. So most of the equipment of the planetary probes is designed to sample, taste and analyse on the spot. The only long-range thing about them is their radio messages back to Earth—and even these are not very strong. The furthest messages so far came from the Jupiter probe. They took 45 seconds to get here and arrived with a signal strength of one quadrillionth of a watt—an amount of energy which would have to accumulate for 19 million years to power a 7½ watt light bulb for a thousandth of a second.

Nevertheless, the sensors and TV cameras on these spacecraft have provided unique data, and more than one surprise for astronomers.

These craft all carried specially adapted video cameras to send back their pictures. Mariner was designed to record cloud cover and operated (through a 1.5-meter telescope) in ultra-violet. Its pictures were later printed with blue filters to further enhance cloud markings. The Viking cameras, on the other hand, operated in normal light. Their pictures were transmitted in monochrome, but by using colour filters (violet, green and red) for different scans, and superimposing the results back on Earth, full colour pictures were produced.

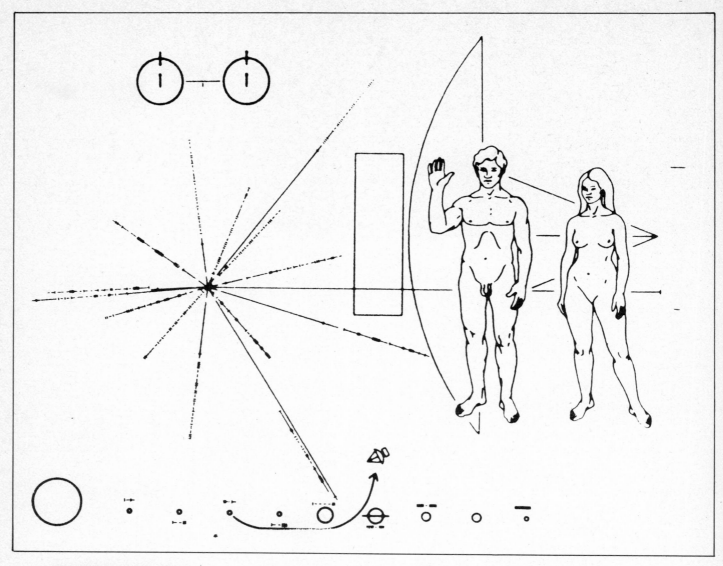

OVER AND OUT

Two formal efforts have so far been made to communicate our presence to the rest of the galaxy by sending messages into space. Whether or not you believe they will be picked up, it remains an interesting possibility.

When the Pioneer 10 spacecraft left the solar system in 1974, after its flypast of Mars and Venus, there was a small gold anodised aluminium plate attached to the side (above), in the hope that someone, maybe a million years hence, will be curious enough to recover the craft.

The 450,000 watt radar output from the S-band radar transmitter at Arecibo can be concentrated into a narrow beam 100 times more powerful than the total electric power production of all the generating plants in the world. If there is a similar instrument anywhere else in the galaxy which is turned in our direction, Arecibo would be a radio beacon 10 million times brighter than the sun, and the unequivocable sign of intelligent life.

In fact, in 1974, a coded message indicating our presence was beamed from Arecibo towards the globular star cluster called M13:

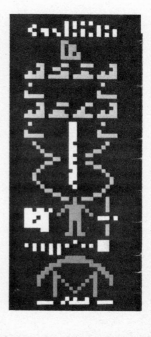

If intelligent, or at any rate technological, life exists there, they may yet decode the signal as: the numbers one to ten, the atomic numbers for hydrogen, carbon, nitrogen, oxygen and phosphorus, the formula for DNA, various population statistics, the solar system (with the Earth raised under a human figure)—and a diagram of the Arecibo telescope.